The Broken Thorns

The Broken Thorns

Dr. Vrindavan Lal Verma

Ocean Books Pvt. Ltd.
ISO 9001:2015 Publishers

Published by
Ocean Books (P) Ltd.
4/19 Asaf Ali Road,
New Delhi-110 002 (INDIA)
e-mail: info@oceanbooks.in

ISBN 978-81-8430-568-5
THE BROKEN THORNS
by Dr. Vrindavan Lal Verma

Paperback edition
First, 2019

Price
₹ 400.00 (Rupees Four Hundred only)

Printed at
R-Tech Offset Printers, Delhi

Preface

'The Broken Thorns' is English translation of a well-known historical novel 'Toote Kante' written by Padma Bhushan, Dr. Vrindavan Lal Verma, the great Hindi novelist who rose to literary heights by his inimitable style, deep insight into human character and sense of history. He could encompass the life and times, the trials and tribulations, the joys and sorrows, and the cultural and social milieu of bygone ages of India's history within a panoramic presentation of the cavalcade of historic characters like Rani Laxmi Bai of Jhansi, Nana Saheb, Sadashiv Rao Holkar, Nadir Shah and numerous others who not only come to life, as it were, in our mind's eye in a flashback but relive their glorious or ignominious lives all over again and leave an indelible impress on our hearts and sensibilities.

The translation into English of his historical novel 'Toote Kante' is a humble homage to the memory of Dr. Verma, the grand master of storytelling who delved deep into the annals of Indian history to create and recreate great human characters and their vision of life.

It is the story of a dancer at the Moghul Court, who with her matchless beauty and artistic accomplishments, had captivated the hearts of the Moghul Emperor Muhammad Shah and the infamous invader Nadir Shah who had taken a fancy to take her along on his way back to Iran. However, Noorbai made up her mind not to leave her country. The realistic picture of the agony of the country in the grip of disruption and unrest, serves as a backdrop to the romantic love between Noorbai and Mohan a Jat guard and a commoner, the latter making the secret and dramatic escape, from the Red Fort, of the former possible.

Mohan, the Jat hero of the novel is a remarkable common man who leads Noorbai to elevate and sublimate her life at Vrindavan by singing devotional songs addressed to Lord Krishna. Noorbai with her transformed spirit finally symbolises the magic touch of the liberal Hindu philosophy of adjustment and assimilation, without whose operation the broken thorns of divisiveness sticking deep into our body politic, even now in the present turbulent times, cannot be dislodged or dissolved easily to make us a united nation i.e. India of our vision . Her self-abnegation in throwing gold and jewellery into the river Yamuna re-establishes that spiritual values are supreme in life.

—I.C. Srivastava

Acknowledgement

I am grateful to Late Shri Satya Dev Verma, son of Dr. Vrindavan Lai Verma, for entrusting me with the translation of 'Toote Kante' in English. He waited patiently for about three years to enable me to finish the work. My father-in-law, Late Shri P.C. Saksena, IAS (Retd.), a close associate of Dr. Verma, encouraged me throughout my endeavours. My wife, Archana, daughter, Snigdha and son, Palash have given me sustained support and made it possible for me to take up this work.

Shri Rama Kant Varma, grandson of the author, Dr. Varma prodded me to complete the work in time for publication by Prabhat Publishers and I am thankful to both him and Shri Prabhat the publisher.

Introduction

The original theme of 'The Broken Thorns' (Toote Kante) had been prodding my mind for quite sometime. When I sized up and assessed the information available in the published books with a view to gather adequate background material, I was not satisfied. In the books of history I found, in small or large measure, the description of facts relating to the sweeping assault of Baji Rao on Delhi in 1739, the merrymaking of Muhammad Shah and his courtesans, the hauteur and mischief of Meer Hasan Khan Darbari, the ambitious plans of Nizamulmulk and Saadat Khan and their invitation to Nadir Shah to attack Delhi, the rise of Jats and the widespread breakdown of administration, etc., but I could not lay my hands on any analytical information about the general economic condition and the rise and decline of the culture of people and the intellectual progress made in those times.

The common citizenry of North India was afflicted by many troubles and sorrows. The common man suffered trials and tribulations. Either he cried or burst into songs of joy. What would he sing? How and when was he inspired to sing? There were festivals and folk-songs to relieve his frustrations and defeats and to give him some contentment. He gave vent to his pent up feelings and thoughts through them but derived moral strength from the sermons of saints and spiritual leaders and from path of devotion which served as nectar for the dejected hearts. How he acquired his moral fibre through them cannot possibly be encompassed by the vision and imagination of a student of psychology. How deep was the impact of exposition by saints, spiritual leaders and poet-turned saints on the folk culture and progress can be gauged little by the description found in the famous books of history in Persian language.

Rai Chaturman Kayath, in his treatise, 'Chahare Gulshan' which he wrote in 1759, has drawn character sketch of saints and monks while Bahadur Singh Bhatnagar has thrown light on the lives of poets, artists and saints in his book 'Yaadgare-Bahaduri' (1817). We have several books of history about the times of the Emperor Bahadurshah (1719-1748). Anand Ram Mukhalis has given an eye-witness account of the attack of Nadir Shah, in his book of history, 'Tajkirah'. It is in the fitness of things to mention that Nadir Shah did not have, in him, Iranian blood and was actually a 'Turk'. A majority of his Kazilbash sepoys were 'Turks'. Frazer, then stationed at Ahmedabad, had written a book 'Nadir Shah' which was published in the year 1742 in London. Mirza Mughal, an intimate friend of Frazer, who was living in Ahmedabad used to receive letters from the private secretary of Sarbuland Khan of Delhi. Nadir Shah had appointed Sarbuland Khan to go on a looting and extortion spree in Delhi. Hence whatever had been written in those letters can be believed. I could come by this book by sheer luck but it does not contain, as vivid and elaborate a description as can be found in the 'Tajkirah' of Anand Ram Mukhalis. Anand Ram was one of the scribes of the Emperor Muhammad Shah.

Elliott and Dawson have devoted only 22 pages (76-98) on this theme in their monumental treatise 'History of India as Told by its Own Historians'. What else could these authors do? The original manuscript was not traceable anywhere. Lt. Perkins had translated 38 pages in English and of these also, Dawson had left out 16 pages, because they contained description of the beating of Anand Ram by Nadir Shah as also the looting carried out by the latter. Little did Dawson realise that the student of Sociology and the story-tellers would find a mine of information in these pages.

This led me to search for Anand Ram's 'Tajkirah'. I wrote to the well-known historian, Dr. Jadunath Sarkar who referred me to Maharaj Kumar, Dr. Raghuvir Singh of Sitamau and thus this search became a story by itself. Dr. Raghuvir Singh sent me a copy of some of Dr. Sarkar's letters and I discovered in them, a reference of Anand Ram's book, a copy of which was found in the collection of Oriential Public Library, Patna. It took a year to obtain a copy of the manuscript. During the communal riots of Patna-Bankipur, the copy prepared for me was also burnt by the rioters and it was a matter of sheer luck that the original could be preserved and a copy made from it again, which was sent to me through the courtesy of Dr. Raghuvir Singh. I am indebted to Dr. Raghuvir Singh and Dr. Jadunath Sarkar too. In 'Toote Kante', one of the 'Rubaiyats' of Omar Khayyam has been rendered in Hindi and made use of suitably. It has been translated by my dear friend, Shri Maithili Sharan Gupta and I find myself unable to express my gratitude to him.

However, I cannot forget the kindness of Maulana Sahib who read out to me the Hindi translation of 'Tajkirah' in several sittings because I do not know Persian language and, to say the least, even Urdu is a little beyond me. Then comes the contribution of the book 'Bayane Bukai' written by Khwaja Abdul Karim Khan Kashmiri. This book contains description about Noorbai. Dawson has devoted only 15 pages, (p. 124-139) in his aforesaid book about the contents of Bayane Bukai. This is a large volume of great importance. One of its copies is preserved in the Lahore Public Library. I could secure a lot of worthwhile material from this book and I should like to express my thanks to a Muslim friend from Pakistan, whom I cannot name.

Initially, a brief character sketch of Noorbai was brought to notice in the book 'Later Mughals' (Vol. II, page 371) by Irvine in which Irvine has, among other things, mentioned as .follows :

> "The conqueror allowed himself some relaxation after his arduous campaigns. Dances and songs were performed before him. One Indian dancing girl named Noorbai so highly fascinated him by her musical powers and ode in honour of him that he ordered her to be paid Rs. 4000 and taken to Persia in his train. It was with the greatest difficulty that she could save herself from this last mark of his favour."

Noorbai was extemely fond of singing stanzas and poems of Soordas, Nanddas and Raskhan besides ghajals. It is quite possible when Noorbai sang one of the stanzas, Muhammad Shah had explained to Nadir Shah that the praise and adoration of Kanhaiya was in reality meant for Nadir Shah himself.

Earlier Noorbai used to grace the *'Mehfil'* (assembly of music), organized by Saadat Khan. After some time, she found her way to the court of the Emperor Muhammad Shah. It hurt Saadat Khan who became more inclined and favourably disposed towards Nadir Shah, leading to the finale as described in the novel itself. In the opinion of one historian, Saadat Khan already weakened, took poison and committed suicide as a result of the ill-treatment meted to him by Nadir Shah. However, I can only accept the fact that he committed suicide.

Muhammad Shah was defeated and humiliated by Nadir Shah near Karnal. Later, Nadir Shah was escorted by Muhammad Shah himself to the Red Fort of Delhi as his honoured guest. He put forward a demand of Rs. 20 crore as compensation for all kinds of losses. Muhamadshah presented to him the gift of Noorbai alongwith 400 slave-maids as a recompense of that loss. Nadir Shah accepted this gift but he remained adamant on his demand for Rs. 20 crore. There were riots in Delhi. Nadir Shah perpetrated such atrocities which reminded of the 'Day of

Judgement and Deluge'. At long last, he was persuaded to return to Iran with a wealth amounting to Rs. 70 crore besides 'Takhte Taaus'.

Shri Abdul Aziz in his book 'The Imperial Treasury of the Indian Mughals' has vividly described the loot ordered by Nadir Shah (p. 552-557). About 4000 slave-maids also found themselves in the siege mounted by Nadir Shah around the Red Fort. Noorbai was endowed with exquisite beauty as well as art of music and dance. Whatever might be in store for her in Iran, she thought, she would not be able to imbibe the melodious rhythm of the Brij music and art. She made up her mind not to leave India, her country, and hence she ran away, making her escape from the Fort. Among the guards at Red Fort there were quite a few Jats and Rajputs. One of them helped her escape and breathe a life of freedom.

After Nadir Shah had left Delhi, during the course of return journey, one day he lost his hold on four thousand maid-slaves. From Iranian custody, they achieved their freedom at the hands of Nature. After 57 days of tyrannical acts and hellish atrocities, Nadir Shah set out for Iran on 5th May, 1739. He had, in his possession, gold, jewels worth Rs. 70 crore, 4000 slave-maids, 130 scribes (for the maintenance of accounts in Iran), 300 masons, 200 blacksmiths, 200 carpenters and 100 sculptors. He had a mind to build in Iran, a new and beautiful city like Delhi, which he had reduced to ashes). One day it rained cats and dogs on the bank of Chenab river which received floods. Two thousand Iranian soldiers were swept away and met their death and it became impossible to continue the journey. The slaves took advantage of this golden opportunity and fled from the scene.

When Nadir Shah was in Delhi itself, Noorbai ran away. Delhi had not witnessed manslaughter or rioting of that nature earlier. Hanway, a European traveller has brought out the real reason for the rioting and manslaughter. I am in agreement with the same, and have made it the basis in this novel. Munshi Sadasukh Dehalvi in his book of history, 'Muntkhabut Tawarikh' written in Persian, has criticized the efforts made by the Perian historian in concealing the real events in jugglery of words and in the misty clouds of metaphors and similes which they indulged in with a view to please their paymasters. Sadasukh had written his book during the year (1817-1818). He has mentioned at one stage, "I do not aim at pleasing any king or Emperor. Instead, I wish to earn the admiration and praise of impartial and honest people. I do not want to distort the history by falsehood. I fear no one nor am I tempted to seek anyone's kindness." I also concede that it is the correct attitude.

Having achieved her escape from the Red Fort, Noorbai joined the band of non-believers. What else could the biased historians mentioned by Sadasukh describe? Had Raskhan lived in those times, he would have spoken the truth or had it been the poet 'Kare' of Datia, he would have done the same as Raskhan. Only two lines of his would suffice to show his spirit:

> "Oh God, the Master of Hindus, even though we have no claim on you, as the Master of all the world you have to shower your Grace on us and save us as well".

How was Noorbai able to reach the place of pilgrimage in the Brij region? When Delhi was receiving the onslaught of Nadir Shah, his sepoys carried out killings in the neighbourhood of Delhi around 30 to 40 miles and in the midst of all that how could she make her escape possible? But undoubtedly, she could make her way out of the tempest of fighting and brandishing of swords. How she was transformed into another human can better be understood by the following rendering of a stanza from Tulsidas:

> I have heard, the Lord Purifies the sinner.
> I am sinful and Thou art purifier of sins.

This is a nice combination; the scriptures certify
That you have salvaged sinful persons like the hunter.
The prostitue, the elephant and the sinful Ajamil.[1]
In addition to these, how many more you have brought ashore
From the ocean of sin; who can count or recount
Those who chant your name knowingly or unknowingly
For them, the hell turns into heaven.
Like a slave, this devotee Tulsidas comes to your portals.
Kindly give him your blissful shelter.

The famous author Aldous Huxley has brought out a unique formula about Bhakti Marg in his book, 'Ends and Means' as follows: 'it is too perfect by half'.

Had I been a philosopher, I would have possibly remarked something more on this. But as a storyteller whatever I could glean from history, I have put down in the novel 'Toote Kante' by taking historical facts as a camouflage. Whatever impact the poet-saints like Nand Das, Soordas, etc., had on that non-Hindu singer, the character of Noorbai in the novel is a mirror and reflection of the same, which also indicates the sustained development of that influence. All the same, the novel 'Toote Kante' encompasses something else too.

Jhansi
27th August, 1954

—Dr. Vrindavan Lal Verma

1. Ajamil – According to a legend mentioned in Hindu scriptures, Puranas, Ajamil, who was a sinner all his life having committed innumerable sins, found his salvation at the hands of God. When he called out the name of Narayana, his son at the time of his death-pangs, God saved him from condemnation and hell as He was pleased by Ajamil's chanting of 'Narayana', an appellation of God himself.

1

It was the beginning of the month of Chait.[1] Even so, there was nip in (the air and some clouds hung by the sky. South-west wind was sweeping all over the place. Gooseberry was in full bloom and cappris was about to blossom. 'Flame of the Forest', Palash had already shaken off its leaves. The branches were shooting with flaming flowers and numerous buds. Mustard crop had matured and the ears of wheat were yet to ripen.

The sun was rising. The sweet, earthy smell of wheat-fields borne on the wind was wafted towards the hillocks of Fatehpur Sikri mingling as it did in the small gooseberry flowers.

With a long stick in his hand, Mohanlal was walking along the fence of a wheat-field. He wore a torn and twisted turban on his head and wrapped himself in an unclean sheet of cloth which covered his stringed tunic. One of his shoes was worn out and torn. The wrapper sheet showed holes and splashes of colours of 'Holi',[2] recently celebrated. Part of his Dhoti[3] covered one of his legs while its other side barely touched the knees. Mohanlal gazed wide-eyed, at his swaying crops, knitted the

1. Chait – Chaitra, corresponding to March-April of Christian calendar, is the first month of Hindu calendar. It is the season of harvesting and hard work for the farmer.
2. Holi – A Hindu religious festival on the day following the full-moon in the month of March; people greet one another heralding new Hindu calendar year sym-bolizing spring-fun, colour and hope and festive mood. People throw coloured water and dry colour before hugging one another on this day.
3. Dhoti – Long sheet of cloth worn by men below the waist in India, especially by Hindus.

narrow forehead and, with folded hands, greeted the sun-god. He sneezed and cleaned his long smooth nose and breathed fast, heaving his wide chest. He thought:

'Oh God! Why this sneeze? What an omen is this?' To overcome the ill-omen, he tried to bring about another sneeze; basking himself in the rays of the sun, he inhaled fresh air carefully but could not succeed. Mohanlal turned towards his house, massaging and feeling his forehead. 'I should start harvesting today itself; any delay might herald hail and rain,' he thought.

Tucked in the midst of groves and bushes, his house thatched with straw-mats stood on a hillock. Beside the house, there was an enclosure rounded by a fallen mud wall on one side and a thorny bushy fence on the other. On one side of the enclosure, there was a verandah resting on pillars of mud and wooden planks. A pair of oxen were tethered to the mud-pillar. One of them was old and the other young but weak. In another corner, a buffalo fresh from her first calving, was roped. A lad of seventeen or eighteen was milking her. Outside the verandah, a woman was making cow-dung cakes for the hearth. Nearby was a shallow pit filled with rubbish, ash and cow-dung.

The house had two exits —one opening in the front and the other in the enclosure at the rear. Mohanlal took off his shoes at the front door, placed his stick against the wall and came into the enclosure.

He asked the woman: Anything to eat, there?'

'What? At such an early hour? Haven't made dung-cakes yet, nor could I skim the milk; buffalo is yet to be milked; besides, you have not washed yourself.' The sharp-tongued woman would have continued in this vein but Mohan interrupted her.

He spoke, 'Well, I can see that myself. But is there anything left over since last night?'

The woman moved away and stopped making dung-cakes. She pulled her veil with a finger sticky with dung. She knitted her brows below her big eyes and gasped through her nose. She was 'Roni', a weeping woman by name but her features betrayed no sign of depression or crying.

Roni replied, 'There was nothing left for me. You and your brother devoured all the loaves. How few were left over for me?'

The man who was milking loosened his grip of hands; his lips quivered to say something but he said nothing, and went on milking the she-buffalo.

Mohanlal's eyes, bloodshot with night-watching of fields flashed with anger; abuse welled up in his throat but he fumbled and muttered to himself 'Oh Ram! To what a devilish shrew am I wedded.'

Mohan nonchalantly walked towards the Milkmen. The woman rested one of her hands on mother earth and the other on dung.

Mohan said, 'Tota, we should plunge ourselves in harvesting wheat after eating something.'

Tota hummed, 'Yes', and carried on with milking.

Mohan continued, 'Clouds are gathering. I am afraid, it might rain or bring hail. Whatever crop has been saved from the tyrants or robbers, may be ruined by rain-god.'

'What, today itself? The crop is not ripe yet and in many beds, ears of wheat are still green.'

The woman shouted, 'Where do you see it green and unripe? Only a small bit may be half-ripe. Don't be slack about it.'

'This is why I had asked for something to eat, but you made all that fuss, Roni.'

Roni retorted, 'What else could I say? Should I tell you to empty the jar of grains? Do you mean without sweeping dung and without grinding flour, making loaves would be possible?'

Roni had got married only a few months back. But her sharp tongue and shrewish nature had added to her years apparently.

Without waiting for any reply, Roni replied, 'There is some roasted grain. Take a handful or two, drink a tumbler of water and plunge yourselves in reaping the harvest. Loaves will be ready by mid-day and I shall bring to the fields.'

Tota had finished milking. Just as he was about to throw some fodder in front of the buffalo, Roni burst out, 'Go and put some curd in the milk and then turn back for putting fodder. If the pail is touched to earth, everything will be spoilt.' Roni had a hurried glance at Mohan to pry if Mohan's appetite had turned to milk.

Mohan said, 'Tota, you may go and put some curd in milk while I put some fodder here.'

Tota turned to pick up the pail full of milk when Roni again spoke, 'Put this milk in some other pot. One there contains curd which has to be skimmed.'

'Yes', — said Tota and went away carrying the pail.

Mohan suggested to her in an humble voice, 'Alongwith the roasted gram, I should take some curd and then be off to harvesting; what do you say to this?'

'And then go to deep sleep. Can't you make out that I shall make dung-cakes first and after washing myself, I shall grind flour; then it will be time for skimming the milk? All this will take at least two-three hours; what will you do in the meanwhile?'

'While I make dung-cakes, Tota will skim milk and meantime you may finish some other chores.'

'You might as well wash face on my behalf.'

'Why should you lose your temper since early morning?'

'Why are you trying to provoke me yourself? You and your brother may divide chores between yourselves, I have to do the grinding.'

'I have done that too and can do it even now.'

'All this appears to be an excuse for not gathering the harvest. Every one has reaped his crop and also hidden foodgrains in the house. But you have an altogether different frame of mind. Someone will take away the harvest, reap it stealthily and then you will repent and curse yourself.'

'No, we go right now and harvest and shall stack it all in barn ('*Khalihan*'). But I put it to you—Can't you speak more softly or in a lower tone?'

'Oh my God, Ram — What a misfortune it is? Wherefore did my village-elders dump me here? May the entire village be burnt down — my curse on it. May those shameless souls be damned!'

Roni wiped her eyes with the edge of her clothes even though no tears trickled from them. Mohan bit his lips but uttered nothing. Tota came upon the scene.

Tota said, 'Dada',[4] let us go with our sickles; we have to cut down the entire crop today.'

Roni taunted, 'Ha, what a big field it is? I can myself reap all the grains of that small patch of field. Can't both of you finish off even that much?'

Tota smiled a little. Mohan suppressed his pent-up breath and went inside the house in search of a sickle.

Tota queried, 'Sister, where have you put roasted gram?'

'I'll give it', said Roni and shook off dung from her hands as she went into the house. Tota stood there.

Roni returned in a moment and said, 'Brother, why are you idling here? Lift all the dung from below the buffalo and put it beside the dung-pan.'

Tota busied himself in collecting dung without any murmur. Roni turned back into the house. Mohan had yet to find out the sickle.

Roni spoke, 'You can't find out things which you yourself kept away somewhere? It baffles me to see you immersed in daydreaming. Go in the other room where hang many a sickle from the pegs.'

Mohan went into the room to fetch sickles.

Roni quickly poured roasted gram into her cloth wrapper and came out shouting into the enclosure. 'If you have found sickles, come out here in the enclosure.'

4. Dada – Appellation for elder brother.

Roni was a lass from a village situated at some distance from Fatehpur Sikri. Her mother died while she was still a child. Her father had brought her up. Father was penniless and worked for wages to make both ends meet. Suddenly, he died. The villagemen took care of Roni in the best possible way. She had grown to be of a marriageable age, but no householder was willing to accept her despite her pretty looks. The small house of Mohan located outside the ramparts of Fatehpur Sikri and his small farm with a pair of oxen and a buffalo were rated a large property for Roni. The village elders got her wedded to Mohan.

Mohan had no one in his family except Tota who was a distantly related brother to him. Tota owned no house nor had he any farm of his own. Both of them lived like real brothers. Tota was always a great help in managing the farm.

—✻—

2

They could somehow lay their hands on roasted grains, but could not munch it at home. Roni busied herself again in making dung-cakes and cautioned them, 'Take a jar full of water to the fields and get down to cutting; take your breakfast and drinking water also there. But if you are having breakfast here, someone will take away all the crop.'

Mohan felt he would be more at ease in the fields than at home and accompanied by Tota, he went out.

Sun shone straight over the heads. It was a bright and intensely sunny day. Both of them took off their tunic and dumped it on the fence of the field and filling their girdle with grains, they got busy in harvesting. Mohan's sinuous, fleshy muscles showed while he was cutting and Tota's slim, wiry muscles were popping back and forth. Husk and ears of corn were flying and clinging to their neck and forehead. There were some gram plants scattered amidst wheat-corn. Tota took them out, root-and-all, with one hand, crunched and chewed them along with seed-coats.

Mohan interrupted him. 'Why not munch some grain and have respite too. One should not mouth corn standing in the field.'

Tota, still busy in cutting, spoke, 'I won't take, Bhaiyya; we shall munch gram later on. Let the work be done with.'

Both continued with harvesting for full one hour. Tota held back his hand and said, 'Well, let's have some bite'. Mohan refused to budge, 'Let's continue for some more time.'

Tota said, 'We are going to have some loaves for lunch very soon.'

Mohan chuckled feebly. 'It's not even mid-day just now; flour may not be out of the grinding stones as yet, how can we expect the loaves right away?'

Tota plunged himself in cutting the crop again. An hour later, Mohan put his sickle aside. Sitting on his haunches in the clean, mowed space, Mohan said : 'Tota, how long will this harvest last? I am fed up now. I wish to secure a job somewhere. You may take care of the household. I shall return only after earning a bit.'

'What would I do here, alone?'

'You and your Bhabhi (sister-in-law) will be here together. How can I bear the unshared burden of your Bhabhi's mouthful talks? Be that as it may be, it's just a matter of a few days', said Mohan.

'How, where would you go away, Bhaiyya?'

'I would like to be in a nobleman's brigade, in Agra or nearby".

'Yes'.

They engaged themselves in crop-cutting once again. They were thirsty. They had a look at the sun. The sun was not shining over the head. Holding back their hands, they looked at each other's face. Speechless, they went to the fence and put their hands on the girdle.

Tota braced himself up and said, 'Why not get busy again with a gulp of water? We'll have loaves in an hour's time.'

But Mohan had untwined his girdle by then.

'My belly is aflame with hunger. Mere water will not overcome the appetite. Eat some grain and then take water', said Mohan.

Tota also untwined his girdle and started munching. After he had chewed half the quantity, he said, 'The other half will do for the afternoon, as dinner will be served late tonight.'

Mohan nodded his assent. Both of them again tucked gram in their girdle, drank some water and were lounging. Mohan spotted some shade below a nearby tree.

Mohan entreated, 'After a gulp of water I feel like lazing. Last night was a sleepless night for me; what do you say to taking some rest under the shade.'

Tota was not tired yet, but he acceded to the request of Mohan. Both of them were squatting under the shadowy tree. Mohan used a piece of sod as his pillow and stretched himself. Tota followed suit and used another piece as his pillow and lay there stretching his feet. Mohan turned his side and was asleep. After a little while, Tota was also sleeping.

The sun, it appeared, had slid upwards over their head. As cool breeze slowed, sleep overcame them. Roni arrived at the fence of the field. Spotting neither of them in any nook or part of the field, she glanced quickly from one end to the other. Her eyes fell on both of them resting there under the shadowy tree. Gnashing her teeth, she walked to the shade of the tree; sound of her steps could not wake them up. Roni had a quick look at the big and small pebbles of clay lying there. She had a mind to hit at Mohan's back with one and at Tota's chest with another. But she, somehow, restrained herself.

Her deep breath indicated her eagerness to come to a decision quickly. At long last, she struck upon the only way out. She raised a full-throated, shrill cry.

'Be damned, both of you, Go to hell. Set on fire all the crop. Dispose off the yoke and oxen and flee to the hills. Fie, shame upon you, sluggish fellows.'

They did not hear her cursed words of 'damnation' — already knew all this — but their ears could catch all that she was saying then.

Mohan begged — 'We were tired'.

'Sleep longer than that and let the crop disappear from the fields.'

Both of them maintained silence. Roni's temper rose. Tears trickled down her eyes.

'Unlucky as I am, I lost my parents. Oh, what dead wood I am yoked under.' Roni continued in this vein and sobbed.

Guilty as he was, having slept over, what else could he do? Mohan pondered and ignoring sign of penitence in Roni's tearful eyes, he proposed to Tota, 'Wash yourself and start the cutting; we have to put all the grain in the barn before it gets dark.'

Tota nodded and rose. Roni felt that her pique and grief had no effect on them. She calmed herself and wiped her tears. Her eyes were red and throat hoarse. With a shake she put aside the loaves making the cloth-cover free. There was a semi-liquid dish made of pulse 'Urad' in a bowl. A little was spilt on the bread. Underneath was some butter. This, in no way, whetted Mohan's appetite; it only added to his irritation.

He said, 'I would break your bones and ribs some day so that you know what Mohan is like.'

In a split second, Roni perceived the terrible eyes of Mohan but she could not humble herself easily. She knew her own tricks. She rose.

Roni threw a challenger, 'Come, come. You will kill me, that's all. What else? I am only too willing to die.'

Mohan had no desire to beat her; even so, he made an advance. Roni turned towards home. But she went on babbling.

'The day I am no more in this world, only dogs will make themselves merry in the house.'

Ignoring her forebodings, Mohan picked up the bread and the bowl of pulses and squatted there for the fill. Having done with eating, they busied themselves in work. Well before dusk, they had reaped the field and whatever ears of corn had been leftover, they gathered. Then they put all the harvest in the open air barn.

—✵—

3

Both men squatted for respite in the barn and munched the leftover gram from the girdle. At the same moment, there was some commotion at the outer gate. They were shaken by all kinds of anxieties and forebodings — might be, they were the agents of the money lender or the sepoys of local Recovery Official or it might be, they were robbers.

Roni came out running. She untied the buffalo and the calf, removed some of thorny bushes from the outworn wall, and put them back as soon as she had turned out the she-buffalo. She spoke in a shaky voice, 'Recovery sepoys are here'.

Roni returned inside the house and started shifting and rummaging things. Mohan and Tota put back gram in the girdle as usual. Startled, they stirred out. A good lot of sepoys were gathered there. At the head of the crowd, the leader, Naik with his bulging, swinging belly stood there.

Naik spoke in an authoritative tone, 'You have put all the harvested crop in hiding. Land Revenue dues are outstanding for years; you don't worry for paying the same?'

Mohan replied in a hoarse, beseeching voice, 'Master, we have not threshed yet. Where, you think, can we hide the harvest and the grains? Time for payment of revenue is still far off.'

Naik warmed up, 'Far off. You don't have to kid about that. Last year, you did the same trick of putting us off; this year also you are pretending. We know everything — you got married, had all the pleasures, and have squandered everything on festivities and rites. If we bide time as suggested by you, we shall not gain a single grain.'

'We have not squandered anything', Tota replied in a tearful voice.

Mohan entreated, 'Take away whatever you like; we shall, somehow, make both ends meet.'

Tota, still holding out, said, 'What is there in our house?'

Naik flew into a rage, 'You, shameless son, an idiot rustic. Take off the ornaments of your wife and put it all here.'

Roni's voice was heard from inside, 'We don't have even rags to wear, ash to smear and cover our bodies, what to speak of taking off ornaments.'

Naik blurted, 'We shall find out everything.' He ordered some of his comrades— 'Go inside and take possession of ornaments. A she-buffalo may also be there, take that also, even oxen should not be spared.'

One of the commands of the Moghul emperors was that neither cattle nor oxen belonging to farmers were to be taken into custody, but this command was respected during the reign of Shahjahan— somewhat also followed in the times of Aurangjeb, but during the reign of his successors, the writ ran on paper only.

During the regime of Mohammedshah, that paper law was in shreds and rotting.

A few in Naik's band entered Mohan's house and made their way to the enclosure through the back door, where there was no buffalo and only oxen were browsing.

A sepoy shouted 'There is no buffalo here'.

Roni cried loudly, 'We never had a buffalo. Did we ever possess a buffalo?'

Mohan gasped, 'If we possessed a buffalo, we would be wanting nothing".

Naik raised his voice outside, 'Hold them and bring outside'.

The sepoys advanced towards them. 'Why do you catch me? I'll come with you just like that'. Mohan said.

Both of them came out. Roni started crying, 'Oh what a misfortune to have been married in a family like this, in which there is no grain to eat nor clothes to wear. To what a damned place have I been thrown in by those childless, wicked fellows. God damn him who has turned me into a worm of the hellish gutter, here.'

Naik replied, 'She is making excuses. Get on with the search; there must be ornaments inside.'

Sepoys entered. Roni came out wailing. Rays of the sun lingered in the sky. Naik observed that Roni wore nothing except some rough, dirty dress, a few glass and bell-metal bangles. Inside there might be ornaments, Naik weighed.

Sepoys came out after the search. No ornaments were found. In an earthen jar, there was about two seer of roasted grain, in another some grain and some unskimmed curd in the earthen milk-pan.

Naik was elated over his discovery. He asked, 'Where did you get curd from? And who gave this unskimmed milk. If you do not possess a buffalo, did it fall from heavens here?

Roni readily answered, 'I asked for some from the village.'

'Ha, Ha'......Naik burst into a loud laugh which made his tummy shake.

His colleagues also laughed.

Mohan looked at each one of them as if to find out a little human touch in any one of them.

Peeping through her veil, Roni also observed all this.

Naik perceived her pretty face, washed with and glistening through tears.

Naik added with all seriousness, 'Don't you know, what powers we have. We can whip off your skin, can tie you to the trees, set your house on fire and to the house-wife......'.

Mohan's eyes flashed with anger. He said, 'Let it be now, Naikji. Take away all the grain and the oxen too. God Ram has endowed us with our arms and legs. We shall make our living elsewhere.'

Naik was aghast but he was not used to losing his authority so easily.

He burst out, 'I can teach you a lesson right now and send you to hell. I thought of leaving some grain for your food but you are so impertinent, that it will serve you too well if your hands and feet are cut off. You think you are the only man to possess a woman. Many well placed men have been brought to dishonour by me. You are a small fry to me. Owner of such a small hut as it is, a handful of grain, a pair of puny and sickly oxen, you like to boast as if you are a 'King.'

Mohan could not help saying, 'I am unlucky in every way".

Naik observed that Mohan was not obstinate. He was becalmed. Roni continued to sob.

Naik said, 'Carts are on way here, three-fourths of the total crop will go to the state enclosure. We are conceding one-fourth for you. When you have done with winnowing, we shall take half as our customary share, and the rest for seeds and your good.'

'Take all', Mohan replied in a choked voice.

'Hm-Hm', Naik's tearing voice was heard.

Roni begged with folded hands, 'My lord, they are very foolish. Forgive them, we shall die of starvation. We have none to look to.'

It appeared that Naik was softened a little.

Mohan turned his eyes upward, which sighted the palace built by Akbar for his mistress who was a 'betel-woman', the upper portion of Salimshahi Gate and 'Birbal Palace'.

Naik commanded, 'Get me some water'.

Roni went inside. The sepoys looked at the roasted gram. 'Do you like to eat some', Naik asked his men. One of them replied, 'Dry gram' — I wish there was some jaggery to go with it.

Roni returned with a pitcher full of water and heard it all.

Putting down the jar, she said, 'We have not seen jaggery for years in this house'.

A sepoy said, 'We are not so greedy as to go for dry gram'.

They gulped water. After a little while, the sun went down and disappeared in the horizon. Two carts were seen coming out of the fortress of Fatehpur and carried away three-fourth of the crop. Mohan's oxen were also taken away alongwith the grain.

Naik went away saying, 'Our customary share — we are still leaving behind. If you try to be clever, I will lash out all flesh from your body and fill it with straw.'

—✻—

4

A little later, the moon rose in the sky. The cool, sweet breeze blowing through the harvested field also bore the fragrance of the flowers, but there was no fire in Mohan's hearth. The unskimmed milk touched by strangers and thereby polluted, was thrown away. Roni had put back roasted gram, flour and the grain where they had been kept earlier.

Mohan could not muster courage to tell her to cook food and Tota was too dazed to speak.

Moonlight was spreading. Breeze was cooler and sweeter. Taking a quick glance at the swinging shoots of corn shimmering through the moonlight, and still-wet green manure of dung, Mohan proposed to Roni sitting in a corner and sighed loudly, 'We cannot do without taking some bread'.

It seemed as if someone had pinched her deeply. Roni sat up and shouted, 'Oh yes, why should you not eat bread? What a big achievement it is for you today.' Long since I had been telling you to reap the harvest and tuck it away after winnowing it, but you paid no heed to it. You lousy, lazy man. I would have jumped into a well and then you would become a murderer but knowing full well that you would enjoy yourself all the more after my passing away, I am content to live longer. You are dying to eat some bread but you are not ashamed of yourself. There they are, shoots of corn devour them all and go abegging thereafter.

Mohan spoke in a low voice, 'Why this outburst of abuse on me? What have I done to you?'

Roni remonstrated, 'Well what have you done. You might as well give these leftovers to them?'

Mohan suppressed his welled-up anger, 'Make some loaves if you wish to. If you don't want to, never mind but don't go on with this chatter.'

'You could not face upto those forefathers of yours and you always remonstrate with me, every now and then'.

Mohan also became bitter, 'My father knew how to strike like a soldier; God knows, how many heads he might have cracked and I can also do the same but — .'

'You can strike your own woman like this and none else'.

'Who will call you a woman—a woman who- ' said Mohan.

And an unworthy son of your father as you are, you are also a coward. You can babble at home only. Outside, you shrink like a mouse before a cat. Your chivalry shows only within the four walls of the house and this enclosure.'

'Unworthy son? Coward? Hm? Well, I won't stay any longer in this house or the enclosure. Home which has such a housewife as you are, cannot house any one like me.'

'I know not how many times I have heard all this but you never stirred out to earn.'

Tota intervened, 'Brother, let it be. Food will be ready in a little while and then we shall see what is to be done.'

'You will break stones? What can you do except striking your chest?'

Mohan raised his voice, 'Enough of it now" and rose from his seat. Roni too was on her feet.

She spoke in a hissing tone, 'Come, Come. Beat me. Kill me. I myself do not want to live any longer.'

Tota stood between them.

Choked with emotion, Mohan replied, 'I am not such a mean creature as to strike a woman but mean as you are, beating is the only answer. Tota, I leave here immediately and may never come back. If I come back, I shall do so as a proud son of my father whom this damned woman has abused. Take care of this household.'

Roni was going to retort but Tota entreated her not to.

'Brother, brother?' Tota called him aloud, but Mohan turned his quick steps towards the hillocks and mounds of Fatehpur Sikri.

The moon rose and shone high in the sky. Wind was laden with cool, sweet fragrance. Mohan briskly trudged on a track. At his back, the tall and ancient palaces of Fatehpur Sikri shimmered and seemed to be mocking in the cool moonlight. Shadows of the massive buildings lingered on the barn, huts, cow-dung cakes and moist rubbish heaps.

Mohan did not look back even once.

He walked in the wilderness. Beetles droned.

Birds fluttered their wings in fear behind thorny thickets. Mohan's worn-out shoes raised the powdery dust of the track, which glimmered a little in the moonlight and again settled down on the ground. Mohan was walking fast but knew not where he was going.

Tota burst into tears after Mohan's departure.

Roni replied, 'Ha....Ha; seems, he won't come back at all. Go and look for the buffalo. We shall hide it again before moving. Loaves will be ready in a little while. Both of you may, then, take your meals. The trouble is that we shall be left with nothing after grinding the corn. What shall we do then?'

Tota cleared his throat and nose and replied, 'Brother told me in the afternoon that he would go away, seek a job somewhere and come back after saving some money from the earnings.'

'...' 'What a tall talk! If he were such a go-getter, the family would not have faced such a ruinous condition.'

Tota gave no reply. Blaming the Naik and his sepoys for the plight of the family, Tota went out to trace the buffalo.

—✻—

5

Tossed between his resolutions and weighing various alternatives, Mohan arrived at Agra, close to the encampment of Saadat Khan, the Meerbaxi of Muhammad Shah, the Emperor of Delhi.

At first his eyes were dazzled to see the grandeur and splendour of the cantonment. He was bewildered to watch the elephants, the horses, the bright, gorgeous equipment and stores, the flags and colourful dresses and the invaluable ornaments worn by the chiefs. He found common soldiers also in good health and enjoying themselves in good clothes. Looking at the cannons and a herd of elephants, he felt a desire welling up within. 'I can also achieve something, once employed in this cantonment', he thought.

His clothes and shoes were torn, his beard and moustache smeared with dust and sweat. He sized up his own situation and muttered, 'Hum' to himself. Overlooking his sorry state in life, he puffed air into his chest and walked up to a bright, colourful tent.

The sentry went up to him. He asked him, 'Who are you? Why are you loitering here? Do you have an eye on some article here?'

Mohan braced himself and answered fearlessly, I came here to get a job. My father was also a sepoy.'

'What is your Caste?'

'Jat, Thakur'.[5]

'Do you possess a horse?'

'No, I don't. Do all the elephants and horses belong to sepoys?'

'Do you know how to ride a horse?'

'I do.'

A middle-aged Mohammedan commander came out. He was wearing gold ornaments. He sized up Mohan from top to toe. Mohan was tall and well-built, but his face was somewhat shrivelled. His eyes fixed between a large forehead and a long nose, looked awe-inspiring. The commander was impressed by his eyes. The commander questioned him;

'What was your occupation till now?'

'Tilling the land and farming'.

'What happened to your farm? Where did you live?'

'In Fatehpur Sikri'.

'What happened to your holding?'

'I was not interested any longer'.

'Well ! I may recruit you in my squadron which forms part of the royal army. You know how to wield a weapon.'

'Yes Sir'.

'What weapons?'

A stick, an axe, a pickaxe, etc'

The chief burst into laughter. Mohan was not overawed but he lowered his eyes.

The chief said, 'Do you know how to wield a gun or a sword?'

Mohan answered, 'I shall be able to learn; it's not so hard to learn. One who knows how to handle a stick or axe can handle all'.

---

5. Jat Thakur – A landowning class among Hindus, inhabiting North India especially Uttar Pradesh, Haryana and Rajasthan.

The chief smiled and added with some surprise, 'How is it that being a Jat, you did not care to train yourself in wielding a gun and sword?'

Mohan said, 'Father died when I was a mere child. I started by grazing others' cattle. We had a small holding of our own. As I grew up, I began to till the land.'

Mohan was enlisted in the army and his pay was fixed at ten rupees a month. He was given uniform and weapons too but had no money to sustain his body.

Having arranged for his lodgings, the chief exhorted, 'Whatever little you get save something for a rainy day. Well! You may get wages every month or once in two months, but it may fall in arrears also.'

This caution did not take away Mohan's fervour arising from the new-found favour.

He threw himself heart and soul into work. He was amazed to see other sepoys relaxing, drawing a pull at hookah, and merrymaking in dance and music. He thought, they must have mastered their work long back. Other sepoys observing his devotion to work adjudged him to be a cynic.

He was culling and collecting every small bit of skill in his work.

His urge to forge ahead of all others spurred him constantly. Even everyday look at grandiose environment, gorgeous clothes and jewelled ornaments did not attract or enthuse him to engross himself into them but he sometimes mused whether he would ever possess enough riches and ornaments. Well then, and then alone, he could raise his head high to face anyone, go anywhere. Where? His imagination did not conjure up images any further.

—*—

6

A few days had passed since the mischievous *jamadar*, the head sepoy and other sepoys had committed excesses, they found more and more clients to fleece- Once again, a *jamadar* and some sepoys had turned up to recover dues. Having received the dues, he said obligingly, 'Well, you had a buffalo which you possess even now. Anyway, we are conceding this to you as a measure of relief.'

Relief was granted to retain the buffalo but they did not possess oxen. Roni was worried, so was Tota. Mohan would come back one day with some money which would fetch the oxen, thought Roni. Tota was sure that Mohan would return quite long after. It might be that he got himself enlisted in some army. What would happen if he was killed in a battle? Tota was not unnerved by this thought. He thought, he would acquire oxen in partnership with someone, 'I would repay it with my labour but how shall we meet our need for grain until the harvest'. Roni did not worry about corn so much. The buffalo was giving enough milk which converted into butter would fetch food-grains.

Tota walked towards the village after milking the cow. Roni readied milk for making curd and went to take care of the buffalo after washing herself. Patting and fondling the buffalo, she hugged her.

The buffalo breathed heavily in long gasps mooing 'Hm-Hm' in response. Roni's face reflected her graceful looks and her lips bore loving smile while her eyes glistened with joy. Clasping the buffalo, she patted her back, moving her hands all over it. She started removing lice from the buffalo which, receiving great relief thereby, mooed loudly. No sooner had she moved away a little than the buffalo turned towards her and bending her horned head, it seemed to call back Roni to pat and fondle her again. Roni burst into laughter. Her teeth glistened like pearls.

'Well, may I hug you again, scrub your back? Look, I would not fondle you too much; otherwise, you will become indolent and frisky. What are you bellowing and begging for? Come, come I'll give you some leftover milk mixed with cold bread. Go and come back home after grazing before dark. Well.. Well!'

It seemed that the buffalo followed Roni's remarks. She started giving a jerk to the string. Roni again clasped her. The buffalo turned her head and began to lick Roni's leg. Roni let her do it for a little while. But when Roni felt her tongue to be a little scrappy, a soft sensation filled her body and she jumped away from the buffalo bursting into giggles. The buffalo again started mooing. Roni's face was lit up with joy. She went in and brought back an earthen pot mixing into it cold bread and whey. Placing it before the buffalo, she began sweeping and collecting fodder. Nearby lay dung-cakes and wet dung-heap. If he was here, he would have asked for his breakfast. She did not allow Mohan's memory to overcome her. But the thought struck her, if he did ask for breakfast, where could she produce it from? She would not let the buffalo starve anyway! Of course, when the flour was ready to be kneaded after grinding, she would have served him breakfast. He would take whey in the meanwhile. What would be left for Tota and me in that case? How hard-working he is! Well, he also toiled and sweated! Ah, he was not so hard-working. How sharp was his tongue! He never addressed me 'Roni', blended with love. He would be loitering here and there! Roni ground the flour, made bread out of it and took it for Tota, who had already left for work. She found nobody, those days, to vent her anger on.

—✻—

7

Saadat Khan was camping near Etawah with his troops, when he received the tidings that a massive Maratha force had attacked and looted Firozabad and Etmadpur near Agra—only eleven miles from Agra! In Saadat Khan's camp, there were fifty thousand troops besides artillery, etc. Saadat Khan rushed and arrived near Jalesar where Maratha force was already camping. Earlier, the Maratha force had clashed with Mughal army, comprising twelve thousand troops. Moghuls had to beat a hasty retreat. Their commander knew that Saadat Khan was moving fast to reinforce his troops. The troops withdrew in the thick of fighting in the direction from which Saadat Khan was coming to join him. Marathas pursued them hotly. One morning, when Maratha troops were preparing themselves to fight the Moghuls, they found themselves confronted with Saadat Khan's fifty thousand soldiers. Marathas were outnumbered. The larger detachment of Maratha forces led by Bajirao was marching in the valleys on the eastern bank of Chambal. Mistaking it to be that massive Maratha army, Saadat attacked it with full vigour.

For some time, Marathas gave them a determined fight but when they found themselves vastly outnumbered and realised that they would be encircled and killed, they were swept off their feet and retreated. Each one of the soldiers was left to his own to retrace path for himself. Pandemonium broke out. Saadat's cavalry gave them a hot chase. Among them, there were quite a few from the platoon to which Mohanlal belonged.

Mohanlal's platoon followed the Marathas up to Etmadpur. On the banks of the river Yamuna, Marathas were further thrown helter-skelter. The same thing happened to the followers who were pursuing them. One Maratha squadron consisting of a thousand troops marched back on the upper bank of the river Yamuna. Fallen apart from his group, only one Maratha horseman had barely advanced to plunge himself in Yamuna, when two Moghul horsemen surrounded him —one of them being Mohan and the other a Mohammedan. The Muslim horseman was a little ahead of Mohan.

The Muslim horseman shot an arrow at the Maratha horseman, which pierced his horse's neck. The horseman fell on the ground alongwith the horse which was then throwing up its legs as it lay dying. Lying under the horse, the Maratha began to moan as if he was about to die of a fatal injury.

Mohan's comrade-in-arms dismounted. Mohan followed suit. Mohan's companion unsheathed his sword. Amidst the vast sprawling expanse of the high banks of Yamuna could be heard the rising sounds of horses' hoofs, gunshots and the screams of the wounded.

Mohan's companion pulled out the Maratha horseman and heaved his sword for a blow.

The companion said, 'Inside the saddle and in the clothes there must be money, ornaments and other booty.'

The Maratha replied as he lay groaning, 'I am wounded. Do not kill me.'

'But you are our enemy.'

'I am a Muslim too.'

'A follower of Marathas, the marauders. How do you call yourself a Muslim.' The sword would have beheaded him but for Mohan's intervention. Mohan foiled his blow by pushing away his friend's arm with his strong wrist.

The friend blurted angrily 'What's this?'

Mohan retorted, 'The wounded can't be killed.'

'Is he your father?'

'My father is no more, but this fellow may not be killed.'

The Moghul sepoy withdrew and changing his position when he was about to strike a blow on Mohan, the latter also unsheathed his sword quickly.

'Ungrateful wretch', Mohan's comrade burst out and brought down the blow. Mohan saved himself. The Moghul sepoy again shifted his position to aim another blow. While he was about to come down on him, Mohan again averted the blow. He had no desire to kill his comrade as far as possible. It occurred'to him that his comrade would come to his senses and the fight would come to an end within moments. Both of them came very close to the Maratha sepoy. The Moghul sepoy was positioned closer to him.

In the twinkling of an eye, the Maratha soldier roared like thunder and his dagger piercing the Moghul sepoy's chest on its side emerged from his intestines. Another split moment and the dagger flashed forth after sawing through the back of shoulder blades and the middle-line. The Moghul sepoy writhed with pain as he fell. Mohan aimed a blow on the Maratha sepoy adding, 'Oh! so you are not injured!'

Jumping back, the Maratha soldier replied, 'I have no enmity with you.'

'But you have killed my comrade. Be prepared now.'

The Maratha soldier sheathed the dagger to his side, 'I shall not strike any blow on you.'

The Moghul sepoy breathed his last.

Mohan became desperate. His grip slipped as he lowered his sword. After a moment's silence, he heaved a sigh.

He said, 'You committed a wrong.'

The Maratha said. 'Did he do something good to me?'

Beyond the shores of Yamuna, the commotion was louder and it seemed as if some men had been encircled.

The Maratha soldier retorted, 'If you wish to kill me, hurry up, then, as I don't want to be taken prisoner by the Moghuls. They will kill, declaring me an infidel.'

Mohan gasped again and replaced the sword into its sheath.

Mohan asked, 'What are you going to do now?'

He replied, 'I shall go back to Poona, my home town, shower my blessings on you and if I get another chance, I would serve again in Peshwa's army.'

The hullabaloo of battle grew louder and came closer.

'I have children to look after! Small ones! I want to go back to them right now.'

'Isn't this pretext of children similar to the trick that you had displayed feigning to be injured? Mohan replied without any smile.

'I had no way out! But God be the witness that I have children.'

The Maratha soldier eyed the dead Moghul soldier's horse which was grazing on the bank of Yamuna.

'All right! Go!' Mohan glanced at his own horse which was also browsing nearby.

Pulling out weapons and articles from the dead body of his horse, the Maratha soldier rushed towards the dead Moghul's horse.

Mohan intervened, 'Don't take him. Go back on foot. This is a horse from our army.'

By now, the Maratha sepoy had reached near the horse and slipped on the same in a sweep. He said, 'There is no other means left to me, by which I can rejoin my family.'

Spurring the horse before taking a plunge in the water, he said, 'My greetings to you! God bless you! My name is Shubrati. If ever we meet again, I shall try to repay this debt.'

He made his horse swim across. It was time of sunset. Mohan mounted his horse and went near the dead Moghul soldier. Never before had he fought in a battle!

He mused, "Should life come to its end like this?'

Slowly he made for the upper reaches of the river. He turned back. He could make out the faint outline of the Maratha soldier, who was making his way across the river. Facing him at some distance, the large army of Saadat Khan marched ahead escorting about one thousand Maratha soldiers by encircling them on all sides. Mohan also joined them.

He announced, 'One of our soldiers is lying dead at the bank of the river. A Maratha soldier has killed him.'

The removal and disposal of corpse was arranged. The Moghul army marched away raising shouts of victory.

—❋—

8

Saadat Khan and his cavalrymen were overjoyed with their victory. They recovered from Maratha forces some booty, a portion of which was sent to the Prime Minister and the rest divided by the nobles among themselves. Soldiers were showered with praise and promises were held out for rewards in future. For each family of those who were killed in battle, a sum of five rupees was set apart.

Saadat Khan called for celebrations. All commanders were invited. Soldiers celebrated the occasion in their platoons.

In Saadat Khan's huge tent, dance and music dominated the occasion. For those fond of drinking, good quality liquor was arranged.

The chief of Mohanlal's platoon also joined the festivities. He had enlisted Mohanlal as one of his select bodyguards. He ordered him to go with him. But it was a big question mark for a soldier of his status as to how he could get into that 'gay-gathering'. The chief was very happy with Mohanlal's loyalty and devotion. Mohanlal was curious to know what constituted a '*mehfil*'. His commander, somehow, managed Mohan's sneaking into that tent.

Sardar cautioned him, 'Watch everything in silence and sit in a corner.' Mohan himself had decided, of his own, to do the same.

It was quite late in the night as its first part was already over. The tent was floodlit with a number of torches which sent up smoke to the roof of the tent. The smoke spread in wavy stretches as it struck the roof. The commanders reclined on huge pillows and bolsters. Mirbaxi Saadat Khan sat on a high pedestal. Sardars had, before them, silvery smoke-pipes with water-base bowl and others, who were drinking had bowl and jugs for pouring wine. On one side there were gorgeously dressed dancing-girls alongwith accompanying musicians. Whispers and undertone voices of Sardars could be made out, but silence tempered with discipline and good manners pervaded the atmosphere.

Instrumentalists had produced the desired symphony from their instruments. The singing girls sat with their jingling anklets.

First of all, a youthful captivating singer was given the chance to start the first singing round. The singer named Noorbai stood up.

The sounding-rod struck the chords of sarangi[5A], the palms played on tabla.[6] The dancers sang a ghazal[7] in Persian.

—❋—

9

From the ruins of Fatehpur Sikri, stones and bricks were being removed and with its mudplaster, a house was being built. The house under construction, which was quite simple and crude, was within the shadowy range of palaces which Akbar had built with great fondness and which had been abandoned by him with equal indifference.

Tota was engaged as a labourer in the construction of this house. The house had nearly come up and only the top of the wall remained incomplete.

In the afternoon, the labourers were granted a break for food. Roni had brought tiffin for him; Tota washed himself and sat for taking food. Among the workers, there were a few women who were also taking meal during the break. Roni began to converse with them.

'The sun is rather scorching, these days; the whole body must be aching due to heat.'

'How to make one's living?'

5A. Sarangi – A loved, short – stringed musical instrument from India.

6. Tabla – Small drum-like instrument generally played as accompaniment with other musical instruments.

7. Ghazal – A lyrical song or poem composed in Urdu or Persian language.

'I agree. Well, it is so; when will this wretched unending work be over? My feet get heated on way.'

'Then why do you come here? Prepare some food early morning and pack it into Tota's belt.'

'There are other pressing things to do in the morning.'

'Finish them afterwards.'

'There is sweeping of cow-dung, and then, there is the buffalo. Don't you have buffalo of your own?'

'If we had milch cattle, you think, we would still come here to work lor wages in this scorching heat.'

'Is your house quite far off?'

'What has it got to do with distance? Wherever one finds work, one has got to go.'

Roni wished to ask many more questions but those women preferred to eat well and then take some rest than answer all her questions.

After the meal, male workers lay under the shade of tree while women workers took rest under another tree. Roni also thought it proper to take a nap under a tree. She wanted to talk but other women wished to keep silent. As they were unable to sleep instantly, they sang a 'rasia'[8] song to invoke sleep; Roni also joined them. Roni's voice was sweet but other women did not have such an endearing voice.

They took amiss Roni's joining their chorus. Hence they pretended to sleep by keeping mum while Roni sang all by herself for a moment. When she observed that her singing had no effect on them, she addressed them: 'Oh! dear, sing a while and then go to sleep thereafter.'

Thereafter you would have run back home and we would go on carrying mudplaster. Will you work on our behalf? Let us sleep.'

'Ha, what work is it?'

---

8. Rasia – A romantic love song sung as chorus to commemorate the romance of Lord Krishna and Radha.

'You get corn in your feet by trudging this distance from your home. How can you carry mudplaster? Go away, don't shout like this?'

'Oh! dear, what women? What a voice have they got?' Women workers got up and sat on their haunches. Their eyes were blood-red. One of them, said 'What we are can be revealed in one go? What a 'Chaudharin'[9] you are!'

'Well, a Chaudharin I am! Unlike you all—wives of cobblers and undertakers, 'Doman.'[10]

Roni's pent-up craving for picking up a quarrel was dammed for a number of days. Finding an outlet, it burst out and Roni, it appeared, gloated in this quarrel. Women workers used to fighting physically, besides engaging in a wordy duel appeared to challenge her.

'You are an impostor to behave like the wife of a big businessman! A Brahman woman's mannerism you have got? Why don't you relax at home? You are starving; this is why, you force the lad to work for wages and now you come here to boast. Run away from here!'

Roni was not to be cowed down like that. 'Barren woman, I shall pull out your tongue if you blurt out any more.'

'Come, let me see how you pull out my tongue?'

The workers got up from the ground. Roni followed suit. The men who were resting beneath the tree also got up. Tota came up running and other labourers... too came there.

'What's the matter? What's the matter?' was the remark made by many persons.

One of the women workers told them: 'Look at her! She asked us to sing filthy, rustic songs. When we refused, she started abusing us. She threatened to pull out our tongue. Come here, now we shall tear up your swinging breast!'

---

9. Chaudharin – An appellation for the wife of farmer, especially of Jat community.
10. Doman – Means wife of a low-caste Hindu, who looks after cremation rites and cremation grounds.

The labourers intervened. Tota tried to persuade her by touching her feet.

Roni went off blurting in a bristling, heated tone, 'I would never come to this murderous place. Even if I come back, I would arm myself with stick and axe to return only after slaying and killing those murderous women.' The labourers shouted aloud, 'You are a murderer yourself and so have been your seven generations preceding you.' The women labourers were about to rush towards her but were stopped by their menfolk. Tota was already begging of Roni to pacify herself. She went away.

The labourers got back to work after sometime. The worker beside Tota started talking with him, 'She is very quarrelsome; this is why, her husband has left his home and hearth.'

'What was her fault? Those women must have said something provocative, which prompted her to put up this fight.'

'Why did she want them to sing rustic, dirty song? They all had broken off singing. She went on singing, God knows what. Just after this, the quarrel arose.'

'I have never heard a dirty song from her.'

'So this is why she had come here to give us a song.'

Tota clenched his teeth and stopped talking.

—❋—

10

Before Saadat Khan could arrive at Mathura, Baji Rao had set out from the valleys of the river Chambal. Both Saadat Khan and Samsuddola were vying with each other in enjoying feasts and dances while Baji Rao rushed close to Delhi after covering 40 miles per day. Then they received the news. Both of them wound up their camp and marched towards Delhi.

They carried with them plenty of heavy luggage and other equipment including the camping equipment for dancing girls, elephants, heavy artillery, countless bolsters and pillows, hookahs, torches, pipe-drums, hookah-bearers, slaves, slave-women, women's quarters. However quick they tried to be, they could hardly hurry up with so many to be escorted? Fifty thousand soldiers accompanying them could, however, gallop away the distance to Delhi and reach there in time, but who was to protect all that equipment after they had gone away? Presuming that Baji Rao was carrying his artillery also, what would cavalrymen achieve all by themselves? On the other hand, if Baji Rao attacked the unguarded equipment, what would befall them?

'What distance would they cover at a breakneck speed?' pondered Mirbaxi and Wajiruddola. They were as much anxious as they could be. They had to stay put at night. After the fighting in the day, sleeping, eating and drinking were as much important.

Hence all this should continue and the fighting too might continue in its own way. It struck both of them that the fort at Delhi had a large number of cannons, twenty-twenty five thousand sepoys, and an unlimited amount of ration —well, their inner voice poked in, 'there were a large number of boats in the river, which would easily carry the Emperor anywhere he liked to go away from Delhi'. But their own fate loomed large before them as their flow of thought was lost and they quickened their pace in order to reach Delhi.

It was discovered one day before departure that a large quantity of supplies had been left behind. There were opium, wine and food articles in them. Tempers ran high. Some horsemen were sent back. The news came that Jats had surrounded the equipment and supplies, and then the carts were on way again. They were delayed by one day.

Saadat Khan told Waziruddola, "What kind of a fellow is this Badan Singh Jat? Since the time Maharaj Jai Singh conferred on him the title of 'Brajraj', 'Jats' mischiefs are on the increase."

Wazir replied, 'He has scant regard for any one except Jai Singh. How fawning and faltering his speech is, as if he is a farm-labourer. I shall take care of him after tackling Marathas.'

When carts carrying opium and supplies, etc., arrived, they thought of advancing. Saadat Khan lost temper on cart-drivers. After abusing Jats, he awarded punishment to drivers, 'If they had driven fast, would there be any delay? Give them a thrashing by whip.'

'We did not delay anyway; instead of cooking and taking food twice, we took only once. Horsemen went ahead of us and robbers surrounded us. We protected the luggage and equipment in spite of receiving a lot of beating and thrashing at their hands. What else could we do?' was the reply of the cart-drivers.

Their reply was not heeded and they were whipped mercilessly. The drivers soliloquised, 'May God bring destruction to the Wazir and the Emperor. They don't give us enough to fill our belly and now our backs are not spared by them.'

—❋—

11

Baji Rao was determined to destroy Delhi completely. Before arriving at Delhi's outskirts, he camped for an overnight respite at some distance from the city. Before retiring to bed, he thought over various matters pertaining to contemporary politics and future plan of action. Still engrossed in thought, he recalled a conversation held years before, in the presence of King of Satara with his representative and minister Shripati Rao.

Shripati Rao had told Baji Rao, 'It was presumptuous and impudent to attack the areas lying north of Malwa. No sooner was the attack mounted than the entire force of Delhi would repulse it. You should, first of all, regain and consolidate the portions of Shivaji's Kingdom lost earlier. In Maharashtra itself, many a nobleman and Jagirdar are indulging in mischief and fight.'

Baji Rao concluded that the reply given by him to Shripati Rao had come true. He recalled his reply, 'Whatever Shivaji the Great had achieved, we should not only follow but should carry forward that tradition. If Shivaji held this view, he would have suppressed Golkunda and Bijapur afterwards and, similarly, would have made inroad into Karnataka later. The noblemen and chiefs of our region would get an opening to make progress, only by coming out of it to lead campaigns. Now the time has arrived when alien rulers should be expelled from the land of Hindus, for which purpose our efforts should be directed towards the regions inhabited by Hindus so that saffron flag of Marathas would start flying from the river Krishna to river Attak.'

Sahu had, then, extended a zealous support to him, 'You will surely hoist that flag on the Himalayas; you are the eldest son of worthy father.'

What Baji Rao had attained so far was a matter of great pride and satisfaction to him. But he mused also on this fact that 'Holkar had sacked Udaipur, while other chiefs plundered various parts of Rajasthan— it was against the interest of all.'

And what would result by reducing Delhi to ashes? How were the flames arising there going to be controlled? Who would do the job? These questions arose in his mind besides the questions of the boundaries of states, beyond the territorial integrity of Maharashtra, called the foreign land, the domination of which was called Mulkgiri, the term fully signifying the expression 'foreign land.'

Many chiefs of Delhi were vying with one another in carving out kingdoms of their own. From beyond the 'Hindustan' through the Khyber Pass came a continuous trail, big or small, of greedy, barbarous marauders and from the oceanic passage swarmed forth the French, the Portugese and the Englishmen, against whom the tortured native population felt itself quite helpless. In face of all that — this determination to destroy Delhi! Would it be a wise and discreet act to set on fire the capital of the Emperor—the Emperor who was to be made a facade to crush the provincial chiefs and other high officials for the attainment of 'Independence' or 'Mulkgiri'.

Baji Rao shook off his torpor. He altered his plan and resolution. 'But what to do now? How to humble the pride and dignity of Delhi chieftains?'

He determined himself on another course of action and set out with his entire army. Apart from light artillery, he carried no heavy equipment.

—※—

12

In the palace at Delhi, festivity prevailed especially in the portion called Rangmahal. Rangmahal was suffused with odours and fragrance. Across the soft woollen carpets, the jingling and clanging of anklet rings mingled with the tapping of Tabla and the patterns formed with henna - hue in elegant, dancing-feet increasingly stirred the smile playing on the lips of Muhamad-shah, also called the Rangeela or the great merrymaker. The pretty damsels touched the brimming wine again and again, poured out of long-necked jugs in the gold goblets with their delicate fingers before they could raise them to the lips of the Emperor. Muhammad Shah was absorbed in listening to sweet jingling sound of anklets of those nubile damsels, tapping of Tabla, endearing clanging of cymbals, the style and movements of dances, sweet symphony and rhythm of song and in the wine poured out from the bejewelled hands of the maids.

That very moment, there was a commotion at the outer gate of the Red Fort. This gave the first jolt to the singing and dancing. Muhammad Shah spoke in his drunken voice, 'What mischief is this?'

The dancers and damsels listened with rapt attention to the tumultuous noise coming from the side of the gates.

The tumult was increasing every moment. 'I am damned—damned! Robbed and condemned! Save us! Give us shelter'!

The Emperor knitted one of his eyebrows in style. He said, 'What a time have these impertinent and illiterate ones chosen for raising full-throated slogans! How much shouting? It is piercing the ear-drums! Silence these unmannerly people.'

The staff bearer went to the gate and came back gasping for breath.

'Your Honour, there at the gate are gathered innumerable subjects of Delhi, some of them are grievously injured as well.'

The Emperor raised his eyebrows again. He said, 'After all, what is the matter? What is the cause of it all? Even though they are injured, yet this is.no disaster. This is a common occurrence now and then on the streets of Delhi. These rustics must have indulged in unmannerly behaviour with some commanders, who must have slapped them. Could these donkeys not come next morning to seek justice?'

The tempo of the tumult went on rising.

'They had big spears.'

'Long, pointed swords!'

'The strong-muscled horses which crushed all.'

'We are being killed! Looted! oh! oh!'

'Elephants were injured!'

'Camels were killed! A few elephants were taken away. Our camels were also taken away.'

The commotion did not subside at all in spite of efforts. The gaiety of the majlis was disturbed by a discordant note. The dancers and damsels became a little sulky and reluctant, the instrumentalists put aside their instruments.

Muhammad Shah flew into temper. He went up to the second storey of the drummer's seat, bowing and swaying himself on the way. One of them was called Meer Hasan Khan Koka. Though an Iranian, he liked to be addressed and accepted as a Pathan.

In those times, the quixotic nature of Pathans, their arrogance, rustic manners, barbarity and boastfulness were acclaimed as chivalry instead of being termed folly. He was good-looking; he had committed some murders on the streets of Delhi. Muhammad Shah had given him the title of 'Khan Jahan Bahadur Kokaltash Jafarjang' having projected in his imagination, the ultimate of manliness in his special qualities.

Meer Hasan Khan shouted at a high pitch.

'Don't make noise. Come out with your complaints, one by one.'

The noise subsided with great difficulty.

One of them shouted, 'We had gone to sell clothes in the fair. We were robbed of everything.'

The other fellow shouted at a louder pitch, 'A wealthy person riding an elephant came to my shop to buy ornaments. He was a Pathan. He was killed and his elephant wounded.'

A vegetable seller screamed, 'We, vegetable vendors have been robbed of our goods. The entire stock of onion was carried away by the marauders. They did not leave behind even one sprout. A hair dresser shouted, 'I was dressing hair, the robbers ran away picking up all my scissors and razors.' Another shouted hoarse, 'They drove away quite a few elephants.'

Then all of them made such an uproar that nothing could be made of their complaints.

The Emperor got it conveyed to them, 'They must be Mewatis. They alone make such small unorganised raids around Delhi. Why did these Delhi men take their valuable wares to Mehrauli and Nizamuddin? Proper arrangements will be made tomorrow.'

Some thought over the matter. Nizamuddin, located at a distance of six to seven miles from Delhi — the capital of Moghul empire — was called an 'abandoned place' by the Emperor! But none could openly decry him. Within moments, the screams and sobs were turned into murmurs and whispers. The Emperor was fretting and fuming over the disturbance created during his merrymaking. He burst into laughter observing their screams and shouts turn into murmurs.

His courtesans joined him too with subdued laughter. Among Delhi-men, those who were standing close to the drummers overheard this comic dialogue. Some of them came forward.

One of them prayed with folded hands, 'Your Imperial Majesty, the supporter of poor people? Baji Rao, the Maratha has arrived with a large army near Kalkaji Temple in Mehrauli. His sepoys have committed this plundering and killing. Mewatis do not carry such long spears and their swords are also not that long and pointed, My Lord, the Protector!'

The Emperor burst into laughter. 'Baji Rao so close to Delhi! In south-west direction, Saadat Khan was already there with thousands of cavalry men and heavy artillery and he has already wiped out Marathas near Etmadpur. In south-west, Ghaziuddin, the son of Nizamulmulk was all set to repulse the attack with twenty thousand cavalrymen and innumerable cannons. A large contingent of Wazir Samsuddola is stationed on the way. Baji Rao has penetrated such large armies and come to Mehrauli near Kalkaji Temple! Just to plunder scissors, razors and onions of these people! All this is incongruous guesswork of these unmannerly people! This is a guesswork of cowards! — formed the train of thought in Muhammad Shah's mind and his imagination run riot made him forget the taking away of camels and elephants.

Pretending to be arrogant, Meer Hasan Khan spoke in a well-mannered style, 'Protector of the World, you have not bestowed upon this humble servant the title of Jafarjung for nothing! If Baji Rao has really entered Mehrauli, his death has drawn him to it. Protector of the Poor, if you command me, I shall produce him here pulling by his ears or should axe him into two pieces or turn him out of Mehrauli.'

Sardar Nijamat Khan, singer, was also standing nearby. His artistic intuition prompted him to think, 'If Baji Rao has really reached Mehrauli, Jafarjung would not be able to achieve any of the three alternative objectives.'

He prayed to the Emperor, 'Jehanpenah',[11] All this sounds discordant — this wailing commotion of Delhi people. May it please Your Honour, someone may be sent to find out as to what's the matter'. Muhammad Shah relished the liberty taken by Meer Hasan Khan for he had listened to the stories of Meer Hamja with great interest, but the remark made by his music teacher and exponent of Khyal's traditional style of music seemed to have greater impact on his mind.

Delhi people were consoled with words 'Don't worry! Whoever has troubled and tortured you will be crushed to the bone. Your losses will be recompensed, after recovery, to the fraction of paisa. Keep patience for the night.' The crowd was turned away from the gate after cajoling, consoling, rebuking and shooing.

Muhammad Shah felt relieved that the unfortunate accidents of the fair were pushed beyond the agonising pale of probing and enquiries at least for some time.

But as soon as he reached the lonely, restful spot called Shah Burj. Meer Hasan Khan spoke to him, 'Jehanpenah, I am itching to give a trial of strength to my swords in the ruins of Mehrauli. May it please Your Honour to command me.' Muhammad Shah again recalled the event in his mind's eye.

He said, 'After all, What was all that? It is possible that Jats and Gujars also can indulge in mischiefs but not so close to Delhi. May be, this trouble has been started by Mewatis.[12] But what will these damned fellows do with elephants? Why should

11. Jehanpenah – A form of salutation addressed to the Emperor — denotes that Emperor is the shelter-giver to the whole world.

12. Mewatis – An ethnic sub-group of Muslims living in parts of Haryana and Rajasthan states of India.

they have named Baji Rao? Meer Bakshi had sent word that Baji Rao's army had been wiped out.'

Niyamat Khan, the singer prayed 'Jehanpenah! There is something black at the bottom somewhere. Your Grace may be pleased to order an enquiry.'

Muhammedshah replied quickly, 'This is what I am also thinking.'

Meer Hasan again entreated to be allowed to show his valour with his sword but it was decided to allow him to do so only after the completion of enquiry.

By mid-day next day, no further news came from Mehrauli, although it was hardly seven-eight miles from Delhi. The spy took his own time to consider the pros and cons and to get ready. He could leave Mehrauli only in the afternoon and was able to return about mid-night.

The Emperor had not gone to bed yet. His orders were that the spy should be produced before him as soon as he returned — it gave a little more fillip and time to singing and dancing.

He had a definite doubt that there was something wrong and disturbing somewhere. The mischief monger was proving superior to the mischiefs of Mewatis. Could Mewatis indulge in the loots of elephants and camels? But Saadat Khan's epistle was a proof that this plunderer could not be Baji Rao himself.

The spy had gone to Mehrauli disguised as a beggar. He produced from his bag and placed before the Emperor the roasted gram and the half-crushed red chillies.

The spy submitted in a well-mannered tone — 'Jehanpenah! I have collected this alm from the cantonment of Marathas.'

Muhammad Shah was bewildered. His forehead was perspiring and his intoxication was overcome.

He could not help saying, 'These dammed ruffians are used to munching dry gram and chillies!' He became silent.

Meer Hasan made bold and said, 'My Lord, these semi-clad, starving ones will be blown to pieces which will be carried with the air and scattered all over.'

Muhammad Shah was tongue-tied.

The spy had to continue his speech: 'Jehanpenah, an attack will be mounted on the city tomorrow morning. They are fully prepared today, their commander is Baji Rao himself.'

The Emperor's voice opened up. 'Marathas have come! Baji Rao too has come! It is unbelievable! Saadat Khan had completely destroyed them at Etmadpur. How have they appeared from the airy nothing? How could they make it to this place? Where is Mir Bakshi, left behind'?

Meer Hasan was one of those men who mistake their self-praise and boasting indulged in by them, long before the trouble had come down on them, as their sole strength.

He said, 'Jehanpenah, they may be Marathas or others, your sovereign power, My lord, has so much impact that your humble servant, as I'm, can humble them to dust with a handful of men under my command.'

Niyamat Khan, the singer said in his sonorous and sweet voice, 'Oh', Protector of the people, they are Marathas themselves. Mewatis cannot mount an attack on the strength of dry-gram and red chillies nor can they take away elephants and camels.'

On being contradicted thus, Meer Hasan raised his eyebrows a little with slight movement of lips and drawn-in nose but he could content himself with a little murmur without adding anything more. He knew very well that Niyamat Khan was a superior confidante of the Emperor.

The spy further submitted, 'Your Honour, the Protector, nobody can sneak into Delhi from that side. Hence no news can trickle. Only in the guise of a beggar, I could get across somehow and get back too. What I have given is absolute truth. Their Commanders indulged themselves in loose, unmannerly talk. The sepoys followed suit.'

'What did they say?' Muhammedshah asked curiously as if he was listening to some kind of a story.

He replied, 'They conversed about plundering and burning of Delhi. They are very wicked and mean, Your Honour.'

'Yes', said Muhammad Shah and lost himself in thought.

The spy thought that the Emperor was keenly interested in listening. He added, Jehanpenah, one of their noblemen was feeding his own horse while another was brushing his horses; yet another was bathing his horse. Some sauntered freely, their pyzamas tucked up or with only a Dhoti worn on their body.

Muhammad Shah shouted, 'God damn them! They were feeding and brushing their horses and they call themselves Sardars. If Meer Hamza was here, he would have finished them in a flash. Farmers and vagabonds have become sepoys and the heads of coolies and labourers their commanders.'

'Dash it. Meer Hasan, my head is giddy and I am going to have sleepless nights. What is to be done now?'

Hasan burst out enthusiastically, 'Your Grace, the Protector, I can see through now. Some escapees from the royal forces have turned up this side. They will all be disposed off by tomorrow morning.'

Muhammad Shah replied listlessly, 'Well, you are there to display your valour. Warn other chiefs as well. May be, the Mewatis would also join the Marathas. Call the Sardars and caution them here and now. What would be the strength of Marathas?'

At long last, this wise question was asked. The spy informed, "The Marathas' number runs into thousands."

'In thousands', Muhammad Shah expressed his surprise as wisdom dawned upon him.

The spy was asked to sit at one side and Sardars were sent for.

Muhammad Shah felt relieved having sent for the chiefs. He addressed all those present in his audience, 'Until the time,

Sardars assemble here, let us have some story about Heer Ranjah[13] or Alif Laila.[14] If some one remembers the stories from Sua-Bahattari[15] or Betal Pachisi,[16] I would like to listen to one cr two as I cannot get sleep now. If discussions with Sardars come to an end in time, I would hear morning recital in Ragini style of music.

Except Meer Hasan, everyone was shivering within but stories were related for the entertainment of the Emperor. The storyteller eagerly awaited the arrival of the Sardars so that arrangement for self-defence might be ensured. Muhammad Shah had a hobby for listening to legends and stories. He used to make up for his lack of qualities of manhood by listening to the stories containing improbable valour of Alif Laila, Heer Ranja, Hatimtai[16A], etc. He heard the war stories of Mahabharat too, not for inculcating any teaching or moral in himself but for the sake of going through the feeling of lack of qualities turned into a fulfilled experience which he considered an entertainment in itself. No sooner did he feel tired of stories, he sought diversion in dance and music.

---

13. Heer Ranjha – A popular love story or folk origin, from the state of Punjab, it portrays the passionate love affair of Heer-a Punjabi damsel and Ranjha, her lover, who did not hesitate in offering any sacrifice for his lady-love.
14. Alif Laila – This is a collection of one thousand romantic stories initially written in Arabic (authorship not known) and later translated into English under the title, The Arabian Nights' Entertainment. These stories of love, separation, adventure, travels, intrigues, magic and romance have a variety and charm of their own.
15. Sua-Bahattari – A collection of seventy-two stories narrated by a parrot to its companion Myna, these ancient folk stories of love, fidelity and infidelity were originally published in Sanskrit under the title 'Shuka Saptati'. They were later translated in other Indian languages also as 'Kissa Tota Myna'.
16. Betal Pachisi – A collection of twenty-five stories described as having been told by a ghost-spirit to the legendary king VIKRAMADITYA. These stories of ancient Sanskrit origin are available in many Indian languages.

16A. Story of a prince Hatim who embarks on a journey to seek answers to seven questions and after finding answers to all he will be able to set free a woman and a fairy from curse.

The stories were barely over when quite a few Sardars and title-holders arrived there. Some were bewildered, while others tried to dissimulate sober appearance despite their quaking fears. The Emperor had just finished listening to the heroic deeds of gods and valiant men who were vaguely recorded in the misty pages of history.

After hearing the spy, the Emperor was heard telling Sardars, 'I would like to face the enemy forces from the front ranks of the battle line.'

All those present were filled with a thrill of joy. The Emperor was eulogised with showers of improbable glory and fame, all of which was hypocritical. Words of counsel were passed on and exchanged. Discussion and arguments were held.

The Sardar heading the artillery called Meer Atish said, 'My Lord, the Protector of All, will come out to give a fight to these wretched soldiers recruited from among the labourers and farmers! This humble creature had accompanied Nizamulmulk in various battles and is fully conversant as to how to overcome these Marathas.'

Meer Hasan did not relish his arrogant boast but his own belief that Maratha army was a mere hullabaloo of farmers and labourers who, after the battle, improvised their swords and spears into ploughs, sickle and hammer was confirmed.

After a short while, the blood-curdling, spirited bravado of the Emperor cooled down. Resolutions, suggestions and prayers were offered mutually with great gusto and candour in the course of stormy discussions.

Big-sized cannons should be fixed at the strategic position near Mehrauli and Marathas should be beaten hollow to make them flee the battlefield.

'But it would take at least three days to lay the strategic stronghold.'

'The heavy cannons loaded on camel should be despatched to the back of Mehrauli alongside of Tughlaquabad.'

'Marathas in thousands must be like swarms of locust, which would be floored across the ground by the artillery fire.'

'I wish we would have the actual count —that would straighten every thing.'

'It is no use! Cannon fire is not to be fed with figures and numbers.'

'Muhammad Shah wished to evade being informed of the exact number. Besides, the spy could not have given the exact figures.'

Home side strength was being assessed now.

'In Delhi itself, there are, amidst us, twelve thousand fully equipped cavalrymen and twenty thousand strong infantry besides plenty of cannons, both large and small. Under the cover of artillery fire, if both the cavalry and the infantry advance, not one among the Marathas would be able to escape.'

And if they crossed Yamuna to mount attack on the fort, what would be the outcome because Maratha Sowars even after withdrawing 30-40 miles, return to launch an attack?'

'Suppose, we may attack them tonight.'

'If they are aware, they would bypass us to force an entry into the city before dawn in order to ransack it.'

Shutting ourselves within the four walls, we must fight with cannons. The forces sent to Doab[17] are about to return and in this way, the Marathas will be surrounded and given a thorough thrashing.'

'It is no manliness to fight from within the fort.'

'May be, Marathas would have come there after defeating Doab forces.'

'My God! Under these circumstances, the Emperor alongwith the paraphernalia may have to be sent away in boats to Agra or elsewhere; otherwise, we may be forced to accept the terms of treaty set by Marathas.'

17. Doab – The area alongside the banks of the sacred rivers, Ganga and Yamuna; literally two waters.

'Impossible! The royal force is very large but with all the heavy equipment, their arrival has been delayed.'

'We must find out the whereabouts of Doab forces and likely time of their arrival.'

'But Marathas are about to set upon us at dawn.'

Muhammad Shah got a shock. He said, 'There is none amidst us like Meer Hamza; otherwise, Marathas would be wiped out in no time.'

After a little pause, one of the Commanders said, 'Trenches may be got dug on the outskirts of the city. Men bearing guns and small cannons may be deployed therein. At one side of the trenches, cavalrymen may lead in the forefront, followed by camel-laden artillery and infantry. Both planning and strategy may be used. To provide support to all forces, there are cannons on the parapet of the fort. This stratagem is feasible and can be accomplished easily.'

At least, this counsel prevailed. But it was unpalatable to Meer Hasan.

Among the bodyguards of the Emperor, there were two squadrons of Rajputs having strength of 750 sepoys. They were bent upon fighting in the front ranks. Three thousand artillery men and a thousand riflemen were left behind to take charge of the defence of the fort and security of the Emperor. In the event of facing defeat at the hands of Marathas who would then enter the city, boats were arranged 15-20 miles upstream and downstream in Yamuna to enable the Emperor escape alongwith the ladies of the harem. The royal eunuchs were despatched to the houses of the nobles and chiefs, to give them advance warning. The palace-guards became alert.

Next day and the following night were spent in preparing for the fight. A message was sent to Baji Rao, according to protocol, extending invitation to Marathas to send an emissary. Baji Rao declined the invitation politely. He wrote, 'I am apprehensive that my army may create trouble in Delhi city! Hence I am withdrawing a little.'

Baji Rao got a strategic reconnaissance carried out in the neighbouring region and himself surveyed it.

Before the next morning, the Emperor's army was fully prepared. Trenches were dug in vast stretches and cannons were placed in them. Behind the cannons were riflemen, backed up by cavalrymen.

But the Marathas were not to be fooled as to come gallopping in swarms to face the cannons.

Meer Hasan Khan alongwith several others of his group were detailed to guard the palace. He was in charge of a band of gorgeously clad troops. He was quite impatient to fight, so were his comrades.

Meer Hasan Khan told one of his friends, 'My friend, have we joined the profession of a sepoy only to vegetate in the palaces here?'

The reply came, 'What to do! His Lordship, has confined himself within the palace and he has interned us as well.'

Hasan Khan said, 'The Emperor is a coward. He has hidden himself like a coward, but we are, after all, sepoys. The quality of a weapon is to provide its striking power in a fight. That is a useless weapon which lies sheathed.'

'I am itching to fight.'

'I am itching since before you felt it.'

'Let's accomplish something.'

'Yes, let us go! The old, fatigued Sardars must know that there are still some men of extraordinary courage and valour left in the royal camp.'

Some Sardars were also restless to display their valiant spirit and agreed with Meer Hasan.

All of them wearing necklaces of pearls and jewels, their horses having saddles over-laid with golden threads and their muslin embroidered clothes rivalling the rays of the morning sun, set out from the portals of the fort.

The commander of the forces outside the fort tried to discipline them but Hasan Khan and his comrades were riding high, as if under some charm, on the crest of their adventurous ardour, and were almost crazy to display their bravery. Some Sardars of the outside forces also joined Hasan Khan's troops. The valiant mettle in them was also stirring from within. They defied the command of their general.

Hasan Khan's force swelled to the strength of eight hundred horse-men—all of them riding excellent horses with saddle embroidered in gold and silver. They carried new and top class weapons. The whole spectacle gave the impression that the Emperor was leading a wedding party for matrimony.

The commander of the outside force tried to persuade Hasan Khan, who was not amenable. He murmured within himself some condemning remarks for Hasan Khan and returned to his own place.

Hasan Khan's comrades gossipped among themselves 'He is quite a cowering person.'

'He himself is rotting in the trenches and wants us to follow suit.'

'He would send word to the Emperor in a bid to get orders from him for our recall. Let us go, run ahead and come back with flying colours of the victory.'

'Launch the attack.'

'Not one among the enemy should escape.' Similar voices mingled together.

Hasan Khan and his eight thousand comrades swarmed and stormed towards Baji Rao's encampment.

The sun was ascendant in the firmament. Through the dust raised by the muscled horses galloping in style and their gorgeously dressed riders, the sunrays shone like scintillating flickers of lightning.

From a watch tower, the Emperor espied those rising tempestuous swarms of horse-riders and instantly forgave Hasan Khan and his men for deserting the palace in such a way.

He told one of his courtesans, 'What a fine youngman is Hasan Khan! I wished I was leading them all to give Baji Rao's mean, wicked fellows a good lesson.'

The courtesan politely contradicted, 'Jehanpanah! Your Lordship may only give a signal and innumerable Hasan Khans would come out to lay down their lives.'

Muhammad Shah swallowed this flattering remark. He said, 'Yes! It is so. It is just like that.'

—*—

13

Baji Rao was on a horseback behind a camofiauge in his camp. His beloved Mastani was riding another horse with her feet in the stirrups, apparently ready to run. She was a Muslim. She loved Baji Rao bodily and wholeheartedly, Baji Rao drew inspiration from her beautiful looks, romantic love and physique. She was also armed like a Maratha soldier. At a little distance, the other Sardars on their horseback were all set for battle.

All of them watched the all round glare of Hasan Khan's troops. They noticed, first of all, the dust raised behind them. Having watchful eyes like those of an eagle, Baji Rao assessed the situation, craned back his neck and told his Sardars, 'At long last, they have come out of their nests. They must be having very good horses, new and improved weapons and the equipment in excellent condition.'

Baji Rao fixed his eyes, for a few more moments, on the spectacle. 'The way these people are spurring their horses shows them to be quite novice.'

With a firm voice, he commanded 'Make an advance movement with a handful of horsemen and trap them by feigning a withdrawing movement. We must snatch away their horses, weapons and if possible, their jewellery too.'

Mastani with a smile on her lips intervened, 'This is quite possible.'

Sardars followed every thing. They rushed to face Hasan Khan with two thousand men. They did not face them directly. Instead, they bypassed the royal forces by taking serpentine turns, evading them altogether. Hasan Khan's squadron guessed that they had run away out of sheer terror.

His squadron chased the Marathas in a great speed. The royal squadron was cut off and separated from its main supporting force and the trenches. Their speed was so terrific that it was impossible for them to fire guns or shoot arrows. Even if they shot, they could not have aimed properly. But Hasan Khan and his men were convinced that the fleeing forces ahead of them would stop somewhere.

When they had covered about two miles, Maratha forces turned round and came down on them.

When long spears and flat swords were brandished, Hasan Khan's squadron came to know that Marathas had fled under a well thought-out ruse and strategy.

Well-versed and seasoned in the art of war, Marathas wounded about a thousand Moghul soldiers and killed at least six hundred of them.

Those, among them, who were saved bore the marks of battle throughout their lives. About a thousand horses and their equipment fell into the hands of Marathas. An elephant also was caught. Very few among Maratha sepoys were killed and only one officer sustained injuries. About six thousand Moghul cavalrymen took to their heels to save their lives.

Meer Hasan Khan also fled for life but a Maratha was galloping faster than him. He struck a blow on Meer Hasan's coat of arms and steel-shield. Hasan Khan fell from the horse. Maratha Sardar deprived him of his clothes and plumes of the turbans, etc. He robbed him of his weapons too and left him groaning on the ground. He took away Hasan Khan's horse too.

'May be, some one who turned up this time, would kill him,' he thought, and started counting the last moments. At that very moment, one of his injured comrades came by.

The comrade fearfully said, 'What? Is't Khan Jahan Bahadur!'

Hasan Khan opened his eyes without fear but not without embarrassment. He said, 'Keep shut! Khan Jahan Bahadur is condemned to hell.'

The comrade was anxious to know all about his well-being, 'How are you, Muzzafarjang?'

Hasan again flew into rage and said, 'Spare me these kind words' and glanced here and there. He desired him not to identify him by recalling all his titles.

'Muzzafarjang' his comrade addressed him with anguish.

'All Muzzaffarjangs have been consigned to fire. Go away from here, good man. If some Maratha were to hear all my titles, I would have to pay heavily. Otherwise, may be, I shall be saved.'

The comrade knelt a little and said, 'I wish I would carry you somehow from here, but with a seriously injured hand, I am feeling helpless.'

Hasan Khan was stripped of clothes and left to lie there. If the Maratha rider had come to know that he was Sardar, his fears would have overwhelmed him. He would not be able to kill him; instead, he would have been forced to pay the penalty.

Marathas had withdrawn. Hasan was carried away by his comrades.

Marathas stripped every one from among Hasan Khan's squadron, who fell into their hands and let them lie there. All of them almost naked and in tears went back to city. Cots were brought for the dead and seriously wounded, from Paharganj; when the dead and the wounded were brought back to city, pandemonium broke.

—❋—

14

The entire booty consisting of horses, clothes, equipment, ornaments and weapons was produced before Baji Rao who sent the arms and weapons to the armoury. Shares of clothes and ornaments were given to those who had brought them and the rest deposited in the stores. An inventory clerk made out the list.

Mastani said, amidst laughter, to Baji Rao, 'If these men continue to come fighting on horseback with such clothes and ornaments on, our sepoys would be well rewarded and the treasury would never be empty.'

Baji Rao was enthused-'Of course.' He was not, at that time conscious of his ambition to hoist the saffron flag on Himalayas. He said, 'If our sepoys were well rewarded like this, they would feel encouraged by leaps and bounds.'

Mastani smiled and looking towards Delhi, she said, 'There is immeasurable stock of gold, silver and jewellery in Delhi.'

'The day would certainly come', said Baji Rao supporting the emotional outburst of Mastani. Even as he said this, he recalled his own words uttered before Sahu years before, which dimmed his ardour.

He exclaimed, 'We can't do without heavy artillery power.'

Mastani replied, 'The discipline and decorum of Sardars are more essential.'

This infused equanimity in Baji Rao's mind. He said, 'Indeed, this is the biggest problem, Kanchan. If the Sardars were given small jagirs in Maharashtra, they would be disciplined.'

Mastani wanted to contradict him but a messenger came rushing in on horseback. The messenger informed him, 'The royal forces are coming down on us from two sides.'

Mastani said, 'In the north, our permanent enemy is the red fort. What would be the total strength of the forces of both sides?' He replied, 'Not less than sixty thousand.'

Baji Rao asked, 'What kind of cannons are there?'

He said, 'Large, small and middle sized, all put together will number three thousand. And we have got a much less number.'

Baji Rao said, 'Cannons will have to be met with cannons or we may select an uneven strategic position.'

Mastani gave expression to her determination by suggesting, 'Let us set out immediately.'

Baji Rao commanded them to depart. The tents were dismantled. Stores and equipment were properly stacked and stocked. Thereafter, Sardars took the roll call of the sepoys in their platoons and the whole cantonment was on the move again.

After covering about 20 miles, they ran into the vanguard of royal army. The heavy royal cannons were far behind. Dusk was four hours away. The vanguard of the royal army beat the drums. Baji Rao's army blew the trumpet aloud as if the fighting was about to follow soon.

But Baji Rao was neither eager nor anxious to fight. Even so, a small battle ensued.

Baji Rao changed the tactics of his forces. The vanguard of the royal army also made frantic effort to change the strategy.

A little before sunset, fighting broke out. It was clear that both sides just wanted to carry on the fight till sunset. Then all would have rest at night. The commander of the royal forces decided that he would plan out the strategy at night and fighting would follow next morning; the heavy cannons would arrive at night itself and would be fixed in strategic positions.

Whatever little fight ensued was marked by the change in tactics. The commander of vanguard force assessed that Baji Rao wanted to withdraw his forces without a fight. The commander wanted to pin them down for a fight and planned to encircle the Maratha force from behind. Baji Rao wanted to undo this ruse. He ordered his camel artillery to be in fore-front and fought with the help of rear squadron.

The sun was about to set. Besides, firing in the air shells were fired from guns and small cannons followed by shooting of arrows.

One wing of Baji Rao's forces fought fiercely with the royal squadron.

The Marathas eyed intently one of the riders of the royal force. He was brandishing his sword a little ahead of others. Arrows were showered on him but they all missed him. One Maratha rider rushed towards him with the spear aimed at him. The royal rider evaded him completely. The Maratha rider struck him with a thrust of his spear. The royal rider could not dodge him this time. The spear struck him on the forehead penetrating below his armour at the shoulder. The forehead was covered with turban and a steel headgear. The spear sent turban and headgear flying to the ground. The rider fell on the ground with a jerk and the horse bolted. The blood oozed out from the temple of the royal horse-rider. He became unconscious because of shock. Maratha horse-rider raised the spear aiming at his chest but his arm became motionless as he saw clearly his face. The other riders among Marathas were engaged with the other platoon of the royal force.

The Maratha rider dismounted. He held the reins with one hand and drew his sword after fixing his spear on the ground. He watched the royal rider more closely. He took him on his horse and mounting his horse swiftly, lie got lost in the midst of his squadron.

In this stray fight about thirty men of both sides were killed and wounded when the darkness set in.

The royal vanguard withdrew a little in order to have a swift and intense fight. Baji Rao proceeded towards Ajmer by taking to south-west direction with all the equipment and the wounded. By dawn, the two large flanks of the royal force arrived on the spot alongwith the cannons. But Baji Rao had already covered ninety three miles by that time. A little after sunrise, they had some rest. The royal rider had regained consciousness by then. The royal winner rider was bandaging his wound and a breakfast consisting of onion, roasted grain and half crushed chillies was placed before him.

One of the Maratha comrades asked him, 'How is he related to you, so that you are looking after him so much even at night?'

'My brother!'

'Brother! How come that he is your brother?"

'A brother to me, he is! If sons could be adopted, why not brother also'.

'Is he a Nawab[18] of some place?'

'No, he is not. He is a king!'

'A Raja! Why did not you present him before his Srimant, the chief of Marathas. We would get a lot of money by doing this?'

The wounded soldier replied, 'I am not a Raja —a mere farmer and a soldier, I am!' His nurse burst into laughter.'Hc was a former acquaintance, this is why he was saved,' uttered the other soldier who plunged himself in work.

'Could you swallow these onions and chillies? All this constitutes our breakfast, mid-day meal and dinner too,' asked the Maratha affectionately. Grateful as he was, the wounded replied. 'Why not? When I left my house, I did not possess even this much.'

Are you homesick now?'

'Oh, no.'

'Do you recognise me?'

'I could never forget brother Shubrati and I shall never fail to remember him in future too.'

—✻—

15

Baji Rao's galloping march continued throughout the whole day and he halted at Narnaul only as the evening drew closer. After a night's rest, he set out again and reached Ajmer.

18. Nawab – A Muslim chieftain or a ruler of a smal! Indian state in pre-independent India.

Next morning when Mughal forces in full fury trumpeted their way to mount an assault, there was none to face them. Nizamulmulk was at the head of one wing of the army. Mughal army arrived at Delhi with a great fanfare. There they had passed the night without dances and jingling of cymbals. Baji Rao had run away after fighting only a little. 'Gone with the wind' was the amusing publicity made by Nizamulmulk.

Delhi palaces and streets witnessed immense gaiety and merry-making by this easy avoidance of Maratha mischief.

Baji Rao's camp at Ajmer was short-lived. Baji Rao received the news of the arrest of royal messenger and summoned both the messenger and the one who had taken him into custody. Baji Rao questioned his own soldier:

'Do you know this man?'

'Yes, Your Honour!' answered the soldier.

'Since when? Wherefore? Who is he?'

'My Lord, he is a Hindu, I know him since the close of the battle at Etmadpur.' He nodded and asked, 'How come? How did you come to know him?'

'He had saved my life at the risk of his own.'

Baji Rao was astonished.

He asked the prisoner, 'Who are you?'

He replied, 'I am a Jat.'

Baji Rao said, 'You might be familiar with Shubrati.'

He replied, 'I did not know him earlier, I come from Fatehpur Sikri.'

Baji Rao asked, 'Your name.'

He said, 'Mohanlal'

'What is the family occupation?'

'Land cultivation.'

'Why did you save the life of Shubrati?'

Mohanlal faltered, 'Because one of our horsemen wanted to kill him thinking that he was injured.'

Baji Rao eyed him so as to know more details. He narrated the whole story.

Baji Rao was pleased and added, 'Your wound was small, and has healed by now. If you wish to go home, you may. I won't keep you in custody any longer. You may join my army if you wish to.'

Mohanlal, with his eyes on the ground, pondered. Baji Rao avidly remarked, 'By joining army, you may become a Naik some day by good conduct. Our soldiers also share the booty looted from the enemy.'

Mohanlal's curiosity was aroused for a moment. He thought, 'Who were their foes and friends? Whether *jamadar* the head servant who had taken away his oxen—was not their enemy too?'

He had neither friends nor foes in the ranks of royal army. He looked upon the commander of his platoon with awe and respect, but did not know why and on whose behalf he was fighting. In his mind's eye, he saw the Emperor's life as full of drinking, dancing, merry-making and extortion of farmers. Among Maratha forces, he had a friend who had saved his life. He liked better the good humour and outspokenness of Baji Rao as compared to Saadat.

Baji Rao said, 'Be quick, reply. If you want to remain in my army close to your village, you may, since we are going to Gwalior now, or you may join one of my platoons there, or one here nearby.'

Mohanlal replied, 'I wish to serve you, Your Honour.' Mohanlal was enlisted in Shubrati's platoon. Winding up his Ajmer encampment, Baji Rao set out for Gwalior. He did not halt at Gwalior as he had to plan his campaign against Malwa.

Baji Rao had acquired, in lieu of his raids on behalf of Delhi, the deputy governorship of Malwa, which was virtually a sovereign power. Rendering assistance to Delhi, establishment of independent chiefship in the garb of governorship, inciting revolt — all was accomplished in the name of the Emperor. Nizam's ambition was to carve a big kingdom in the Deccan and to gain Malwa in the bargain in the name of governorship. But due to political intrigues of Delhi, Sawai Jai Singh, Raja of Jaipur was appointed

Governor of Malwa for namesake and Baji Rao, the Deputy Governor as a recompense for an old, good deed so that Nizam's ambitions were hedged into shorter limits as Marathas would continue to keep him on leash and under control from both sides. Nizam's ambition was growing in the name of the Emperor. Baji Rao's Malwa campaign was also materialising in the name of the Emperor even after his raids and looting spree of Delhi.

But Baji Rao had to give up his Malwa campaign. Nizam had started off from Delhi with a massive army and heavy cannons which had no match in the whole of India.

Baji Rao made up his mind to reach Maharashtra well before rains. Mohanlal too joined his platoon in this march. Baji Rao returned home with his army and acquisitions.

Long before this, around 1716 AD, when Saiyyad brothers — Hasan Khan and Hussain Khan were busy plotting for the overthrow of the Emperor Farukhsiyar, they had sought the assistance of Marathas and it was a mere coincidence that Marathas' thrust in north India became an inevitable part of their strategy and Raja Sahu had nominated Baji Rao's father, Balaji Rao as the commander of Maratha forces. Marathas, in return, gained the right of recovering revenue, share in crops, and sardeshmukhi,[19] etc., in the provinces of Deccan.[20]

Nizam turned up at Bhopal after making his way through Kalpi, Dhamoni and Sironj. Many a Rajput king also reached there to assist Nizam. They were the ones who had been victims of Marathas' vandalism in the recent past.

—✵—

19. Sardeshmukhi – Shivaji, the great Maratha overlord of 17th century realised this tax amounting to one-tenth of the total revenue of the neighbouring states over and above one-fourth of the revenue paid to Moghul government.

20. Deccan – The entire South India.

16

After two months, the news came floating somehow that Mohanlal was killed in the battle between royal and Maratha forces near Delhi, and even his mortal remains could not be located and recovered. From the royal army treasury, a sum of rupees five was despatched for the family of Mohanlal but shared, as it was enroute by cashier, treasurer and revenue officer of Agra division, it never reached the family. Although it was a small sum, such small sums made up a sizeable amount for sharing; otherwise, how could officers lead their life in a grand style—full of wine, roasted meat, dancing girls, gorgeous clothes and ornaments.

Mohan's household did finally receive the message. Customary death-rites were gone through. Some quantity of foodgrains was required for Brahmins to be fed and also for charity.

But the household had just enough quantity to see it through only for a few days. Tota had earned some wages which were kept away in a corner hole for a rainy day. The family possessed a buffalo which yielded curd to make their meals juicy and butter for sale to get some cash. A pair of oxen was an absolute necessity. They could manage one harvest by borrowing and sharing with others, the oxen for plough but this could not go on for long.

Tota had none else to assist him in farming. He burst into tears all too often. Roni also cried but it was largely in visualising her widowhood. Roni wished she had someone to console and cajole her but she apprehended some new trouble with Tota's pitiable condition.

She said, 'The dead will not come back by crying. Get to work and think of things ahead.'

He said, 'My arm has cracked already. If I knew he would not come back, I would not let him go.'

Roni was depressed with the thought that she had given Mohan the cause to "leave his home and hearth."

She said, 'How can we feed Brahmins? We did not have enough for charity and rites at the death of my father. Then the villagers had postponed the whole thing for next year?'

He made bold to ask, 'Did the villagers give charity then?'

Roni replied, 'Yes, they did give some things. We'll have to do the same. What shall we save after feasting Brahmins, besides giving charity.'

Tota did not like this suggestion but finding himself helpless to defy her, he submitted to it. The villagers of their class also did not relish the idea. They thought that at least the buffalo could be sold off to gain godly benediction so that the dead would rest in peace in heavenly abode. Roni did not yield.

She told Tota, 'The villagers are jealous of us. They are against our possessing a buffalo. God damn them, their chests may be roasted. They want us to turn beggars.'

Tota had to eke out his life as a farmer with the help of the same villagers. Roni knew it full well and therefore, controlled her tempers.

Tota thought that people of his clan knew Roni already and would not blame him.

The revenue officer arrived in the village on his usual tour. His duties included measurement of land, fallow land brought under cultivation and updating of record but in practice, he came to realise the advance of his share in the crop, from the farmers. He carried a list of outstanding dues and a list of fifty forms of levies. No farmer could ever pay full land revenue and levies. Thus the revenue officers could continue to realise their customary share. Mohanlal's name also figured in the revenue officer's list and the heavy levies outstanding in his name could not be repaid even by ten cultivators.

With a view to please Qanungo the revenue inspector rather than out of any jealousy, some helpless fellows suggested to him the way out to recover dues from Roni by forfeiting her buffalo.

The officer pondered, 'I should recover my customary share and if the buffalo is giving enough milk, it will remain at my home.'

One of the debtor-cultivators who was trying to please Qanungo told him, 'The buffalo is quite wet and Roni has plenty of foodgrains also.'

Another person said, 'Mohan is dead, so the expenses of the family must have been reduced.'

Qanungo already knew about the death of Mohanlal but he did not allow the picture of dead person or animal to flash in his mind's eye.

Mohanlal's name had to be struck off from the record and Roni's entered in his place —this work too called for his rightful share. The same farmer informed, 'Roni had performed the thirteenth-day rituals in the memory of Mohan.'

Roni's miserliness was none of his concern; nonetheless, he did not wish to hear any more about the dead man. He said, 'You are a fool! Am I here to go round collecting foodgrains. This is a process server's job, not mine. Would someone show me the way to Roni's house?'

Somebody escorted him. The official moved towards Mohanlal's house alongwith the sepoys. But someone had already informed Roni about his coming that side. Tota's sorrow melted in the air and Roni had already overcome it. Tota went behind the bushes with the buffalo and its calf. Roni swept the dung under the dry compost and removed all signs of buffalo being there. Then she peeped through the half-shut door and saw the official coming. Roni opened one side of the door and stood behind the other. On the official's arrival, one of his sepoys called forth, 'Who is there inside?' Covering the head with her veil, Roni came forward and faced them as her eyes peered through a narrow passage made wide enough by her fingers through the veil, she said, 'What's the matter? Please tell me.'

The official remonstrated her, 'Land revenue is in arrears, the levies too have not been paid by you. All the land has been left untilled. Where is the buffalo?'

Roni started crying aloud, 'We have been robbed of every thing that belonged to us. Fellows carried away foodgrains at first, and then the pair of oxen were snatched away. We neither had a buffalo then, nor we possess it now. If we had a buffalo we would not starve. Oh! I have none to support me.'

'Where is Tota?'

Roni seated herself with a thud as if she had fallen and started weeping bitterly. She kept on the veil cover as she went on with her monologue. How well-built was my husband. How he worked hard. Even four men together could not match him. He was enlisted in the army. Ah, what a physique he had, we did not receive even his dead body. We could not cremate him; God knows who took away his corpse.'

A scenario of crows and kites sitting on a tall and stout body came lloating in the air before the official's inner eye; and some invisible thing appeared to hit him but he brushed it aside. He did not have any feeling of compassion. He burst into an old saying, 'Jat hould be taken as dead only after the thirteenth day death-rites,' so as to amuse himself. He seemed to be unaware of his own callousness. Instead he laughed at his seemingly original remark. His companions smiled, for compassion had no use for them. Roni's cries grew louder.

Men shouted, 'Where is the grain stored? How much is there? Take out the grain, else we shall enter the house. Produce the buffalo, otherwise, the house shall be set on fire. Tota will be caught and cut into pieces.'

Roni's only reply was in the form of louder shrieks and piteous cries. Puzzled as the official was, he thought that it was his sepoy's job not his; his coming there personally was a wasteful exercise. But what about the buffalo? He thought.

But every thing—buffalo, grain, land revenue and levies all seemed to be drowning in Roni's loud, tearful wails.

The official said, 'Mohanlal's name has to be struck off and replaced by someone else. Tota is his heir?'

Suddenly, Roni's crying ceased and she replied, 'Tota is no way related to him. There is no other heir except me.'

The official said, 'Give my rightful share and your name will be entered in the record.'

Roni again started crying—'Oh my Arjun-like husband was killed on the battlefield. We did not receive even his dead body. The damned killers threw his body to kites and crows.'

Dismayed by the unfavourable prospect for recovering the buffalo and dissuaded by the constant reference about crows and kites, he decided to leave that ominous place. He left holding out threats, 'I'll see to it again. If you let the land remain untilled, I shall get you killed besides setting the house on fire.'

In the evening, Tota came watching cautiously, with the buffalo and its calf. The buffalo yielded less milk in the pail, the calf having fed itself in the day-time.

Roni told him, 'Better go away with the buffalo behind bushes for grazing and return only in the evening but take care that the calf does not suck milk. I shall go out for work on wages. In the meanwhile, rains will come and the fears about revenue officer's coming would fade away. If we can't make out our living here, we'll go away somewhere else.'

Tota asked, 'Where shall we go?'

Roni replied, 'May be Bharatpur-Deeg or somewhere else, wherever this destructive, tyrannical regime has no sway and there will be 'Jats' like us.'

Tota said, 'There the people have land, cattle and wealth and we shall have to pass all our life working for wages. Work, for wages, we shall — but —.'

She said, 'I shall not pass all my life as a wage-worker.'

'What would be-fall to our land and thatched hut? We shall not secure a well-tilled and developed land at Bharatpur or Deeg.'

In reply, Roni's wishful thinking ran thus, 'Is there none born to do away with these Qanungos, jamadars and sepoys, just as Kanhaiya[21] had wiped out Kansa.[22]

Tota said, 'Keep silent, who knows when...?'

The thought of going away to settle somewhere else was needling him.

—✻—

17

Sahu, the Raja of Maharashtra province had his headquarters at Satara. Poona had not yet acquired the status of capital but was shaping well towards occupying a place of importance. Baji Rao had met Mastani in 1731. On February 1, 1731, he got a palace built for himself and Mastani at Poona at a cost of Rupees 16,000. It came to be known as Shaniwarwada. Whenever he got respite from his campaigns, he came to Poona and stayed there alongwith his soldiers. Mastani kept his company during his campaigns. Baji Rao had to go to Satara on business of state. He was, during that period, at Poona. Mohan too had to stay put there. Shubrati, of course had his home there.

On reaching Poona, Baji Rao ordered detailed statement of accounts of his campaigns to be recorded. A portion of booty was deposited in state treasury. The rest was distributed among nobles and soldiers. The salaried soldiers required to remain in cantonments were lodged there but other seasonal soldiers called

---

21. Kanhaiya – An adorable address and another name for Lord Krishna.
22. Kansa – Krishna's maternal uncle who was killed by Lord Krishna himself. Kansa had put Krishna's parents in prison as he was mortally afraid of their eighth child who, according to a prophecy, was destined to kill him. For details one has to read Mahabharat.

up for duties went home to till their land. They had to return to their ranks in the army for launching attacks and campaigns. Shubrati was living as a soldier in the cantonment. Mohanlal and Shubrati also received their share in the spoils of war.

Mohanlal asked. 'When do we make a move towards North again?'

'Didn't I tell you that it would be roundabout Dusshehra.'

'Is the date not fixed as yet?'

'How can it be fixed so early?'

After the rains, an early, propitious day would be chosen and then, we shall march.'

'Where? Which country will be attacked this time?'

'It is not certain as yet but, may be, it will be north and eastern side."

'Will it be in the direction of Delhi – Agra?'

At first, we have to take on Nizam at Malwa.'

'Then, should we move towards east?'

'Of course not, Bhonsle has a claim on the east. Baji Rao may go that side only to reinforce his strength?'

'Would he not go to Gwalior?'

'Why? Are you feeling homesick?'

As Mohanlal sighed, Shubrati said, 'When I go out, I feel much better and do not feel homesick.'

'You don't remember even your children?'

'No, for my wife is a clever and courageous woman and is able to manage every thing. I am concerned only with earning money,'

Mohanlal suppressed a sigh again. Shubrati was compelled to ask, 'Why do you feel sad? You would not receive that much salary in the royal army as you get here.'

'I feel out of sorts here.'

'Wherefore? You remember your better half, the Chowdharin?'

'This is not so. People here call me damned, wretched fellow. I used to think that people make fun of me because of my coloured turban but when I read a certain disgust in their eyes while addressing me, it hurt me badly.'

'They call every outsider a rangda.'[23]

'Are you also addressed as such? Don't you feel hurt?'

'I hail from this place and now I belong to it. Members of my family know Marathi language and freely speak it also. But, yes...'

'I should also learn Marathi'.

Shubrati laughed at Mohan's innocence and added, 'Even then you will be called a damned fellow. Marathas always treat the outsiders as low-class folks.'

Mohanlal asked, 'What, treating their own sepoys as low-class folks' and added in anger, 'and the practice of untouchability prevails here so much that I am consumed by heartburning. I am a Jat Thakur by caste and do not consider myself inferior to any other caste fellows. Back home, every one regards Jats as high caste people and takes food and drink touched by us but here the situation is quite reverse.'

Shubrati had abhorrence for Hindus' narrow-minded notion of untouchability but could not reveal the same. Even so, he said, 'Caste considerations prevail here so much that Marathas are at loggerheads among themselves.'

But Shubrati, in sheer awe, did not wish to dilate on this subject and hence he changed the topic. He said, 'Perchance, if we could defeat Nizam, we would receive such a handsome prize that you would not mind all this.'

Mohanla's anguish took another form. He said, 'Nizam robs farmers and other poor, innocent creatures; we shall now loot his property.'

'He has accumulated wealth by depriving others; we shall now make clean sweep of his property, but one thing........'

'The farmers and labourers do not gain at all from this.'

23. Rangda – An outsider — a derogatory term used by Marathas for outsiders.

'If they enlist themselves in the army they would gain every thing.'

'Who will till the land?'

'What does one gain from farming? And then there are countless people for tilling.'

'Don't you have land to till at home?'

'No, no; we are sepoys by profession.'

Mohanlal had experienced the happiness of tilling one's own land besides the troubles entailing it. With the passage of time, he forgot the sorrows like a soldier who being reminded of the joys derived in fighting, forgets the wounds of war. The memory of his painful cohabitation with Roni had lost its sharp edge alongwith that of farming. But he did cherish the sweet remembrance of keeping vigil through the night at his farm, his own singing while ploughing the field, the fragrance of margossa and gooseberry flowers floating in the spring-air and the overgrowth of bushes and branches in the lonely spots outside Fatehpur Sikri.

Mohanlal exclaimed, 'These battles don't let farmers till their land; instead, they destroy the crops and render the fields deserted and forlorn. God knows, how many families are deprived of their earning members —the light of their lives.'

Shubrati interrupted him, 'You are a sepoy and a Jat too; even so, you chatter like this.'

Mohanlal had an unflinching faith in his friendship and was convinced that Shubrati would not carry tales.

He said, 'Isn't it the duty of a soldier to protect himself, his land and his family. If a soldier sacrifices his life in harness, such a death surpasses all. But to bring glory to others by killing and looting the innocent is no good; farming is far better than leading such a life.'

Mohanlal's ideals had a limited but clear horizon and expanse. Shubrati did not like all this but he held Mohanlal in high esteem, having witnessed his gallantry as a soldier several times. Hence he did not refute his views.

Shubrati said, 'Well, brother! This is all right as far as it goes but one has to serve as soldier for the sake of belly, like we are doing. Rajas and Nawabs go on fighting among themselves. We have to serve under someone or the other, and remain loyal to him as long as we are in his employ.'

Mohanlal's mind could not absorb this discourse about principles but he had neither words to contradict him nor desire to do so.

Shubrati asked him, 'Are you going to give up your job as sepoy to take to farming again?'

Mohan replied, 'I can't say anything right now. May be I'll do so.'

Mohanlal said spontaneously, 'I think I must serve God for some time. It is said that one who meditates with devotion would be blessed with God's revelation to him.'

Shubrati became serious. During this exchange of ideas on religion, Shubrati's thoughts first turned to vague, pious feeling and then to the family life of Mohanlal.

He said, 'You seem to be worrying about your family.'

Shubrati's manner of speaking was a sweet mix of friendship and truthfulness. The topic which he could not touch upon directly, he brought up indirectly.

'Well, there is some substance, but it is no use mentioning it — you are free from family worries and happy thereto.'

'Let's go to my house some day; I shall offer you jaggery. You would be delighted to see my children.'

Mohanlal nodded assent, thinking of the change from the routine.

—✻—

18

Seeing a tall and stout young man accompanying Shubrati, his wife went inside the house. Children were playing in the courtyard outside. Mohan did not have any feeling surging within him, on watching the children. Children became curious on seeing a stranger but when their father came closer to fondle and caress them, they ran into the inner apartments and started making noise. Shubrati felt quite happy but Mohan was unaffected. Even so, he put up a happy countenance to look as though he was sharing the joys with Shubrati.

Shubrati took him to the inner verandah. He seated Mohan on a sackcloth and went inside to bring jaggery. Mohan turned his eyes towards walls, ceiling and thatched roof. He saw children's shabby but somewhat colourful clothes hanging from some pegs on the wall; on another peg there was a catapult. On the walls were drawn some unidentifiable charcoal sketches which defied understanding besides all kinds of cobwebs—thick ones with wide netting or thinly spread across the thatched ceiling which had a wooden puppet too tucked therein apparently, over-laid with cobwebs but more clear in outline and appearance than charcoal sketches. Mohan's eyes were fixed at it more intently. He thought, it might be a big doll for children but its size was so big that small children could not have played with it.

While he was looking at it and making a guess, Shubrati brought a big lump of jaggery. Seeing him engrossed in looking at the doll, he smiled and told him, 'Here, eat it. There is a kind of sweetness in this doll's story also, which I shall narrate now.'

Mohan took raw jaggery and tasted it. He was eager to listen to the doll's story. He uttered nothing but his eyes betrayed his curiosity and astonishment.

Shubrati's eyes turned towards the inner courtyard when he said, 'Does the doll resemble me or not?'

'Not the least'?

'If I tie my turban on his head and stick false beard and moustaches...?

'May be, then it will somewhat resemble.'

Mohan laughed. Shubrati laughed too and with a glance towards the courtyard, he said, 'This doll has done a big job; this is why, to cherish his memory, he has been tucked in the thatched ceiling.'

Mohanlal's curiosity was aroused further. He asked,'Well?'

'This doll is the instrument of peace and happiness in my household. If we offer prayer to it, we shall not be doing any thing wrong.'

'I could not follow!'

'In my family, the quarrels broke out quite often. Morning and evening, every now and then, we had fierce fights.'

A woman coughed inside in the courtyard. Shubrati said, 'Don't worry, I am telling my own and not your story.' The laughing voice was heard again.

'He is an intimate friend of mine — he saved my life.'

Mohan interrupted him in a firm tone, 'And you saved mine..'

Shubrati remonstrated and went on, 'First, listen to me. Tell me one thing before I narrate my own story; how did you get along with your wife? Did she quarrel, or not?'

No body coughed then. Mohan said,

'Yes, she did?'

'Very much?'

'Yes, very much.'

'Same here, with me! Brother, I was a bit of waste? Those days, I was not yet enlisted in the army and used to shoot birds with a catapult, and also earn something by selling propitious threads and trinkets. She used to remonstrate with me and was right thereto. I was sulking at that time. But then wisdom dawned on me while watching a doll-show...'

The coughing in the courtyard, this time interspersed with welling up laughter, vainly interrupted the conversation. Shubrati was not discouraged.

'I got a doll made partly with my own hands and a bit from my carpenter friend. I dressed him like me, placed him in the courtyard and begged of my Begum that....'

Amidst laughter, the sound of footsteps turning towards the inner room was heard. Shubrati also laughed, and continued, 'I prayed that Begums and queens are prone to flying into tempers and there, someone or the other should fall to their wrath; otherwise, the heat generated by their frayed tempers would consume their heart to ashes.' Hence he prayed to his wife, 'You may strike this image of mine five times, with shoes, every morning and evening.' Shubrati burst into laughter. Mohan too joined his tempestuous guffaws. Jaggery juice stuck in his throat and he was feeling uneasy with the bouts of laughter. Children stood at the door, first a little puzzled and then smiled. Anyhow, Mohan could also overcome his laughter. Mohan said, 'You did an excellent job; such a thing I have never heard before. Its results would have been queer.'

'A big fallout indeed; the doll was not hit at all and the anger too had vanished. The household was agog with pleasure and radiated with children's presence.

'I also gave up giving omen plaques and seals and joined the army. I go out and get back. No worries now! The doll tucked in the thatch raises a smile, off and on, not anger anymore, not a tempestuous one in any case.' From the courtyard, the coughing was heard again. Children turned their glance. Someone beckoned them and taking that hint, they went in.

'You may also try this doll's marvel.'

'Prosperity will smile on you and bring children too in its train?'

'Would this, holy formula work for everyone?'

'It is a sure prescription, why not try it?'

'The same medicine can't cure every disease.'

'Test it and then air your views.'

Mohan recalled the pretty face of Roni, the gathering shadow of anger therein and imagined its remedy in the doll. He could not help laughing.

He said, 'When I get back to north, I shall think of it.'

When Mohan returned from Shubrati's house after taking jaggery, he was not depressed.

—❋—

19

Rains came to an end ushering in Dushehra[24] festival season. The farmers busied themselves in harvesting their crops and the nobles and commanders in the preparatory measure for their assaults and campaigns. The Dushehra festivities included processions and display of mounting attacks. But the festivities were yet to acquire and reflect splendours of Emperor in Delhi and Iranian nobles. The lifestyle of Maratha nobles had just begun to absorb the impact of that grandeur to be felt slowly. The riches of Delhi and the northern region had so far stirred the temptations of Maratha sepoy but the splendour reflected in the external life had not yet made them crazy to indulge in inflated self-glorification. Maratha nobles had, by then, closely observed Delhi Emperor's court and seen, inside out, the palaces of Jaipur and Amber as well.

Maratha commanders had developed Mulkgiri, the ambition of expanding their areas of control besides aspiring for the goal of independence.

---

24. Dushehra – A festival of Hindus falling on the tenth day of Ashwin — the seventh month of Hindu calendar corresponding to September-October — in which the drama of Rama's victory over Ravana symbolising that of truth over evil in life is re-enacted culminating into setting fire to the straw-images of Ravana and his brothers.

Dushehra festival was the culmination of the dedication to those ideals and emotions, which was reflected in the clenched fists, chests charged with the zeal and also in the smiles playing on the erect necks of people.

The farmers were also celebrating by making themselves busy before, harvesting, with all the fun and frolics and dancing, while gazing intently at the clear or hazy, dim directions, at the same time.

In Poona, Satara and other towns and villages of importance, the grandeur of rejoicings mirrored itself in the houses of Rajas and nobles in proportion to their respective status and importance. Betel-leaves and cardamom were offered to people. As the harvesting was over, came the appointed day when Maratha army, armed with long spears and swords, bows and arrows and artillery guns, riding the speedy hilly steeds, gathered under the command of Baji Rao. On a scheduled day, Mohanlal and Shubrati moved towards Ujjain as members of that squadron.

When Mohanlal arrived at the bank of river Narmada, he felt, more than ever, nostalgic about Yamuna. When he bowed in reverence to Narmada, he could not help recalling Yamuna which also reminded him of his household, Roni and his own troublesome period. On seeing his companion, Shubrati smiled. He thought that Narmada had smiled on him. Shubrati did not question him.

Mohanlal, however broke the silence himself, 'I was reminded of the doll in your porch, back home. He laughed while he remarked thus.

Shubrati laughed longer.

'While bowing in reverence to Narmada?'

'Yes, I too can't resist being reminded of that doll off and on.'

'Well, then the family will be well taken care of.'

'I shall go home as soon as I am free from war.'

'I too start thinking at times.'

'Why?'

'Because you are not as sad as you were in the past; you are now interested in things and talk about the current lifestyle of towns in the North.'

'I should like to see Delhi again.'

'Despite being away from home?'

'No, after transacting all business at home, some other time in future. May be, someday, Peshwa[25] shall mount an attack on Delhi.'

'During the last assault, I could not see much of Delhi.'

'Most certainly, this time'.

'God-willing, may it be so.'

'Of course, God's grace will bring about that.'

They crossed Narmada and thereafter advancing across big, small rivers, jungle hills and plains, Peshwa forces pitched their tents in the vicinity of Ujjain. Nizam was camping in Bhopal. Peshwa was determined to engage Nizam and fight to the finish. After a respite of a few days, he decided to descend from Sironj side and fight the battle at Bhopal.

20

Hermits, saints, sages practising hathyoga[25A], naked monks from seats of holy men formed a sizeable segment of Ujjain's population. Many Maratha commanders went to have an audience with some well-known mendicants and to seek some desired godly gift. A number of sepoys also took time off to follow suit. Mohanlal also joined them.

He had seen the roving mendicants in or around Fatehpur, but such a big gathering of holy men he saw at Ujjain for the first time. He also benefitted from the audience with a well-known hermit.

25. Peshwa – Title of the chief of Marathas with headquarters at Poona.

25A. Hathyoga – A branch of Yoga alluding to Hath i.e. force technique in Yoga Asanas.

The hermit chose to remain stark naked except for the sanctified ashes which he had smeared on his body. Apart from three straight lines marked on his forehead, or sanctified rosary in the neck, a water jug at his waist side, a tiger-skin-spread, a small trident, a sacred fire in dying embers he could boast of nothing except a few followers. Mohan observed that people came, had a pull at charas-pipe or offered the same to others, smeared some ash on their forehead and went their way. The hermit expected nothing from others and would even return the offerings given to him. The disciples were under his strict discipline; they were not debarred from taking meal once a day, which was invariably offered by the devotees. Mohan preferred that hermit to other mendicants. Mohan found a name for him 'Trishulanand'.

Trishulanand sported matted hair and beard and his eyes had fiery look. He practised sheershashan[26] with his thin leg and heavy chest supporting a heavy neck. His disciples pointed out to Mohan, 'Guru Maharaj[27] is performing penance to please god Bhairava whom he has often seen in dreams but now seeks his face-to-face revelation.'

'Well?' Mohan asked with reverential awe!

'Well, he will seek God's blessing and gifts for himself and his devotees. This world is full of wicked persons and Guru Maharaj is doing not only this but, God knows, how many other types of meditation and penance,' one of the devotees thus elucidated the goals of the Guru's penance.

Mohan expressed his devotion thus :

'Maharaj is very calm, he gives hearing to the poor whenever he is free. The saints here don't converse with others.'

The disciple went on, 'Whenever Guru Maharaj finds himself free from his daily prayers, he preaches in his nectar-like sweet

26. Sheershashan – Yogic posture which enjoins one to stand on one's head.
27. Guru Maharaj – A form of salutation to senior men preachers of holy order.

voice to all people around but if someone addresses him before his prayers, he flares up.'

Mohan was further taken in by all this. Early next day, he went to see Trishulanand at his seat. There being no discipline or restriction of drill or exercise on parade ground, as Baji Rao's soldiers had already gone through all that, he got some respite. Some eager men seeking boon or his blessings had turned up that day also like every other day. The hermit was going for his bath and morning ablutions. One of the devotees lay prostrate before him. The other visitor withdrew himself a little. The one who received the blow from his leg was quite happy and said, 'I got the gift.'

The hermit (Baba) feeling a bit embarrassed said, 'Be damned.'

'The one who got the leg-blow was still more happy and said, 'This is the second boon' and went his way. Baba's eyes turned red with fire and fury of anger.

'The hermit had his bath, smeared himself with sacred ash and commenced his head upside down exercise. After a full three hour meditation and penance, the hermit was back to his seat. Mohan, in the meantime, had gone back to his cantonment and returned after taking meals. He did not make out any iota of anger in Baba's face and it appeared to him that Baba's eyes, though red, were brimful with honey.

Some men brought him offering of food. The hermit and his disciples had food and drinks to their fill. It was followed by a wordy duel and a chain of intermittent blessings.

The hermit faced no problem in disbursing blessings but he was rather miserly in doing so. The seekers of blessing felt again and again that whenever the hermit struck a blow with his leg, one got the real blessing. Someone was determined to come quite early in the morning while another one decided on some other timing. All of them went away but the debaters of scriptures stayed on. A question-answer session followed.

'Maharaj Kalidasa worshipped God Shiva as the Omnipresent yet quite distinct from other gods; it has been well said that Shiva does not reveal himself to those practising yoga,[28] but devotees can certainly seek him by meditation, which affirms the Bhakti cult.'

'Kalidasa was a poet — not a person practising Yoga — never mind whatever he said; I have full faith that I shall have God's revelation only through Yoga.'[28]

'What is the way out for those who can not practise Yoga? How will they overcome the hurdles of this world?'

'The Lord, Shanker is the moving spirit behind Kartikeya who is the Supreme Commander of heavenly forces. No sooner does Shiva raise his trident than Kartikeya will attack your enemies.'

Whatever may be the substance in this formula, the hermit's strong voice had the desired impact.

But one of the debaters tumbled and mumbled. He said, 'It is rumoured that a devil called Nadir Shah has embodied himself in the world.'

Unruffled, the hermit smiled and said, 'Those who can overwhelm the devilry will also appear before us. I should like to see one who is called Nadir Shah. I shall proceed towards Delhi some time.'

The disciples felt happy and relieved on getting answers to their queries. Mohanlal asked, 'What would be the outcome of the fight between Nizam and Peshwa, Maharaj?'

'Peshwa's victory!' Baba made the forecast without hesitation. Mohanlal felt encouraged but did not ask any question. Thereafter, the earthen-pipes filled with hemp were exchanged freely. But Mohanlal did not share the pull at the pipe and proceeded towards cantonment.

—❋—

28. Yoga – A means of overcoming the defects and imperfections of earthly life and of gaining complete mastery over the mind and senses.

21

Mohanlal's thatched cottage was quite ordinary but his fields were fertile and not far from Fatehpur, his village. The grazing land was also close by but the tyranny of Qanungo and Jamadar hung like Damocles' sword. While Tota was still indecisive, Roni made up her mind. She entrusted her land and house to an aequaintence who was native of the same village. Roni gave expression to her optimism surging below the surface of her frustration: 'By God's grace, we'll be back here when luck favours us again; till then, this will remain as my entrustment with you. You may give us whatever rent of the land you think proper, on our return.'

The acquaintance related his own difficulties, 'Subedar will come back to recover from me the dues of land revenue — wherefore, shall I pay?'

'Didn't I tell you, give us what you deem proper.'

'What do I deem it as proper? What will be left on balance?'

'Maybe, you have nothing left. Won't you give back our land?'

'Of course; I swear by mother Yamuna. You may take back your land.'

'What about the thatched house?'

'If Qanungo and his sepoy spare the house, I shall give back that too.'

'Would these marauders raze it to ground.'

'They may not raze it, but would certainly sell it.'

'Will someone really buy it? Would he not ponder that the house belongs to an ill-fated woman.'

'Well! A Jat may not go for it but there would be many others willing to buy.'

'What will he do with the house, the land being in your possession?'

'And suppose Qanungo and Sepoy give away the land to someone else after dispossessing me of the same?'

'What a tyranny!'

'Tyranny? And Tyranny? They are showering cruelty on us.'

Roni heaved a sigh but burst into hopeful monologue again: 'If God is kind, everything will be safe; otherwise, everything will be lost the way he is gone.'

The familiar farmer was moved by this effusiveness. He assured her, 'No one would grab your land until I breathe my last. My faith will also help me in all this.'

Roni and Tota set out before dawn with some essential articles, clothes, pots and pans.

They were enraptured by the barren, brown hills, leafless Cappris trees and withering green grass interspersed between bushes, where the buffalo used to graze. At the same time, disappearing from view, the thatched hut dimmed further and faded on the horizon.

The boundless horizons beckoned them in all directions; they wished to go far away to such safe distance, where no one would dispossess them of their wet milch buffalo; where they could stretch themselves and their arms in comfort and safety; where they could eat to their heart's content after day's hard work on wages. They could now visualise the limits of boundless horizons beyond this yearning and the boundary marks of these limitless directions they could anticipate only in Bharatpur. They had enough grain and flour to last them until their arrival there. Even so, they were apprehensive that the dacoits or highway robbers might snatch the buffalo which they had somehow managed to save from the awesome, cruel hands of Qanungo and his sepoys. Hence, after leaving Fatehpur, they made their way through and across the contiguous villages. When they arrived at Bharatpur after a few days, their bodies bore the deep marks of that journey but the joyous feeling of victory in having saved the buffalo and the possibility of seeking out a shelter for themselves, made them smile ignoring the weariness of the dust-laden, thin and weakening bodies.

They secured a place for themselves at an old Jat's house. He was a farmer. He had some cattle which he tended all by himself. One of his sons tilled the fields. He was about fourteen-fifteen years of age. Another son was seven-eight years old. His wife was no more. His eldest son, a sepoy had been killed in battle. The old man opened up one day: 'The boy is gone but he served the state very well. The Maharajah of Jaipur had conferred upon Badan Singh[29] the title of Brij Raj. Now there is nothing left for me in this world except for a few fields, some cattle and these children. Now that you have come, you may live here, as my son and daughter-in-law.'

Badan Singh's uncle Chudaman was the ruler towards the close of the 16th century, when Jats seethed under the tyrannical rule of Aurangazeb in his last years. They were forced to indulge in activities which engaged Marathas in the south. Jats were more manly and stout than the Pathans of the border, besides being more hard-working and honest. They rallied under the command of Chudaman, organised themselves and jumped into the fray. After Chudaman, his nephew Badan Singh became their leader. He was so polite and loyal to his community that he did not call himself a 'Rajah!' He raised a large army and collected a vast sum of money. He regarded Jai Singh, the ruler of Jaipur as his 'Chhatrapati'[30] in case of need to fall back upon. Jai Singh bestowed upon him the. tittle of 'Brij Raj' while the poets elevated him to the appellation of Indra.[31] In a way he was rightly likened to god, Indra, for he had so many angel-like women who bore innumerable children many of whom he himself did not recognise. But he probably administered the

29. Badan Singh – The Raja of Bharatpur.
30. Chhatrapati – A sovereign with sway over other rulers.
31. Indra – The mythological king of gods.

people better than what Indra did. Those who were persecuted elsewhere, came to seek refuge under him and prospered too.

The man who gave refuge to Roni and Tota mused to himself; when his thirteen-fourteen year old son attained manhood, Roni — pretty and petite as she was — would make good daughter-in-law without his incurring any expense for this purpose. Hence the old man was more affectionate towards her than Tota.

Tota might not have taken the cue but Roni lost no time in making out. She did not nurture high ambitions; instead she wished to lead a dignified life.

She had no fears about having to work for wages but would not like to be called a wage-earner. After a few days, Roni raised the subject with the old man to allow them to till the fields on crop-share basis. The old man, still keeping to himself his counsel and desire to make Roni his daughter-in-law, yielded to her suggestion.

Tota was not conscious about any unkindness in the old man's behaviour towards him but did not receive any paternal love from him. Roni's behaviour, on the contrary, betrayed a sense of rightful claim.

—✻—

22

Roni had to cook food for three persons at her homestead and there at Bharatpur for five persons. But there she grudged her work and sulked noisily too but here she was not vociferous. In the old man's home, in the inner courtyard under a thatched roof, her buffalo was tied. There was plenty of grazing land around Bharatpur and to take the buffalo out for grazing, his two sons were always available. Tota was helping at the farm as a labourer while Roni looked after the buffalo and its needs. Roni set apart her butter from that of the old man who, however, had no objection to her keeping it mixed up. The old man was apprehensive that Roni might re-marry and have Tota recruited in Badan Singh's army. He tempted Tota to the garden path of a soldier's lifestyle.

Roni had finished making loaves of bread and was, then, serving food to Tota. A nagging thought kept goading his mind. However, he talked to her on sundry matters. When Roni had also taken her meals, he broke the silence suddenly.

'How do you like the idea if I enlist myself in Raja's army?' Roni was somewhat taken aback: 'Wherefore?' She said. He replied, 'It would augur well, I think so: I would earn more and here, of course, everything will go on as usual.'

Roni felt like expressing her 'no' as a matter of right but she refrained. 'Isn't there so much of risk in the fighting?'

'Lakhs of men join the fighting forces as a profession — not all of them die.'

'Here why do you feel out of sorts? What is the trouble here?'

'I am not ill at ease here but would earn a lot more by joining the army.'

'Don't think of this?'

'Why?'

'I won't like to have a lot of money. Whatever we earned here is enough; after your departure, I would be left alone.'

Tota yearned to listen to such an outpouring of feelings. His eyes wistfully looked into Roni's eyes which also betrayed a yearning but if there was something else, he could not fathom. He hesitated a little and said: 'Why don't you remonstrate with me here like you did at Fatehpur?'

Roni could not help laughing but became serious again and said, 'Do you like my shouts and shrieks?'

'I never took it amiss nor shall ever do so.'

'Well then, I shall henceforth, speak in a peevish tone.'

'You may........?'

A smile played on Roni's lips. Tota observed, 'If all places become quiet, we may go back to our home and hearth.'

'We are better off here than there.'

'A home is home.'

'A home can be set up here too.'

'What would befall that house, an ancestral house for that matter.'

Roni's smile vanished; her raised eyebrows for a moment waxed with anger and then relaxed.

Heaving a deep breath, Roni said, 'We will see to it when God bestows us with better luck.'

They were reminded of Mohanlal's sudden departure one night, of the news of his death, the raid by Qanungo and his sepoy. Tota became sad while Roni turned sullen.

'Why do you remain so sad?'

'Not really! Busy as I am in my work, I get tired at times - nothing else', Tota tried to ward off his sadness.

'Why do you relapse into an unhappy mood just now?'

'You should shout and remonstrate with me while talking to me and then I shall no longer be sad,' Tota could not help saying while depression vanished from his face.

'Should I abuse you then?'

'As much as you wish to.'

'Whether you are guilty or not.'

'How often was I at fault at Fatehpur?'

Smile faded from Roni's face again. Roni used to direct her abuses mostly to Mohanlal at Fatehpur and much less to Tota. It seemed to her that Mohanlal was standing before her.

Roni observed the buffalo chewing cud and said. 'Put some more fodder to the buffalo.'

Tota rose to lay fodder for the buffalo. Roni gazed at him with a blank look. Tota looked back while putting down feed for the buffalo. Roni kept on looking at him without batting an eyelid. Tota was spreading the fodder before the buffalo. He looked back and found Roni gazing at him absent mindedly. Tota stared at her for a split moment and tried to read meaning into her looks but could not find any. Roni turned aside her eyes. Tota, having done with feeding, came closer to her; Roni was smiling.

She said, 'You have to swear by me that you would not enlist yourself in the army.'

The veins in Tota's body distended and betrayed his rising passion.

'I swear I shall not join the army.'

'Don't take a vow like that, swear by me.'

'Hm, Hm....No....' Tota took the vow with a slight coy pertness.

He said, 'Grandfather had suggested my joining the army.'

Roni muttered, seething with anger, 'God damn him, burn him. May serpent sting him. His bones may be burnt.'

Tota cautioned her, 'God forbid! None should hear all this.'

If it was Fatehpur, Roni would have flared up but merely said, 'So what? Even if someone hears all this, what harm can he bring to us?'

Roni checked herself instantly. With a slight smile, she sweetly put it, 'Whatever any one may tell you, you should go on ignoring it — now that you have sworn by me.'

Tota nodded his head in obeisance, blended with love.

Roni cast a glance at the buffalo and said amidst her smile, 'You should not toil so much. You get tired and then feel depressed.'

Tota also said with a smile while he looked at the buffalo, 'I don't work that hard.'

'Didn't you say this just now?'

'I did not mean that. Don't say it even casually. I don't like it.'

'You have become extremely garrulous.'

Roni moved towards the buffalo rather coquettishly and from there with a louder laugh, she said, 'Ah! How did you put the fodder to buffalo? You did not untie some of the bundles of grass fodder. Where were you lost?'

"I don't know" was the reply which welled up in his throat, but he could not bring himself to say this.

He said, 'You are not spreading it too well, either.'

'We are unable to finish a task even if we do it jointly.' Roni uttered this amidst laughter.

Tota's heart was full of zest and passion. He wished to say and also hear something more in the same vein but Roni interrupted the flow of his thoughts and said, 'Now you may explain things and dissuade grandfather from sending you to join the army but do not enter into argument or quarrel with him; we should conduct ourselves carefully until we see better days.' Tota's passion was aroused, and he added, 'I will never quarrel with him, more so because he is old and revered. I shall ward off argument and say amen to his advice; in the meanwhile, no one would force me to get into the army without my consent. I shall work harder and sweat it out so as to continue to gain his affection.'

Roni nodded assent with 'Hm'. She turned to one side and went out. The old man perceived that Tota's remarks and conversation were suffused with sweetness and he also displayed a renewed dedication towards work. The dialogue converged to his joining the army but the old man did not enthuse him such as he had done earlier.

The old man told him: 'Badan Singh, these days, does not go about fighting against others but if his sovereign, Jai Singh, the Rajah of Jaipur renders assistance to the Emperor, he will be forced to join the fray, for another great Emperor is reported to be marching from the direction of Kabul to mount an attack on Delhi.'

'Delhi, then, will witness an array of many armies.'

"Yes, it would; but didn't I add 'perhaps'."

'I should, like to put in more labour into the household chores.'

—✵—

23

Saadat Khan showered money and affection on Noorbai besides keeping wide open, for her, the doors of his mansion; she spent most of her time in his mansion. But just as Noorbai alone was not the cynosure of his eyes and passion — his ambition was to secure for himself the highest or the most singular position in the Moghul Empire — correspondingly, Saadat Khan's Kothi was not the only grand place for Noorbai to frequent and aspire for. She gave her love and charms to Saadat Khan but she cherished, at the same time, a deep desire to captivate the heart of the Emperor and thereby extract a fragrant perfume from his burning desire for her.

Overwhelmed by the rising passion of Saadat Khan for her and being embarrassed thereby, she gave an inkling of her yearning only once or twice after the celebrations at Mathura; but realising the inclination and demeanour of Saadat Khan, she never gave expression to her emotions.

Saadat said, 'These bracelets studded with diamonds will add glamour and charm to your tender wrists.' Noorbai ogled sideways, smiled and turned back her head to stretch her arms towards him.

She said, 'Please put them on my wrists with your hands.'

'Well?'

'Your hands will lend grace and glamour, not the bracelets.'

'Turn your eyes to me, how can I put them on your wrists without this?'

'I can't help for I am unable to turn my eyes on you.'

Noorbai screwed her neck further and put the wrist of the other hand parallel to but slightly behind the first one; her waist bent and turned a little in unison with her neck which too received a rhythmical jerk at the same time. The entire body made a wavy movement and her bust bulged as a beautiful solid mass.

Saadat Khan had witnessed such harmonious and wavy movement of her body on many other occasions but rarely in such unique unison. Saadat Khan placed the bracelets on her wrists while Noorbai looked on sideways at his face.

'Let me now have a look at your face'. Saadat entreated her in a soft, hushed tone.

'I have no courage to do so.'

Saadat Khan grinned and took out a gold necklace studded with diamonds and emeralds. He put one of his hands on her shoulder and touching her chin, with the necklace held in the other, he said, 'You will have to come into full view to wear this, of course.'

'Your obstinacy is overpowering indeed.'

Noorbai's smile preceded these words and she turned a full circle to face him. She put her arms on her wrist. Saadat glanced quickly first at her wrists and then on bracelets exuding charm and glamour and then his eyes looked into her wearied eyes.

While Noorbai laughed, her pearl-like teeth shimmered. She bowed her head arid raised her long eyelashes so much that they almost touched the eyebrows. Her face was lit up with a smile and she feigned a coquettish wrath.

Saadat Khan offered the necklace pleading, 'This necklace is meant solely for you.'

Saadat Khan made a move for putting the necklace round the neck of Noorbai. The silken scarf slipped from her head to the long dangling pleats of hair and dropped spreading itself wide. The necklace slowly found its place. Noorbai merrily began to have a closer look at the necklace almost in a frenzy. The smile and feigned anger gave place to keen, curious and prying eyes.

Exuding innocence, Noorbai asked him, 'Must be very valuable, Your Honour.'

Saadat answered with pleasure, 'Not very expensive; it is worth merely Rs. five lac'.

A thought flitted, for a split moment, through Noorbai's mind and vanished : if His Excellency the Emperor is enthralled by my dance and music, there is nothing which he could not bestow upon me.'

Noorbai shook her head with a coquettish nod and spoke with an expressive astonishment 'Merely!'

Saadat Khan was elated with joy. Noorbai showed both the ornaments lo her Ustad[32] and told him the exaggerated value.

'The necklace is worth Rs. nine lac. And the bracelets would cost about Rs. one lac'

Noorbai expressed her own estimated value. The old teacher's eyes glistened with joy.

'God has bestowed upon you numerous benedictions as if to match with your name, light from the Gracious', Ustad said and blessed her thus:

'May your bewitching beauty and art make you the Queen of the Emperor!'

His blessings seemed to buttress, with a loud echo, her high ambition.

With a yawn and stretch of limbs, Noorbai protested in one word 'Hm', which still betrayed her yearning.

'I have no use for such things, I have everything by your blessings.'

Ustad, unable to see through Noorbai's aspirations, expressed his neutral attitude by saying, 'I mentioned it casually.'

Noorbai could make out his neutral tone and made up her mind to seek his assistance and cooperation in furtherance of her aspirations.

---

32. Ustad – A mentor or teacher. At times the term is used for the accompanist (on any instrument) of a dancer.

'Are they excellent singers who go to court for dance, and obeisance in the presence of the Emperor?'

'The Emperor is extremely sagacious and is himself a great connoisseur of dances and music.'

'I enquired of you whether all of them are knowledgeable artists.' 'Of course, they are knowledgeable, and for that matter, who would find fault with them?'

'Even so, tell me, my mentor, whether their Ustad is also a great artist apart from their being great musicians.'

'You know every one, already. What more can I tell you?'

'Even so, who can be a greater and perceptive connoisseur and critic of music than you, Ustad?'

'May God pardon me, for pride goes before the fall of a man; if I may utter the truth, most of the so-called 'Ustads' have to learn a lot even now.'

'And what about the dancing lasses trained by them?'

'Oh, what do they know, apart from blowing their vocal chords hoarse and the monkey-feats? What can they learn even otherwise? The Emperor is enthralled by their good-looking faces, that is all.'

'By their pretty features.'

'Yes, of course? None of them possesses as beautiful a face and features as bestowed upon you by the Creator.'

'If the Emperor, God save him, watches my performance, he will fathom how deep is my Ustad's art — the ocean-like depth that he possesses.'

'Oh, no. I am but a humble creature shaped by God's grace; but I do wish that the Emperor must watch your performance and listen to you at least once. How many years have I spent in grooming you? The trouble is that Nawab Saadat Khan does not brook any delay on your part in loving him.'

'Ustad, you can accomplish any thing.'

Ustad's fingers were engrossed in scratching his head. Noorbai looked ardently and expectantly. Ustad started coughing, Noorbai's eyes now gazed at the necklace and bracelets.

Turning back her face, she said, 'Nawab Saheb loves us. Here we are living in great comfort. But the only nagging thought is that I should present dance performance and steps taught by you before the Emperor himself.'

Ustad said, 'Well, yes of course. I am also thinking on the same lines.'

Noorbai helped Ustad to work out his ideas and alternatives. She said, 'You can accomplish anything. I wish Nawab should not come to know of this move from anyone; it will be a surprise move if the royal summons are received all of a sudden, one day.'

Ustad cleared his throat in a mellow tone: 'Your reputation will be enhanced and I shall be saved from the confinement of Harem,[33] we shall stand to gain a lot there.'

Noorbai again glanced at her necklace and bracelets and Ustad's eyes followed hers. He added: 'If the nightingale gets into the rose-bed confines, there is no harm.'

In a flash, the picturesque scene of her own singing of the Persian ghazal[34] 'Nightingale and the Rose' unrolled in her mind. Ustad's lyrics echoed in her ears, 'if the rose-bed yearned to confine within it the nightingale, the latter would not have any other wish.' And she herself had begged of Saadat Khan only this much. In the meanwhile, Saadat Khan had, besides the ornaments, given her his love too.

'Well, there were so many rose-beds in the Emperor's garden. Even so..........'

Turning her back, Noorbai gave a smile and said, 'The freedom here is worth it and better than the confinement there;

---

33. Harem – Ladies' apartment in royal household where concubines and wives lived together.
34. Ghazal – op. cit. 7, p. 43

it is a far cry still as there is no starting point in sight; even so, you may try and make a move.'

Ustad nodded in agreement. Noorbai was able to hide her joy.

The full picture and portrayal of Noorbai's bewitching beauty was carried to the ears of the Emperor Muhammad Shah and the alleged barrier lying in her way up to the Emperor was also brought to his notice.

The Emperor sent for Saadat Khan by royal summons. Noor's joy knew no bounds, mixed as it was with her apparent effort to suppress the same. Saadat Khan mistook that Noorbai was saddened. Saadat Khan tried to make out excuses and dilly-dallied too. Ustad's secret efforts made the Emperor obdurate and also irritated him. The helpless Noorbai arrived in the Emperor's palace one day. In tears, she presented herself before Saadat Khan but no one could make out whether these were tears of joy or sorrow. He fretted, fumed and was overcome with grief but all in vain. The tale of his overwhelming sadness too was borne to the Emperor's ears in an exaggerated and impertinent form. Consequently, Saadat Khan lost his title of Meer Bakshi and the Emperor conferred the title to his powerful rival. Noorbai was admitted to the Harem.

Saadat Khan was smouldering within. Nadir Shah had conquered Kabul. Saadat Khan and some angry, alienated nobles invited him to attack India, which Nadir Shah accepted. He mounted the attack.

Nizam was campaigning in the South to enlarge his Sultanate (Kingdom). He arrived in Bhopal to have a clash with Baji Rao who had already girded up his loins and was itching for fight.

—❋—

35. Rajahs – A common name in Hindi language for Kings, nobles and rulers of areas not controlled or ruled by the British in India.

24

Nizam had overrun the region of Bundelkhand before settling himself in Bhopal fort. Some of the Rajahs[35] of Bundelkhand had joined him there with a view to keep their kingdoms intact. A few Rajput Rajahs also allied themselves with Nizam, in order to safeguard their own kingdoms.

Nizam possessed numerous huge and heavy cannons and artillery guns besides innumerable animals to serve as carriers. Baji Rao carried no such heavy burden. Nizam had to play his counter moves to meet the tricky game of Baji Rao.

Marathas had, in a way, imprisoned Nizam in Bhopal. The watchful and sharp Maratha cavalrymen blocked the supply-line running to Bhopal. Nizam soon realised the shortage of supplies. Marathas thought that they would soon take over Bhopal. They mounted the attack. Nizam's heavy cannons spouted fire balls and Marathas had to beat a hasty retreat with a large number of casualties. Thereafter, Marathas started fighting with extreme caution.

A large contingent of Maratha forces was engaged by the Portuguese at Poona. Nizam's son advanced from the south to render assistance to him at Bhopal. Baji Rao devised and managed to counter this. Nizam's son could not reach Bhopal. Marathas reinforced and strengthened their siege. Nizam and his fellow-fighters started starving. Nizam decided to come out from the fort, to fight.

Nizam wanted to join his son in the south with his huge and heavy equipment, a large army and retinue accompanying him.

He had received a letter from Muhammed Shah to the effect: 'Drive out the disbelievers from Malwa.'

He had also inspired Baji Rao with joy and pride by his letter which ran like this: 'Nizam's loyalty has tilted- he wants to carve

36. Sardeshmukhi – op. cit. 19, p. 73.

a kingdom for himself....Crush him and Sardeshmukhi[36] and tributes of all the six states of the Deccan will be yours for ever.'

Muhammed Shah thought that with one stroke he would divide and make them both fight to the finish and meet their end.

Marathas started troubling the Nizam's mobile cantonment. There were minor skirmishes intermittently, rendering a few casualties on both sides.

Under the watchful eyes of a smart contingent of about one thousand and two hundred Nizam's soldiers, supplies of foodgrains, butter-oil, etc., were being transported from one direction. Nizam's entourage and encampment could not cover a distance of more than four-five miles a day, while Marathas were past masters in swooping upon their enemies and covering a distance of about fifty miles before taking any respite and in repeating their performance all over again.

One of the Maratha bands descended upon the Nizam's cavalry-men. Mohanlal and Shubrati were members of this band.

Nizam's horsemen were all set and put up a brave fight but were swept off by the guerrilla tactics and hilly hatchets of Marathas. Maratha squad was smaller in number than Nizam's squadron. The Nizami commander hazarded a guess that his men would surround the Maratha squad and finish them off. Marathas pretended to have been encircled and then fanned out in small groups. Nizam's squad divided itself into small bands and gave a chase to those fleeing groups of Marathas.

Marathas came like dustorm and also passed off like storm but turned back again in likeness to whirlwind, closed in as their long spears and swords made a clean sweep of the Nizam's troops who were divided into smaller bands by then, leaving behind a handful of Nizam's soldiers who reported to the Nizam's mobile cantonment, of their loss of equipment and supplies besides the casualties sustained in their fight with Marathas. Many a noble of Nizam felt the agony.

'Everything was carried away by Marathas. They left nothing behind.'

'Nothing absolutely.'

'What! Could not save those carts which carried...'

'No Sir, not even those which carried the drinking jug and the barrels....?'

The commanders pondered — with what great difficulty those articles had reached Kabul from Iran and were taken to Lahore from there. The Persian wine, 'Shiraji' and its many varieties had been carried through an arduous journey. There was dancing and merry-making at night in the encampment but the wine which went well with and inspired all, had been taken away by the Marathas.

The spirits of the commanders were downcast.

'Those fools would be drinking only the local liquor and now this wine of ours free of cost mixed with the other one.'

They could do nothing but repent and sigh on what had transpired. There was plenty of grain and butter-oil for the commanders but the carts laden with butter-oil and grain, which had been taken away would have been used for feeding the soldiers. The commanders were concerned more with the wine but they could not reveal their despair on its slipping away from their hands. Instead, they gave vent to their rue only on the loss of foodgrains.

The Maratha squad having taken possession of the goods sped away. The articles were laid out before Baji Rao and a list was made; it included even jugs and barrels. All these were distributed among Maratha commanders. Baji Rao too received his share.

'Does Peshwa also consume liquor?' Mohanlal asked Shubrati. 'The high and mighty do drink and also take meat', Shubrati told him. 'Despite being a Brahmin?'

'So what! He is a commander also!'

'Yes, of course; but this liquor was being taken to Nizam's encampment.'

'There may be many more liquor-consumers there, who surpass in riches and splendour all these on our side here.'

On one side, the articles were being disbursed; on the other, the wounded among the Maratha troops were being taken care of and nursed. One had his fingers snapped while the other had lost one of his hands! Yet another had lost his leg and become lame. The bleeding did not stop in the veins of a few others. Their deep agony was suppressed and absorbed in the satisfying realization of the commanders expressed by them as follows.

'A lot more soldiers of the enemy have been killed.'

'The wounded have also been far too many.'

'We have snatched away and robbed them of all their food supplies; hence the entire entourage of Nizam would starve themselves out.'

'Whatever articles and equipment we are getting now would last for months.'

'We shall secure new Jagirs[37] now.'

Nizam was perpetrating a lot of bloodshed in the south in order to found a new kingdom for the benefit of his descendants and Marathas were indulging in raids and guerilla strategy so as to carve out Jagirs for Maratha commanders and also to enable farmers in Maharashtra to till their fields in peace and comfort.

The tyranny meted out by Aurangzeb and his descendants was meeting its nemesis in those forms.

In all this, Mohanlal could not make out any thing except his own means of filling his belly.

The battle lasted only a fortnight or two. Nizam was forced to sign a peace agreement with Baji Rao and was made to accept the latter's terms for peace. Now the area lying in north upto

37. Jagir – Grant of land from the sovereign ruler to a chieftain for services rendered in the past.

Yamuna and upto Narmada river in the Deccan came in the possession of Marathas for the purposes of recovering tributes and revenue and for dispensing the Jagirs as well.

During the course of negotiating the peace treaty, Baji Rao came to know that Muhammad Shah and his counsellors had issued a fiat with a view to eliminate him and his infidel companions while Nizam was informed by his own sources that Baji Rao had received a royal decree that Nizam, the rebel should not be permitted to set up his kingdom, the 'Sultanate' in the Deccan.

Both gnashed their teeth. Nizam received another command from Delhi which ran as follows:

'Nadir Shah has crossed the river Indus and is moving towards Lahore; reach Delhi with military reinforcements.'

Nizam had signed the treaty with Baji Rao. He had heard many bits of news floating in the air about the power of Nadir Shah. He was well-aware of Baji Rao's promise and the distance between Delhi and the Deccan; he had firm belief that in case Nadir Shah did reach Delhi, he would not advance beyond Agra and if at all, he did, Marathas and Rajputs would join hands to meet his challenge. He visualised his and his fellowmen's interest being served by Nadir Shah's onslaught on Delhi. He set out for Delhi with his army and military might at a leisurely pace. Before reaching Delhi, he received reports of Nadir Shah's takeover of Lahore.

—✵—

25

The report of Nadir Shah's crossing into India's borders was received by Baji Rao also. Baburao Malhar, his envoy at Delhi had sent him a letter, informing, 'Nizam and the Emperor display apparent friendship but within their hearts, they bear grudge and ill-will against each other. Saadat Khan and Nizam, who are intimate friends had urged Nadir Shah to attack Delhi. Intriguing and cunning as both are, they are deadly against Marathas. After getting Delhi ravaged and plundered, they are inclined to invite him to Deccan to fight against Marathas.' The envoy had also pleaded that keeping in view the smaller number of men employed for his protection, some more should be sent up to Delhi.

Baji Rao put off his move to advance towards Delhi, stayed on in Malwa and got busy to consolidate his position. He sent a small squad to strengthen the guarding of his envoy. Mohan and Shubrati belonged to this squad which was asked to take the route lying via Ujjain instead of Kalpi-route. They made a short stopover at Ujjain to rest for a while. Mohan, finding some respite, went over to have Darshan[38] of Baba Trishulanand. Baba was busy doing 'Sheershashan'[39] after his morning ablutions. One of his disciples informed that Baba extended his time for 'Sheershashan' from three to five hours.

Having finished his 'asanas'[40] and meditation, Baba offered Mohan an 'asana' (seat) to converse with him.

Mohanlal respectfully said, Maharaj,[41] Baji Rao Peshwa has won his battles by help of your blessings.

Baba's eyes brightened; he spoke in an undertone, 'I had foretold that Peshwa would be victorious. God Shiva's[42] Kartikeya (Shiva's son), is not an ordinary power to reckon with.'

Mohanlal's heart swelled with gusto and he said enthusiastically.

38. Darshan – A glimpse and a face-to-face audience with a greatman or God.
39. Sheershashan – op. cit. 26, p. 90.
40. Asana – Yoga exercise or posture which may or may not include meditation.
41. Maharaj – A form of respectful address for king or any great person including a saint, priest or hermit.
42. Shiva – One of the three gods of Hindu religion constituting Trinity-Brahma the creator, Vishnu the preserver and Mahesh (Shiva) the destroyer.

'Maharaj, there is a lot of commotion and disturbance as reports have come in. Nadir Shah is advancing; may be, he is already in Lahore, what will happen now?'

'Peshwa would not be involved in this war.'

'Will there be a war between Nadir Shah and the Emperor.'

'Yes, of course!'

'Who will win?'

'Whoever will be blessed by Kartikeya.'

'Nadir Shah is said to be extremely powerful.'

'He was one of Shiva's 'Ganas'[43] in his previous life.'

'What, Shiva's Gana, Maharaj?'

'Yes, being guilty he was accursed; now he is coming to annihilate Delhi. He must be a great warrior.'

'But Delhi has both Hindu and Muslim population and it is said that a great congregation of hermits and mendicants is scheduled to be held at Kurukshetra; no wonder, if he torments them too!'

'He won't be able to torment them; he can't bring any harm to them.'

Baba was swaying his body in ecstasy. Mohanlal was further enthused.

Baba said, with his body still in sway, 'My group is also going to join that 'Mela'.[44] I should see to it how dare this Gana raises his head against hermits and mendicants.'

Mohan maintained silence. Baba was further provoked to say : 'If Nadir makes up his mind to torture anyone other than Moghuls, I shall reduce him to ashes.'

Mohan's awe was enhanced; he said: 'Maharaj, I am going to Delhi alongwith my squad. If you happen to visit that place, I shall certainly come to have your Darshan.'

---

43. Gana – an attendant or follower of a god.
44. Mela – a religious fair.

Baba nodded, blessing him to be happy, and added, 'Keep on looking for me.'

Mohan entreated so as to receive a blessing from him.

'Maharaj, I shall go on leave for a day or so to Fatehpur where I have my home.'

Baba raised his arm blessing him, 'May you roam about wherever you like. You won't come to any harm.'

Mohan was thrilled to the core and his joy knew no bounds. He had never felt such great strength within. Paying obeisance and after collecting the sanctified ash in a small cloth-knot, Mohan went away.

Next day, Mohan started off for Delhi as a member of his squad which took the route via Agra. The squad made a stop-over at Agra for some rest as also to get some news of Delhi. The 'Naik'[45] of his squad allowed him only two days' leave. Mohan said to Shubrati: 'I would have escorted you to see my cottage but you won't get leave; I could obtain leave of absence after putting in efforts for days.'

Shubrati said amidst laughter : 'It's all right; if we are alive we shall see it on return journey. Remember the recipe I told you about the 'doll-puppet.'

Joining his laugh, Mohan went away.

—❋—

26

Mohanlal carried some money with him besides a few clothes for male and female-meant for Roni and Tola, for whom he had taken about a kilogram of pudding as well. In his turban, he tied, in a knot, a pinch of sanctified ash which he had collected from the sacred fire-place of Baba Trishulanand. His heart was bubbling with joy for he had overcome many hurdles. In those times, very few could undertake such a long journey as

45. Naik – Corporal in command of a small squad.

he had done. He had fought many battles, in some of which he sustained injuries and in one he was nearly dead. The events relating to all battles flashed back in his memory while he was on his way from Agra to Fatehpur. He remembered, when he had set out all alone that night in this desolate wide world for his own sake, what did he, then, possess? Whatever he had in his girdle he was not bothered about whether he lost that or not; he wished to reach Fatehpur which he certainly would. The sanctified ash from the sacred fire-place of Baba Trishulanand who used to perform 'Sheershashan' for five hours at a stretch, would act as his shield to enable him to overcome all odds and troubles. Tota would come running and hug him with a choked throat, charged with emotion and, well, how long would Roni go on wrangling, he pondered.

He also possessed that prescription given and tested by Shubrati. Mohan burst into laughter and turned around to see if some one was watching him. Travelling alone and engrossed as he was in his reflections and misgivings, he liked trudging the journey all by himself. He felt fearless and determined. That night also he had left home all alone to make his way and to fight on his own against the poverty, despair, humiliation, penitence and sorrow.

The moon had risen in the sky spreading its light while the winter-sun was about to tuck itself at the horizon by then. He made up his mind with a grim determination even to die; now after the golden sun-lit day, as the fading sunlight lingered amidst the approaching darkness, he was determined to hold firmly the reins of life in the palm of his hand and to begin anew his life with his land and plough, his buffalo and his wife — all flashed in his mind's eye! Mohanlal arrived near his home immersed in thoughts surfacing from the depths and colouring of his imagination. Night had descended. But he could espy the familiar mounds, the cluster of tamarisk-shrubs, and capparice trees besides the high trees located near his house. Still his eyes yearned to see the fire-flames shimmering height beyond the barriers of mounds and cluster of trees, or he would like to see the smoke-cover rising and fading above the smoke-columns! But why this restlessness! He thought, he would be there in a few moments but then something seemed to scratch his heart — suppose, Qanungo and Jamadar had dispossessed Tota and Roni of the land and turned them out! He tried to get a feel of the sanctified ash tied at one end of his turban and thereby healed the scratch of his heart.

Making up his speed, he came and stood at the door of the porch. The firewood was not burning outside the house. The firewood of tamarisk tree was fed into the fire which was alit inside the porch. A few persons were warming themselves in the heat produced by the fire and talking among themselves. The fire reflected some light outside the porch. Mohan saw his lengthening shadow at his back. Some persons sitting round the fireside faced the door while others had their back towards it. Among those who were facing the door was the one who had come to acquire land from Roni. Mohanlal was familiar with him.

Mohanlal came at such a fast pace to the door that busy as they were in their absorbing conversation, they could not get to know his arrival.

Mohanlal stood at the entrance of the porch with doors behind him. He was wearing a military uniform and carried an arm and a bundle. With a sharp glance, he looked closely inside the porch but found neither Roni nor Tota. He thought they might be inside. Mohan greeted them with loud 'Ram-Ram'[46] but their ears probably were not receptive to such greeting; those facing him recognised him instantly:

One of them screamed 'Oh, my God!'

Another shouted, 'He would kill.'

46. Ram-Ram – A form of popular salutation using the name of Rama, one of the Hindu Gods and the hero of Ramayana, the great Hindu epic.

The third, preplexed as he was, shouted,

'Oh God ! Save me.'

Faces of those who had their back towards him turned white, they stood up and others soon followed suit; some one picked up the half-burnt piece of wood; others took small and big chips of firewood. One of them overran the fire and jumped to the safety of the inner apartment;

'O...EE., O-O Ugh ! O Ugh!'

'EE O Hu Hu'

'Ugh.. Ugh..'

'Ghi....Ghi...Ghighi!! '

None of them was able to articulate his voice clearly. Reflected in the light of fire, their untrammelled limbs were shaking with jerks and they were roaming helter-skelter in such a manner that Mohanlal was quite perplexed. For a moment, he had a quick glance at their distorted faces; the next moment, in the flickering lights of the flames, he saw the shadow of quick movements of limbs forming a pattern similar to a spider's cobweb on the wall, and also saw their moving arms forming circles made by fire-sticks, fire-wood chips and blocks in their hands. Some bits of half-burnt slicks and chips were thrown at him but no scars were left on his body as the burning pieces flying astray struck the walls or fell outside the door. The embers were flying away and got scattered thereby. Mohan could not figure out what it was all about. All of them rushed towards the interior to get hold of some bigger weapon. Mohanlal advanced a little, 'Brothers, hold on! Don't you recognise me.' Mohanlal shouted.

A bewildered voice floated from inside;

'Yes, oh yes; my God! It is his - his.'

'Oh.....we know it already that it is the same terrible Devil......'

'Hush! hush!

'Maharaj, go, go away we'll dedicate a platform in your honour.'

'Prayers and worship will follow thereafter.'

'We shall arrange to hold a fair too and offer incense or burn a sacred-fire in a pan.'

Ram-Ram,[47] Sita-Ram,[48] Radha-Krishna.[49]

Mohan now could figure out a little. He did not advance further but spoke from inside the porch.

'Brothers, I am not dead; I have come from the Deccan, from the city of Ujjain. Don't be afraid.'

'Jai Mahadev; Jai Shanker![50] Save us', A chorus of two-three voices come floating from inside.

Another voice dominated the previous two, 'Mahakal[51] Mahakal! Those who are killed in battle do travel to south only.'

Mohan contradicted, 'Ugh! What are you muttering? I am not dead; earlier I was merely wounded.'

'Hush! Yes!' One of the voices gasped and challenged him: 'We know how to deal with all kinds of devils.'

Mohan could hear the gun being loaded and his ears could gather another beseeching voice, 'Take sword as well.'

Mohan challenged them with a roar: 'Don't make a fool of yourselves; I am a soldier, you should know.'

'Yes, yes! We too are soldiers though we are not enlisted in the army.

'We shall clean up the mess in this haunted house right now.' The defiant voice roared from within.

Mohanlal's hand spontaneously reached for the sanctified ash given by Trishulanand. He could muster up courage to gurgle out, 'Where are Roni and Tota?'

---

47. Ram-Ram – Here, instead of form of greeting, recalling God in an aid to man in a state of awe or terror.
48. Sita-Ram – Sita, the wife of God Ram. The pair of words denotes dimurvate of gods worshipped together.
49. Radha – Consort of Lord Krishna.
50. Mahadev & Shanker – Other names of Shiva.
51. Mahakal – Shiva's temple at Ujjain. Literally means 'The Great Wheel of Time'.

The voice from within replied, 'Ran away towards Bharatpur; they must have got married.'

'Marriage!' Mohanlal's head reeled. It seemed to him that the fire in the porch, his own shadow on the wall and firewood pieces — all were shaking and shimmering in the shadowy lights. His ears again caught the tapping sound of the loading of the gun.

'Marriage!' he repeated softly when his dizziness waned.

Somebody spoke inside the house, to another person, 'Fire a shot from here; the ghost will run away.' Another voice was heard, 'We aim the gunshot at him by taking a defensive position here. The ghost will vanish and make his way to south whence he came*.

'Ram! Ram! Sita Ram! Radhey Krishna! Mohan's dizziness ended and things became static. He could make out a gun-barrel at one side of the door which opened in the courtyard inside and also saw the glow-worm like faint light of the about-to-burn-out muzzle-powder. Mohanlal was, in a moment, out of the porch and found shelter by the side of the wall. The persons in the inner courtyard found out that he had vacated the porch. They went forward with firm footsteps and with drawn out swords.

One of them said, 'Maharaj, go away to your abode quickly; else our gun, the symbol of Bhawani[52] will spout fire just now.'

Mohan said from his hiding, 'Brothers, don't be perplexed; don't get frightened; I am not dead.'

The gun-man's defying voice came muttering through the clenched teeth: 'Yes, yes, we know every thing. The horrid ghost-devil combine to speak such voice. The elderly persons were not wrong when they said so.'

Mohanlal could snatch a side-look at the determined movement and sweep of gun followed by swords, hatchets and

52. Bhawani – Synonym for Kali/or Durga, the two warrior goddesses who killed demons and devils and eliminated evil from the world. Here gun symbolizes the spirit of the goddess overcoming devils.

sticks towards the front door. He moved for a better hiding. He said, 'Don't commit this folly.'

The same voice cut short his remarks: 'The gun has not fired as yet; if it had.....by now........'

Mohanlal ran and hid himself behind a tree and spoke from there itself: 'I am hungry as I am coming from Agra.'

They found a cover of the front door of the porch. The fire was dying out but a little light flashed outside in the dark. Mohanlal watched the gun and its stalking shadow jutting out of the door.

One of them put it politely: 'O God, we are going to offer you incense and butter-oil weighing one chhatank',[53] which will meet with your appetite but you must leave this place now.'

'All of you have taken over my land.'

'Baba,[54] when Poni and Tota come back, we shall give back the land and every thing besides some money. Come, now you must leave.'

'But I am not dead, my brothers!'

One of them counselled, 'All demons speak alike. Fire gun with a loud bang, which will make him run away. Tomorrow you may give the offering of incense and butter-oil besides showering flowers and leaves on Lord Shiva.'

Mohanlal with a deep suppressed breathing said,

'I am going away but when I turn up tomorrow, you would regret it.'

The reply came: 'We shan't be a mere few. Then, the whole village will I turn up; besides, the government sepoys and their innumerable guns would be there to meet your moves.'

Heaving a deep breath, Mohanlal vanished slowly in the darkness. A frightened man's voice was heard, 'Look how this demon has left, exhalting and raising gust of wind.'

---

53. Chhatank – An earlier weight equal to about 50 grams.
54. Baba – A generic term for monks, mendicants and hermits.

Another person mingling some doubt in his voice said softly: 'Perchance, it might be real Mohanlal! He might have been saved from death in battle.'

'Fie! The commander of the force had sent the message about his death on time. But that witch, Roni did not perform the last rites in a befitting manner; this is why, he has turned into a demon.'

The speaker was reprimanded: 'And if he turns up in daytime....'

'We shall face him with guns and cannons and also we shall be able lo see every thing clearly and thereafter we'll proceed very carefully after fully sizing up everything.'

Throughout that night, none of them was able to get a wink of sleep. They kept themselves awake by keeping the fire burning and were ready lo swing their arms into action.

Mohan turned back towards the familiar cluster of tamarisk trees and thickets.

He was lost in his thoughts:

Roni and Tota had run away from the land of forefathers! They got married! Where would they be living? What was there for him at Fatehpur now? When I reappear before my acquaintances in daytime they will certainly come to believe that I am not dead but why should I come back to show them my face....to what purpose? They went away! Probably, the sepoys of Moghul government had driven them out. They were married! Oh, my God! Despite my being alive! But, may be, they also mistook me to be dead.'

'But.......But.'

Mohan could not make up his mind as to what he should do. He held firmly the sacred ash tied in his turban. His heart and mind were now more at peace and stable. It was a biting cold but he had enough winter clothes and some fried sweets made of flour, which he had carried for Roni and Tota, in his bundle. Mohan had got used to different kinds of calamities but this exceptional one created by Roni and Tota was becoming unbearable for him. Now the chill of the cold and the acuteness of hunger had become more intolerable. He went to a nearby but familiar pond of water. He had his meal and water and wrapped himself into clothes for a short nap. As a Maratha soldier, he was not used to long and deep sleep but it was part of his usual sleep to get up after intervals with a sudden jerk and surprise. He rose from his deep slumber after two hours; when he uncovered his face, he saw the stars shimmering and twinkling; slow-moving breeze, it appeared to him, was shooting sharp arrows at him. Mohanlal seated himself, looked at his weapons and stood up. He thought, 'I should return to Agra this hour and would proceed to Bharatpur from there? But why? Wherefore? Fie! No, he would proceed to Delhi with the same squad! What should I tell Shubrati? Would convey anything. When I see Baba, I shall tell him also something else! I shall see to it! Mohanlal took the road to Agra with a firm mind. As a sepoy from Maratha army, he could cover a distance of fifty miles on a horseback for a campaign and return another fifty miles — could he not rush back a few 'Kos'?[55] It seemed as if Mohanlal had got a renewed strength and was infused by a new vigour and vitality. He thought he would arrive at Agra by daybreak but he found himself there pretty early before dawn. After a few hours, his squad set off for Delhi.

Shubrati expressed his pleasure, 'It is very well that you came back so early.'

The corporal of the squad said, 'You probably came to know that Nadir Shah has occupied Lahore. He is already on march towards Delhi and we are required to set out for Delhi immediately.'

55. Kos – About two miles – a term used in North India.

Mohan nodded his assent to both of them in a wearied tone. When this squad reached Delhi, Muhammad Shah had already left Delhi with his large and heavily-laden encampment and entourage on way to meet the challenge posed by Nadir Shah.

—⁕—

27

Delhi, the capital moved with and followed the Emperor of Delhi. Muhammad Shah with his massive army and a large retinue and encampment had marched towards Thaneshwar to prevent Nadir Shah's conslaught. Bajirao's envoy and informer followed him, rather was compelled to do so. The squadron to which Mohanlal belonged also followed suit. Mohan having settled himself in his small camp went out to look for Saadat Khan's particular squad in which he had been recruited to launch his soldier's career. He went there in daytime and not at night. The captain of that squad immediately recognized Mohan; his complexion had darkened and his physique become more slim. Despite his Maratha uniform and outfit, he gave himself away.

The captain of the squad looked around, raised his eyes upward and then stared into the eyes of Mohan. It was still daylight and rays of the sun lighted the surrounding while his soldiers moved about.

After greeting him, Mohan said with a smile, 'Did you also take me to be a ghost?'

'No....no....Hm, yes', the captain replied.

'I am no demon or devil. You can see for yourself.' Mohan reassured him.

'Certainly not; I am forgetting your name.'

'Mohanlal'

'Yes, you were wounded. I recall,......dead.'

'I did not die; was merely wounded.'

'Oh yes, yes; well, what happened then?'

'Then I was taken prisoner by Marathas. I was treated and I got well. I landed a job with them. What else could I do?'

'Oh, you did the right thing', the captain said.

Suddenly, captain asked him casually, 'Have you been to your home?'

Mohan raised his eyebrows but maintained his cool and added. 'Yes, I did go there but the people there....'

Naik interrupted him, 'What happened to the money? Money was despatched according to convention taking you to be dead; what did they do with it?'

'How do I know?'

'Money will have to be refunded.'

'You may take the refund. I came to reassure you that I am not dead. Besides, I wished to find out the whereabouts of members of my family and came here to get some clues.'

'We have to investigate, of course. The government money can't be allowed to be squandered like this.'

Your office would certainly be in possession of the acknowledgment and receipt in lieu of payment. They must be available in the office of the Qanungo and Cashier.'

'You can enlist yourself in my platoon again if you so like'.

'I am all right there; if I don't get along there, I shall come back to you.'

Mohan returned to his encampment. The captain included this matter in his miscellaneous and current pending work. The news travelled via Delhi to Agra in due course. Those who had embezzled and shared the money did not bother at all. There was neither commotion of fear nor any confusion among them, for this was a routine affair. But this news was pitted against the conviction that Mohan had turned into a ghost and was seen not once but several times at Agra, Delhi and God alone knew at how many other places. After some time, the news reached places around Bharatpur also.

Tota told Roni, 'Bhaiyya's ghost has been seen at Fatehpur and other places, I do not know how many.'

Roni's beauty blended and matched well with her robust health. Her imagination cherished yearning of love and her emotions assumed softness while her dress bore the distinctive mark of her effort to adorn herself. She had not made up her mind yet. On one side was the old man's growing desire and on the other, the passionate advances of Tota.

When Roni saw Tota approaching her, her eyes betrayed her welling-up passion and her lips bore a smile in keeping with the same. Tota came closer and she found him sad and frightened; this subdued the passion rising in her eyes. But she smiled all the more as she wanted to make fun of his grim looking face. When she listened to Tota, she was stunned and asked a spate of questions: 'What? Who said this? Where was he seen? When? Who saw him?'

Tota told her with a sore throat, 'People saw him at Fatehpur in our own thatched cottage; they exchanged words with him. He asked our present address. Then he was seen at Agra, Delhi and Mathura.'

'Oh God! Ram...Ram.... Sita Ram', Roni chanted the holy mantra several times.

In the meanwhile, the old man who had heard their conversation also came there. Thus he knew the reason of their fear and cowardice. He said, 'Why do you lend your ears to such a rumour! All this talk is a gossip. You did perform all the funeral rites?'

'Very well, indeed!'

There is nothing to worry about and shiver: 'I know all the tantras[56] and mantras'.[57]

'Do the devils and ghosts appear in day time too? 'Never.'

---

56. Tantra – The spiritual magic practised by a class.
57. Mantra – Holy formula of hermits and monks, whereby they claim they can call up souls, spirits and ghosts.

'But I was told, he was seen at Delhi and Agra.' All this is a gossip.'

Tota kept quiet. Roni, however, spoke in a suppressed tone, 'Someone might turn up here too; I have suffered all life. Now.... now Oh my God!'

The old man assured them,

'Don't be perplexed. No ghost or devil has been able to withstand my mantra and tantra.'

'This wretched creature has no guts to come here. He will never come! You should live on joyfully, as sportingly as before. Your future is extremely bright. You won't face any trouble in this home of mine.'

Roni mustered up her sinking courage and busied herself in chores. Tota wanted to see her in her usual jovial self but she could not regain her gay 'spirit'. Tota could not entirely banish fears from his mind and hence put off his efforts to keep Roni in good humour by persuasion.

Roni, while busying herself in her work wished in her prayers that hours of the day would extend. After the fall of the night, darkness spread and the homestead would become lonesome. She guessed, he had left home for fear of her abuses and was killed in battle. If she had not ill-treated him in the manner she did, all this trouble would not have been caused.

'Oh my God, pardon me! I shall now live a life like Savitri[58] and Ahalya,[59] save me now! I am afraid he might pounce upon my chest with his mouth, nostrils, eyes and ears emitting and blowing flames. Oh God, protect me, now!'

---

58. Savitri – A Hindu heroine (from mythology), who by her deep devotion and loyalty to her husband could bring him back to life after death had snatched him away.
59. Ahalya – A Hindu heroine (from mythology) who had been accursed to turn into stone by her hermit husband Gautam who doubted her chastity, after she had received visitors disguised as her husband in the latter's absence.

Roni's heart was thumping with restlessness. She was determined not to go out or sleep alone. All of them started sleeping in a big room.

—✻—

28

Nadir Shah had already occupied and taken control of Lahore. Then he headed towards Delhi. Muhammad Shah too proceeded in that direction in his full regalia and splendour. Nadir Shah sent word, "The administration of your border province is in shambles, I came to set right the same; I shall return after receiving 'your gracious favours'."

The Emperor was also keen to have his face-to-face 'Darshan'. He presented his compliments thus, 'I am coming to receive you'.

Saadat Khan and Nizam were fully seized of the situation. They apprehended that there would be no occasion for any clash and their interests would be served without any effort. Nizam needed Nadir Shah's help to carve out a kingdom for himself while Saadat wished to become Mir Bakshi[60] of Delhi on permanent basis so as to dethrone the Emperor and declare himself all-in-all. Noorbai's abduction was pricking into his flesh like broken thorns. Having landed in the pleasure palace of Muhammad Shah, Noorbai never turned back nor did Saadat Khan ever regain the position of Mir Bakshi.

Muhammad Shah's encampment was set up with tents and layers of canvas sheets, which demarcated and encircled the area around. Saadat Khan had been deprived of Noorbai but his sighs and pangs of love for her remained embedded in his heart. He tossed in his bed, his mind vacillating between disgust, despair and sorrow, still, the charming face of Noorbai, it seemed to him, appeared and fondled him when he was turning sides in bed. What would be her fate there? He thought, 'I had won her

60. Mir Bakshi – One of the titles and a position conferred by the Moghul Emperor on a commander of his confidence.

hand and love with great effort by overcoming her coquettish whims, and airs. What would be befalling to that grace and elegance in her beauty. It might be that she was being robbed of the same in some tent or behind some canvas-curtain. Whose eyes would be ogling and converging on her eyelashes, towards the bend of eyes-brows, the suppleness of her neck and on the rhythmic, subtle movement of her heaving limbs? And what pretty legs, their complexion far surpassing the hue of henna! And the tinkling of the little ringing bells tied to her feet, which vied with the fifth crescendo of the Sarangi[61] and sublimated its harmony! The melodious even notes of Tabla[62] synchronising with the rhythmic tinkling movements of the dancer, seemed to recreate the atmosphere of a sleepy nightingale singing sweetly. From behind gleaming veil and long skirt, the sheen of her smile playing above the pearly, lustrous teeth seemed to be in rapturous love with lips adding to her beauty. He recalled the diamond-studded necklace and the pretty bracelets! Oh! fie! they were not too costly. But — but what did he gain? What did she give in turn? The Emperor, damn him, robbed me. But, then, what could he do if his own coin turned out to be counterfeit. Never — never ! That great rogue has held her back and does not allow any news of hers to trickle down to me. But then she could run away and come back. But how? May be, the chief eunuch (Khwajsara)[63] or other sentries would have killed her! The days of her release from bondage are coming closer — Nadir Shah, the warrior is advancing fast — then and then! But why did she offer to present her performance before the Emperor herself? What did she miss here? I spared no pains for her! I did every thing to please her? I do not lag behind Emperor as dilettante of music and her artistry? Oh! It is extremely difficult to make out a woman's frame of mind. That innocuous ogling! That matchless

61. Sarangi – A string musical instrument played by hairy rod.
62. Tabla – op. cit. 6, p. 43.
63. Khwajsara – Chief of the eunuchs.

smile!! No......no, the accursed Emperor is to blame squarely, Nadir Shah....Nadir Shah....I shall become Mir Bakshi again and Noorbai will be mine.......thus wrapped in restlessness, he went to sleep.

—❋—

29

It was not cold inside the royal encampment; the firewood logs were burning- the Persian carpets were spread within tents; apart from the shawls frorm Kashmir, to add to the warmth, there were several kinds of wine filled in wine-jugs and soft hands of the angelic damsels holding up the gold goblets for drinking. Outside the royal encampment, barring the commanders, the sepoys were managing it somehow to pass the night on their own. If the firewood provided warmth to their back, their chest and belly remained sticking out in the cold. It was such a biting and chilling cold that soldiers' clothes could not match and overcome it. The cold weather was likely to linger on for a month more; the sepoys were itching to fight against Nadir Shah – they thought that either the cold season should come to an end quickly or the demonic Nadir Shah's onslaught was warded off somehow.

That night, Muhammad Shah was to judge for himself as to who was the best singing and dancing girl – whether it was Noorbai or some other damsel. There were quite a few and all of them were beautiful, vivacious and brimming with youthfulness; but Noorbai was confident of her beauty as well as artistic qualities. Those running in the competition relied more on their luck than on the sound judgement of the Emperor.

It appeared to be a mart of glamour and splendour. Muhammad Shah had earlier witnessed, several times, the bending, bowing and the wavy movements of the dancing girls besides their ogling The mention of the gay abandon of nightingale's singing in the garden seemed rather stale and out-of-time to Muhammad Shah. Beauty seemed to embody itself, in that garden, in the form of beautiful damsels. Muhammad Shah continued to gulp his goblets of wine, while girls danced through the night. As he poured his wine, his judgement faltered. He looked for a new turn and rhythmic face in dance movements and the latest elegance, expressive of emotions. More goblets of wine went down the throats as the yearning for novelty also mingled into and was drowned with the incessant flow of wine in the psyche. The pretty dancing damsels raised their voice and gave sharper twists and turns to their supple bodies with an intended effort to sublimate their beauteous looks and handsome bodies. For a split second, a serving maid's hands seemed to touch the quivering lips of the Emperor when graceful movement of the artists expectantly waiting for that moment of acme vanished from the focus and gaze of the Emperor. Muhammad Shah uttered a word of admiration in a soft voice with a slight swing of his head. Those angelic maids were sore and sulky about the flow of wine from jugs and from thin hands but they were expecting a quick turn of luck as well from the same — it might be that the Emperor would like something appealing thereby and pronounce his judgment accordingly.

Noorbai's turn came last. Her firm conviction and confidence in her own exquisite beauty and artistic qualities had begun to waver but she was also aware that despite several pegs of alcoholic drinks, some iota of 'merrymaking spirit' still remained at Muhammad Shah's conscious level. She showed off elegantly and gracefully, her bewitching beauty and virtuosity. She projected her beauty into the graceful dance sequences and blended her mellowed voice in pleasing ragas!,[64] sweet tunes and simple musical rhythms, which harmoniously mingled into a unique composition. Muhammad Shah's tipsiness had increased and there was nothing else but his customary expression of admiration 'well done' and an uncertain nod and sway of the head. Noorbai was thoroughly immersed in her assiduous

64. Raga – Particular permutation and combination of musical notes.

performance and single-minded devotion to art; the Emperor's intoxication relapsed into meditation.

'Butter-oil lamps may be lighted,' the Emperor remarked. As the music was stopped, Noorbai got a shock.

'That's a good one! Go on', he said. Noorbai again engrossed herself in her performance.

After a short while, Muhammad Shah said, 'What are the rates of butter-oil in Delhi?'

Music came to a halt again and every one kept quiet. The Emperor repeated the question, 'What is the rate of butter-oil?'

One of the maids cleared her throat and said, 'One Rupee a maund'.

There was silence again. Noorbai stood all set on her toes as if she was about to give a new dimension to her art.

The Emperor said, 'I shall order the butter-oil lamps to be lit even in the ruins of Delhi after I have vanquished Nadir Shah – Go on '...Noorbai, well! What were you singing?... any way!......A new song, a new style of dance – straight one or with a twist will do at the moment.'

The damsels — artists who had already given performance of their art got a shock. Their hearts seemed to suggest to them that even if the Emperor had ordered them to dance bare-bodied, they would have willingly done that or would do so wearing only a dress made of flowers. They glanced at the maids sideways with their eyes. Their attention was focussed on the Emperor's beckoning hands expectantly. The red-hot wine, poured out of the jug, reached the lips of the Emperor. Noorbai began to dance and sing her number.

'Sing us a Kanhaiya![65] – song, Noor! a song about the Kanhaiya or Brij.[66] "Why not act like a Gopi"?[67]

---

65. Kanahiya – op. cit. 21, p. 78.
66. Brij – The region around Mathura and Agra in U.P. state, where Lord Krishna spent his early life and youth.
67. Gopi – Milk-woman in ancient Mathura, who adored Lord Krishna and danced to the tune of his flute on the banks of Yamuna.

Muhammad Shah's intoxication prompted him to utter this command.

Noorbai was absorbed in her artistic performance. Her zest for dancing made her blush through the smiles playing on her lips and she felt a flowery, fragrant sensation filling her limbs and a wondrous essence inspiring her passionate voice. Her spirits soared in sublimation as she sang with full-throated ease, far above the instant atmosphere and surroundings. She sang the following stanza composed in 'pathos' style of music forming part of a romantic song about the flower and the bee, by the poet, Nand Das:

'Had he no mouth, tell us, then,
who ate the cream?'
Had he no feet, tell us, who wandered
from forest to forest?
One who applies collyrium to the eyes
One who held the mount Goverdhan
on finger-tips
Is very much the son of Nand and Yashoda,
The Prince Krishna, the Lord of Brij'.

In the beginning, she, merging her inner self in the song became a Gopi and seemed to present, before every one's eyes that paragon of the earthly exquisiteness which is the fountain of all imagination - 'Kanhaiya' of the Brij. She became infatuated instantly oblivious of what she was doing and where.

The image of 'Kanhaiya of the Brij' receded to the back of her mind for a while and was replaced by 'about-to-weep' face of Saadat Khan in a gesture of praying apparently for her favours but prepared to shower all his riches for her sake. All of a sudden, she started acting as a Gopi. The Emperor's head swayed and hit against the pillow but he regained his self and in a monologue said aloud 'all praise be to your song and dance'. The 'Kanhaiya of Brij' again appeared before Noorbai in her mind's eye giving fillip to Gopi's emotional outpouring. Noorbai was thrilled to the core with her own passionate exposition. She could feel passion welling up and vibrating within her body. Her feet kept on the rhythm and momentum as a natural corollary of her long periods of rehearsal; her vocal chords seemed to be flowing with sweet musical sound like a nightingale 'pouring forth her heart' as she flies light-winged, without fluttering its wings, above soft-cool breeze, her wings kissing the wind, yet wafting through it with great ease; her voice reminded one of several waterfalls cascading, unceasing stream of water flowing quietly but separately, in a tangent or straight line absorbing within themselves, as they fall, the shimmering rays of the sun on their way to merge into the hushed silence of a lake. She had, before her eyes, 'the Kanhaiya of Brij' alternating with Saadat Khan, the latter ever ready to place himself in her service. It was past midnight — what was the import of the 'pathos' expressed in that stanza composed by the poet Nand Das, and now being sung by her in 'Bihag'[68] style of music. Suddenly, Noorbai's vocal chords quivered and faltered; the rhythmic tune and the singing voice finding expression on 'Murkiyan'[69] style faltered and her eyes became moistened. Despite best effort to keep 'sonorous' balance, Noorbai could not withstand it. One of her refrains turned into sobbing and her cries assumed the form of singing again. The Emperor's hand struck against the pillow as he again burst into his remarks of admiration, more aloud this time. Noorbai sobbed again and started crying; she wiped her eyes with the arms which still bore the bracelets gifted to her by Saadat Khan and then, with rhythmical tinkle-ending produced by small rings tied to her feet in a string, her lips spontaneously sounded 'My Kanhaiya!' These words penetrated, as it were, the frenzy of the Emperor's intoxicated mind. The singing and dancing stopped

68. Bihag – One of the Ragas of North Indian classical mustc rendered during the night.
69. Murkiyan – Particular style of rendering musical notes with flourish.

suddenly and the tune produced by Sarangi floated above all this to, finally, fade far away in a distant direction.

The Emperor's half-shut eyes opened a little more, betraying their moistening; everything appeared to be rhythmical to him. To Muhammad Shah, the pearls hanging from the armlets of the rounded arms of Noorbai seemed to be swinging to and fro.

His voice quivering, Muhammad Shah said, 'A wonderful performance, Noorbai! but why did you start crying?' Noorbai made an effort to control herself.

Muhammad Shah said, 'You invoked Kanhaiya a little while before? Isn't it? Whom did you address?'

Noorbai had, by then, wiped her tears and stood still with folded hands; she said, 'Who else could I pray to?'

'Well done! well said, of course. No doubt.......no doubt, I am Kanhaiya.'

'My Lord.'

'You are just the same in your inner self as you appear to be outwardly; what a wonderful artistic style you possess! You are the greatest artist of the world in this age of ours.'

'Your Grace has bestowed the greatest honour on me.'

'Undoubtedly, I am yours, my beloved Noorbai; you should come and sit with me, for you must be tired.'

Noorbai was not at all pleased to be invited to sit beside the Emperor on the cushioned, high mattress; but the invitation was beyond her expectation.

Noorbai became still and quiet. She entreated, 'If Your Grace would be pleased to hear, I may sing another song.'

Muhammad Shah's intoxicated mind did not restrain his speech, 'Begin a new one'; he said and hinted to maids to pour wine from the long-necked jug.

The goblets were gobbled up. Noorbai began to sing and dance but she could neither conjure up 'Kanhaiya of the Brij' nor the tearful Saadat Khan. Facing her were the maids with their wine jugs and Muhammad Shah whose head swayed after drinking a number of goblets in a row — it was followed by an incongruous and ill-timed word of praise — 'well done'. Finally, the Emperor reclined completely on his pillow, and the singing went on for an hour thereafter for the standing instructions were that the music must go on until the Emperor was wrapped up fully in sleep, losing all consciousness and was carried away by six chamber-maids to his dream-chamber.

In an instant, loud and terrible sounds of shots, bursting of gun-fire, 'kill them; run away resounded the air. The music stopped in this commotion and Muhammad Shah rose from his sleep. His face was distorted and his eyes contorted.

'What's the matter? my friend, – Nadir Shah has been defeated? Light the butter-oil lamps. What's the price' – the sentence could not be completed when the lady-guards entered the tent.

'Nadir Shah has surrounded us, Your Grace,' a chorus of several voices was heard.

Muhammad Shah was still in a state of torpor.

He questioned, 'Is Nadir Shah still not defeated?'

'We have been besieged, Your Grace!'

'His Grace be condemned to hell. Saadat Khan, Nizam where are they? Have they died?'

The Emperor's sleep and torpor — all vanished as he felt a burning sensation in stomach and an ache in the head.

One of the guards said, 'Nobody knows where they are?'

The Emperor commanded, 'Make me lie down in bed. Let me rest for an hour or two; then I shall see. Meanwhile, you should put the commanders and the guards on alert; let them fight fiercely and intensely.'

—❋—

30

In fact, Nadir Shah had not yet mounted his assault but was laying siege of Muhammad Shah's encampment and tightening his hold on the same. That night, a cat jumped over the head of a sepoy who was sleeping. The sepoy in confusion and bewilderment fired his gun, which led to the breakout of commotion and confusion which was worse confounded when several guns were fired. After the hullabaloo, when wisdom dawned on men, they were ashamed of themselves and became silent.

Nadir Shah was a remarkable general of that age. His soldiers wore identical uniforms and were fully equipped with European arms, besides being a thoroughly disciplined force. He wanted to return from Hindustan without getting involved in a battle with the Moghul Emperor. One day, in the outer cordon of the Moghul Emperor's encampment, a few sepoys ran into a small squad belonging to Nadir Shah's army. Saadat Khan and Nizam wanted to avert the fight. Nizam being too old, Saadat Khan went to mediate but at one place, the skirmish did take place. He was slightly wounded and taken into custody. Nadir Shah meted out a good treatment to him but did not let him go scot free. Saadat Khan became Nadir Shah's informer, spying upon Muhammad Shah. Nadir Shah wanted to extort money from Muhammad Shah, for which negotiations were under way. But settlement was not yet in sight.

'The Emperor wants to get away by paying a sum of Rs. 30 lacs. But it is reported that the Emperor has immense wealth.'

'Endowed with riches and wealth as this country is, its wealthiest person is the Moghul Emperor himself.'

'I too consider that the sum of rupees thirty lacs is too little.'

'Yes, too little, indeed, my Lord! It is not even a makeweight. The throne called 'Takhte-Taaus'[70] alone is worth nine and-a-half crore Rupees.'

70. Takhte-Taaus – The famous peacock throne of the Moghul Emperors; studded with Kohinoor, the largest diamond in the world besides other jewels.

'Yes, yes; 'Takhte-Taaus' is invaluable but what about the cash, gold, silver and diamonds?'

'Thirty crore—Yes, thirty crore but how do you reckon it?'

'My Lord, you may send summons for Nizam and then the Emperor will present himself, in your service, of his own accord.'

'I sent for Nizam but he chose not to come.'

He would certainly come; you may like to remind and pressurise him a little; he is a friend of mine.'

Nadir Shah again summoned Nizam and sent a message to the Emperor too. But Nizam got no respite from the intrigues of the Moghul court; secondly, he wanted to go in the presence of Nadir Shah with a large squadron; in case he went there without force, he might be taken by surprise and made to suffer.

A day did arrive when the protocol and courtesies ceased between the two. Muhammad Shah's commander engaged the enemy-forces relying on the strength of sheer numbers. But Muhammad Shah's massive force could not hold their own when confronted with the fully trained armed personnel and the latest equipment which belonged to Nadir Shah. After a lot of bloodshed, courtesies were exchanged again and the sequence continued. Besides, Nadir Shah's grip over the siege had become more firm and strong so as to enable him to pounce upon and have his way. The Emperor was taken prisoner in his own camp. The dancing and merrymaking diminished. The artists and the connoisseurs of arts were mortally afraid. The Emperor in order to easily get away from Nadir Shah did not negotiate peace treaty with him – instead, he invited him to a feast.

Nadir Shah sent word, 'Send over Nizam — he should come riding a mule.'

'Riding a mule! A dreamer of empire-building in the south should go riding a mule!'

The one who colluded in inviting Nadir Shah had to go, for the latter's audience, on a mule's back. It was essential to pay obeisance to the will of Nadir Shah. The Emperor had committed the folly of involving him in a fight. Now he had become a greater terror and force to reckon with and could be relied upon for invaluable assistance against Marathas in the south — Nizam pondered over all this.

His misconceptions were cleared up when he was brought to audience with Nadir Shah.

Nadir Shah said, 'By accepting a defeat at the hands of Marathas and then entering into a peace treaty with them, you humiliated the Emperor.'

'Did I?' Nizam expressed his astonishment.

'Who else could it be then? And in spite of all the arms and the equipment, you surrendered and bowed your head! Why did you have to do this?' Nadir asked.

'The Emperor did not come to my rescue.'

'You took away the entire fighting equipment and the stock-pile of large and heavy royal arms; where was the wherewithal for the Emperor to help you! If the Emperor had adequate army, he would have crushed Afghans on the borders and I would not have come to India!'

To Nizam, for one thing, all this implied that he should not have succumbed to Marathas; secondly, he should have left behind so much strength of the army and the equipment as to enable the Emperor to suppress the uprising on the borders; thirdly, and which is more important, Nadir Shah would not have been compelled to come close to Delhi in order to crush the border-area! Nizam, old as he was, considered Nadir Shah to be his well-wisher; but the fact that he was made to come riding a mule, exasperated him with a desperate anger.'

Restraining himself lest he should be provoked more, he said, "Your Honour, we have a parable in India which runs like this — A he-goat and a wolf were riding the same boat! The wolf complained to the goat 'You are raising dust! I am restless.'

The goat submitted, 'Your Honour, neither is the boat in water nor am I raising any dust.' I beg your pardon, I do not wish to disclose the outcome in the story."

Nadir Shah replied calmly, 'I know stories longer and better than this one but this will neither satisfy your appetite nor mine. How much would the Emperor pay as penal compensation for the battle?'

Nizam replied with a quivering voice, 'Your Honour had already received the message for a sum of rupees thirty lacs, but he would be willing to pay up to rupees fifty lacs.'

"Hm! The throne 'Takhte-Taaus' itself would fetch any thing between nine and a half to ten crore."[71]

'But that is meant to be the seat of the Emperors.'

'You must rest assured that only an Emperor would be seated on that. But I am talking of cash payments just now. The person who possesses a throne worth crores must be a multi-millionaire. I am conceding quite a bit; I shall not accept anything less than rupees twenty crore.'

'Twenty crore!'

'Yes, please; Twenty crores and not nineteen crore.'

'It is extremely difficult indeed, Your Honour.'

'It is all so easy; you yourself possess far more than this sum.'

'Oh, my God ....well! With your leave, I may go and submit this to the Emperor and would also try to persuade him to this sum.'

'No; you need not worry — You may be pleased to remain here as my guest. I shall myself invite the Emperor to a feast here.'

Nizam lived there like a prisoner. The Emperor, perforce, had to accept the invitation for the feast and was compelled to come. He also became desperate and angry. But he made adequate

71. Crore – A crore is equal to 10 million.

arrangements to entertain and please Nadir Shah. Noorbai and other court-singers were part of his retinue; he thought that he would be, anyway, compelled to part with something for Nadir Shah but this way, he might arouse his compassion to elicit a good bargain.

—✵—

31

With the premonition of the imminent trouble, Baburao Malhar, the envoy of Baji Rao immediately left Muhammad Shah's court. His squad also followed him but Mohanlal did not choose to go with it.

Shubrati's voice quivered as he said, 'Well! It seems our companionship will come to an end here and now.'

Mohan said, 'Brother. I do not wish to leave the region of Brij to go anywhere else.'

'What will you do here? In this encampment? This place is not a part of the Brij area.'

'I shall join my old squad for some time... and then.'

'And then you will go home; of course, it is in the fitness of things; if I had my home and hearth here, I would have also done the same. I also wished to go round in Brij area; anyway, it does not seem to be possible.'

Mohan kcept quiet. Shubrati asked him, 'When you went home, did you find peace there?'

Mohan was not inclined to answer this question. Earlier also, when Shubrati had put this question to him, he had evaded it.

Shubrati diluted his regret in parting company and said, "You may not be required, perhaps, to make use of the 'puppet-doll device." Shubrati's face was lit up with some forced laugh. This increased Mohanlal's sadness. He said, 'If you happen to come this side with the envoy or Peshwa himself, I shall try and meet you.'

'Now we are proceeding to Jaipur where we shall stay or make our way to any other state of Rajputana for camping there; thereafter, we shall await and abide by Peshwa's command.'

'May be, you'd go down south directly from there.'

'I am not sure!' The envoy wants to go on a pilgrimage to Mathura and Vrindavan.

'Quite possible! No — it is not likely——but, I do wish to go to Mathura and Vrindavan; let us see, where my destiny leads me to.'

'Why don't you accompany us then?'

'Assuming that the envoy does not visit Mathura and Vrindavan and also does not make any stopover at Jaipur, it will be my undoing.'

'Quite likely! Well, wish you Godspeed! — Ram—Ram.[72] Shubrati hugged him before departure and bade him goodbye, saying, 'Ram — Ram'. He went away with his own squad. Mohan got himself enlisted again in his old squad. The Naik put him on duty with himself.

Mohan was drinking life's elixir as if from a poisoned cup. He thought of picking up a fight against Nadir Shah's sepoys; otherwise, he might find some one to fight a duel in Muhammad Shah's army; he thought, rather wished, he might die on some battlefield and disappear from this world. He, at times, thought, 'I should not get wounded this time; each limb of mine may be sacrificed like in a Johar.'[73] His blood gushed and glowed within his body reflecting a certain radiance; at times, his heart prompted him to go on a pilgrimage of Mathura and Vrindavan to have a Darshan of Kanhaiya. Every now and then it happened like this!

---

72. Ram-Ram — op. cit. 46, p. 117.
73. Johar — A sacrificial pyre for the ladies of royal family, who immolated themselves to save their honour after their husbands had lost the battle and got killed in fighting.

Nadir Shah extended his invitation to Muhammad Shah, which was accepted by the latter. The dance and music programme was arranged for once but was cancelled. Muhammad Shah was already apprehensive. His commanders had no faith in Nadir Shah's overtures.

One day, instead of feast, an open fight broke out. Mohan considered it a good opportunity but being one of the guards commanded by the dastedar Naik, and deployed at harem,[74] he could do nothing; for the harem was frequented by the Emperor. The situation could be likened to the bright light emitted by lightning followed by clouds carrying raindrops. Except for the sounds of cannon shot and clanging of swords, the lascivious and merry life-style of 'harem' remained unruffled, notwithstanding its commotion; nor did any one yearn for something else as it might disturb its tenor.

Khwajsara, the head guard of the harem, told Muhammad Shah, 'Your Grace, a cat has, again, taken a leap over the head of some damned fellow — those ill-fated fellows are bent upon indulging in fireworks.' 'What about those shouts and that uproar; it was time of night and someone might be hurt with a gun-shot!' But after dawn, when the rays of the sun dispelled the hangover of the night and the tidings were received of thousands of soldiers having been killed or injured, Muhammad Shah was unable to make out anything. Nadir Shah sent message for a feast. Nizam and Saadat were already interned in his camp; Muhammad Shah thought that perhaps this fight was the outcome of his men's folly.

Nadir Shah had besieged and tightened his grip on Muhammad Shah's encampment. The soldiers fought the battle very well but those who were supposed to hold the fort failed in their efforts. Delhi's heavy artillery fire-power, sword-power could not match the well-disciplined and experienced Iranian

74. Harem - op. cit. 33, p. 105.

army which had gone through the vigorous drill-practice on the parade ground as well. Twenty thousand soldiers were killed.

Then a feast in the honour of Muhammad Shah was arranged.

Nadir Shah regretted that unnecessarily so much bloodshed was committed just because of the folly of a few commanders of Muhammad Shah. Muhammad Shah, vacillating between doubt and trust and shivering in suspicion, accepted the invitation.

The feast was laid out; a variety of tasty dishes combined with renowned Persian wine were served. But after dinner, a wondrous wine, sprightly and entertaining, which could vie with any wine in the world was presented to Nadir Shah — it was Noorbai. Accompanied by several dancers, she towered above all of them. Nadir was nearly fifty one years old. He had spent the best part of his years in skirmishes, manslaughter, conspiracy and in organising his army and collecting the latest in the weaponry. What he was witnessing before his eyes, he had never seen in his life until then — neither as a drover of sheep and goats nor during his bloody exploits in slaying and slaughtering. On watching Noorbai and other danseuses, it struck him for a moment, 'if he could have a chance (to watch all that without having to fight battles, it would be all right but (then, this battle was brought off only on account of the tomfoolery of people from Delhi.'

Noorbai looked at Nadir Shah, blinking her eyelids in awe. Nadir Shah could see through her fright. He thought — if a beautiful woman did not possess the shy, blushing nature, her exquisite face would bear no charm. Some day, she would be his mistress, he made up his mind.

Nizam and Saadat Khan were also invited to the feast. Nizam was seated prominently while Saadat Khan remained in the background. He was still licking his wounds which had not yet healed up fully. Having withdrawn to one side during the feast, he was relaxing in the background but could not be ignored. Saadat recognised Noorbai — she was wearing the same diamond necklace and the bracelets, given by him. Besides, she sported the Emperor's newly bestowed gifts on her —the scintillating ornaments; Saadat suppressed his rising sighs.

Noorbai began her singing in unison with the sounds of Sarangi chords and the soft-beats of Tabla. Noorbai recited a few Persian Ghazals, the import of which she tried to project by swaying her supple, tender body and the feet wearing the jingling ringlets. She could shake off the gripping fear by singing; even so, Muhammad Shah felt that her movements of limbs had not attained the desired perfection.

Nadir Shah was exclaiming with admiring looks, 'Wah.... Wah!!' Muhammad Shah looked forward to a better performance from her.

Saadat Khan concentrated his thoughts a number of times, 'Are they not the same old graceful dance-steps which enraptured me too.' With such thoughts, his unhealed wounds were smarting more and more.

'Noorbai's singing and dancing was over and was followed by others.' Saadat Khan tried to reason with himself, 'The poor woman! She was helpless indeed; if she did not sing any more, what else could she do? Muhammad Shah had summoned her in custody and having arrived there, she had to carry on singing. Muhammad Shah, God damn him. I shall bring him to ruin.'

Nadir Shah liked the singing and dancing of other danseuses but he cherished the charm, which Noorbai had infused in him.

Nadir asked Noorbai to repeat her performance. Shaking off her awe for him, Noorbai was feeling relaxed by then.

Noorbai's spirits flowed into an ecstasy having such an admirer as Nadir Shah. She bowed in obeisance to Nadir Shah with smiles playing on her lips. Nadir Shah made out that those smiles were dedicated to honour him. Muhammad Shah bemused that Noorbai's bewitching beauty and artistic excellence would be able to rescue the crown and the throne of Delhi.

Muhammad Shah spoke in Persian, 'Noorbai. Sing that song about Kanhaiya with the same elegant gestures.'

Nadir asked, 'Which Kanhaiya?'

Muhammad Shah told him, 'Kanhaiya is a god of Hindus. He reigns over their heart's desires, ambitions, expectations and helplessness — the one who charms the ladies and makes them dance to his tune'.

Nadir dissented, 'Beg your pardon! On the one hand, you have rose and fragrance, the nightingale and its sweet twitter, the graceful and coquettish ladies, the fairies and on the other, that man — what did you call him? Anyway! Let something else be performed. When I go to Delhi, I should see what is to be done about him.'

Muhammad Shah's head reeled. He would go to Delhi! What would he do there? Why does he want to go there? Let us comply with whatever he desires us to do here — it might be that Noorbai's sweet singing and the jingling, stepping sound of the ringlets of her feet would be able to hold back that rising storm and turn it towards the same direction whence he came.

Noorbai began to sing a Persian Ghazal. Her gestures and the ringlets in her feet seemed to concretize and embody the ideas of the Ghazal. Nadir Shah began staring at her with penetrating eyes, and felt absorbed in her sweet singing and passionate, provocative gestures.

Saadat Khan's smarting wounds seemed to be bursting. His pangs and sighs welled up to his lips. He tried his best to suppress them so as to hide them from others.

Making an assessment of Nadir Shah's rising joy, Noorbai brought forth smiles after smiles as her eyes looked sideways or in front while her sprightly body waved into dance movements. She thought, 'Whatever reward I should get during that entertainment, it would be invaluable indeed; the Emperor would, of course, throw offerings' but Nadir Shah, the great Emperor would also bestow upon her gifts — her joyful spirits seemed to suggest all this to her and her artistry supported her spirits.

In the twinkling of an eye, a tide seemed to be rising within the heart of Nadir Shah. His lips seemed to suggest, 'How lovely is that creature; I should like to gulp her down or shut her up in the drinking-jug to drink at leisure from it, or wrap up the whole of her body to be kept in my custody.'

His speech forced itself, 'I have not seen such an elegant, coquettish gracefulness in Iran.'

Muhammad Shah said, 'She is the pride and honour of Delhi.'

Nadir said, 'She would make pride of Persia now.'

Muhammad Shah mistaking that his device was materialising became effusive and expressed himself thus: 'There would be nothing more delightful, to me, than this.'

Nadir Shah thanked him with a smile. Noorbai assumed that the smiles and soft tones as the unfurling of the flag of her fame. She became more sprightly and swift in her movements.

Her last refrain in musical rendering and her ending in the tinkle of her ringlets appeared to be drowning themselves in the whirling crescendo of Sarangi and the rising beat of Tabla. Noorbai's heaving arms seemed to be sublimating the admiring words 'Wah....Wah' uttered by Nadir Shah, who blessed her with a boon by remarking, 'You were the pride of this Empire until now, but you will now become the glory of Persia. You will be honoured far more there.'

The complexion of Noorbai's face changed — it assumed one complexion which turned into another. She bowed her head further down to hide the emotions reflected in her face and paid obeisance more reverently. Nadir Shah thought that she was expressing her gratitude thereby. That very moment, there was an uproar in the midst of the Sardars gathered there.

Everyone listened to it. Nadir Shah saw that Saadat Khan had reclined completely on his pillow with a loud shriek; Noorbai also recognised him. She went and seated herself with a thud in the company of instrument players. Saadat Khan was taken inside his tent to be looked after properly.

—❋—

32

Next day Saadat Khan regained his health and vitality. Nadir Shah called him to his encampment. They began conversation with a reference to his health.

'That fairy-like woman, or whatever you call her, sings very well. Your spirits imbibed her ecstatic singing so deeply that you became unconscious with a shriek' — Nadir Shah said.

Saadat Khan said, 'Your Lordship, an old wound gaped up all of a sudden; its agonising pain made me unconscious.'

'You are all right now, isn't it?'

'Yes, Your Grace, by your blessings.'

'Now you have got to do one thing, which you alone could accomplish.'

'May it please Your Honour to tell me!'

'Your Emperor is an utterly foolish person — as useless as a pumpkin!'

'A pumpkin! Not so, Your Honour.'

'And simpleton too! To that fairy-like woman, he wants me to.......'

'Yes, Sir, her name is Noorbai.'

'Yes....Yes, Noorbai; I should like to return to Persia with the satisfaction of taking Noorbai only.'

'I do not follow, Sir.'

'Is it so hard to follow?' He has made a gift of Noorbai to me. She will be a member of my harem alongwith others.'

It seemed, Saadat Khan got a lump in his throat. Nadir Shah went on, 'Here in Hindustan, I have faced a great ordeal and in recompense to that, I must get a sum of Rupees twenty crore at least. Noorbai cannot fetch that high price.'

'Yes, Your Honour.'

'Why are you mum now? Has any other wound opened up? You should not become unconscious in my presence. Don't you follow? Don't you remember what you had told me.'

'Yes, Your Honour.'

'The old Nizam is rather a weakling. Apparently, he does not even know how to make use of his limbs. I summoned him too but I am told that last night's celebrations have forced him to lie in bed. You should do something! You can! You will be appointed Mir Bakshi. You were suggesting that I should put in a demand for Rs. 30 crore.'

'One of the wounds has started giving me immense pain just now, Your Honour!'

'I know how to treat all such wounds. No pretext will do the trick. Persuade the Emperor. I'll grant you some time. If you are unable to get him round to this sum, I won't spare you. Two days would suffice, isn't it?'

Saadat Khan groaned; Nadir knitted his eyebrows. He said, "Two days' time is more than enough! Nizam should also be out of bed. He will also assist you, but you must start your work right now."

Saadat Khan wanted to say 'yes' and then rise from his seat. Nadir Shah repeated as Saadat Khan was going out, 'Explain it well to the Emperor that his gift of Noorbai would remind me of his gentlemanliness but anything less than Rs. twenty crore would not serve to compensate me for my losses. I wish to leave this filthy place as soon as possible.'

Saadat Khan was under Nadir Shah's surveillance and custody. As he reached his camp, he sent for Muhammad Shah's bodyguard whose squad had Mohanlal on roll. The other commanders had either been killed that day or had fanned out helter-skelter.

The bodyguard came accompanied by Mohanlal. The bodyguard alone went into the tent; Mohanlal was left outside. That camp did not flaunt the Moghul splendour and regalia. The Persian guards were gathered at one side. Mohanlal stayed back there. He could hear most of the conversation under way inside.

'By no means twenty crore rupees can be raised. He is getting Noorbai nevertheless.'

'Nadir Shah is not an infant which could be lured to entertain himself with a toy. Don't talk rubbish.'

'The Emperor himself thinks on such lines.'

'If he has no brains, you people may lend him some.'

'You should come with me; he values your advice more ever since that dame has arrived here.'

'If I could breathe the fresh air of freedom and get out from here, I think the Emperor would be forced to seek shelter in such a place... Of what avail thereafter will be the 'Takhte-Taaus' and the diamonds hidden in the cellars?'

'What are you driving at? You should remind yourself of the loyalty you owe to the Emperor, who has provided you the means to live by.'

'I owe loyalty only to my sword, the soul is bestowed upon us by God and the body belongs to me only.'

"You are mouthing irrelevant things. Even otherwise, you did spoil the enjoyment of last night's 'Mehfil'[75] when everyone was enjoying passionately and had sacrificed his individual desires by adoring and admiring mellifluous voice of Noorbai, her graceful gestures and postures; you swooned at a wrong

75. Mehfil – A special congregation of selective audience for performance of dance and music, or recital of poetry.

time. You should now act with tact. If the Emperor comes to know of this, what would he think of you?"

'Tell him.....carry this to him and inform him that Delhi will not be spared now..... Tell that spoilt, – defiled, nay, frail woman also that.....—'

The sentence could not be completed. He heaved a sigh and gave out a light shriek.

The Persian sentry lifted the curtain and peeped outside. The Emperor's bodyguard was coming towards that tent.

He said, 'Sardar Saadat Khan has been taken ill suddenly. Probably, he is unconscious; send for the Hakim'.[76]

'Unmannered! I am not unconscious yet.....' Saadat Khan sat up in his bed and cried, 'Delhi's Emperor and Delhi's pride, Delhi's cynosure' — He could not go on. He whipped out a dagger lying on one side of his bed and thrust that quickly into his chest. He cried in pain for a while—and then died.

The Emperor was informed of the suicide committed by Saadat Khan and the reason given out was the unbearable pain of wounds. Mohanlal passed on this information to his fellow-sepoys who, in turn, carried the tale to the men and women-guards and maidservants. Noorbai also received the news of this incident but in an exaggerated form. She could not express her own emotions before any one. Only one thing she could bring up to her lips, 'I shall not go to "Iran — I won't go to Iran in any circumstance — I shall not go anywhere forsaking my country.'

Before it was evening, she took off from her person the bracelets and the necklace given by Saadat Khan and put them in a box — lest perchance the soul of the dead enters the ornaments. Noorbai slept very little that night.

And Muhammad Shah slept much less than Noorbai. The bodyguard could not help revealing the demand for payment of Rs. 20 crore although he tried to mitigate its intensity.

76. Hakim – An equivalent of a physician in medieval times.

With Saadat Khan's death, Nadir Shah thought that the period of two days set for making payment could not be enforced. Nizam was unable to move about; so, Nadir Shah sent his emissary to remind Muhammad Shah about the sum of twenty crore rupees. He did not convey any message about Noorbai whom, he thought, he could possess anyway and thereafter preserve for himself.

The Empefor expressed his inability in very polite language, in words full of courtesy and solicitude. Nadir replied immediately in equally, rather more courteous manner, — 'It is all right, are your hospitality, your gift of Noorbai to me, beautiful and pleasing scenery of your country not charming enough for me? Now I wish to see Delhi as well; after a stopover of a day or two, I shall set out for Persia; after drinking in the beauty of Noorbai and her music in your company, I shall return to my kingdom with her within a few weeks.' What was implied in all this became partly clear to the Emperor, but how could he contradict him? He had to agree to all this. Noorbai was shaken to the core. The entire cantonment including the Iranian one which had besieged the Emperor's own cantonment marched towards Delhi.

—❋—

33

Nadir Shah had set his eyes on future while Muhammad Shah did not look beyond his nose. He imagined and persuaded himself that Nadir Shah would be preoccupied and engrossed in music, dance and merrymaking and thereby soon forget and forego the levy and claim of twenty crore rupees; Nadir Shah had planned that Muhammad Shah should keep himself thoroughly immersed in merriment and drinking rounds from morning to evening, so that he could capture Delhi without losing a single

77. Naga – 'Naked' hermits who abstain from clothes and shelter and are known for their insolent and indifferent behaviour towards people.

soldier and thereafter he would turn to the Emperor in order to extract money and riches.

The full complement of personnel in the cantonment enjoyed themselves en route and reached Kurukshetra. A fair was in full swing during that period. With the spread of the news about the arrival of Nadir Shah's army, the people in the fair dispersed and disappeared except for a few 'Naga'[77] Sadhus, who were adamant not to leave. One of them was Trishulanand.

The encampment of Iranian soldiers was set up away from Hindustani soldiers; even so, quite a few Iranian soldiers and Hindustani sepoys developed esprit de corps. A majority of Hindustani soldiers were Muslims. Among the bodyguards of the Emperor, the Hindus were predominant.

Mohanlal took time off to see the remnant of the devastated fair at Kurukshetra. A few Hindu sepoys and soldiers followed them.

Trishulanand was free from his morning ablutions. When Mohanlal came to see him, he had just seated himself. He sat after paying obeisance to him. Mohan thought that Baba had already recognised him but the former's eyes did not betray any sign of recognition.

Mohan reminded him, 'Maharaj' —

Baba interrupted him, 'Who are you?'

Mohanlal told him, 'Maharaj gave me some sacred ash as 'Prasad',[78] which is still tied in my cloth. It protected me a lot but.....'

'No ifs and buts, you may keep it and take some more from this Dhuni[79] (fire-pit).'

'I shall take it, of course. You didn't recognise me. I was a member of Baji Rao's army.'

'Baji Rao won the battle and would be victorious again.'

78. Prasad – The offering made to God and distributed to the devotees.
79. Dhuni – A pit or bucket made of soil for keeping sacred fire burning for a long time.

'You told me that Shiva's Gana has embodied himself in an incarnation. He is marching towards Delhi with his entire cantonment.'

'May be! He will wash the sins of Delhi and then go back. How are you concerned?'

'Can't he be forced to go back from Kurukshetra itself.'

'He has come to take a dip.'

'They take bath infrequently and that too.... in this cold weather!'

'Who are you? Are you trying to assume responsibility for the whole world — Go away.'

Mohan observed that as compared to the day spent at Ujjain, Baba had become Tamasi.[80] He touched the ash tied in his cloth so as to appease the temper of Baba.

He said, 'I came to serve you!'

Baba replied — 'What service! Have you brought something? Brought some corn?'

Mohan loosened his grip over the knot containing ash and said, "Haven't brought corn but came only to get some 'Prasad'."

'Here take this sacred ash and run away Baba told him as he reached for the fire-pit. Mohan said a little firmly: 'I'll certainly take the ash but kindly help protect Delhi. Nadir Shah's soldiers don't distinguish between Hindu and Muslim soldiers while slaughtering them.'

Mohanlal took the 'prasad' of ash. Baba said, 'If he indulges in tyranny, he will be destroyed.'

'How? When?' Mohan spontaneously asked the question.

'I shall do it! I shall destroy him. Do you have any more questions?'

'Nothing.'

80. Tamasi – One of the three lifestyles as clarified in Yoga philosophy. One who is engrossed too much in worldly affairs having belief in drinking, eating and merrymaking.

Mohan saw that Baba had closed his eyes. He kept sitting, maintaining silence. After a little while, Baba opened his eyes again. His eyes were red. He said, 'Are you going now or, I will have to pick up my rod?'

Mohan did not relish this. One of his arms twitched for action but he controlled himself immediately.

Mohan and his fellow-sepoys were on their feet immediately and departed from there. They went in one direction while from the other side, a few Iranian and Hindustani soldiers turned up there. Baba was unmoved, so were his disciples but their minds were unhinged a little.

Iranian soldiers began to converse with their Hindustani companions.

'They are all naked and that too in this cold!! These damned fellows have thought of facing the biting cold only by smearing ash on their bodies.'

'They are Fakirs[81] — Hindu Fakirs.'

'A few Fakirs remain naked, stark naked back home in our native place too but they can perform miracles also.'

'These too can do the same.'

Iranian soldiers did not believe this, but they chose not to tease those 'Nagas'. They started looking closely at fire-pits and the tridents fixed around them — what was contained in the tridents? Some of them removed the tridents from their fixed place and started examining the same. The Nagas were exasperated. Trishulanand flew into anger.

'What are you doing? Get away! Don't defile the place! I shall reduce you to ashes!'

Iranian soldiers could not follow the language but they were able to make out the import. Hindustani sepoys could understand both the language and its import and were overawed.

81. Fakirs – Mendicants (and monks) equivalent to Hindu hermits or Sadhus.

One of them said, 'Baba, we beg your pardon. These people are not aware of your powers as they are outsiders.'

Baba wanted to concretise his anger but did not know in which form he should express it. Baba's eyes fell upon the swords hanging from his small tent erected close by.

Iranian soldiers wanted to enjoy themselves with their child-like innocence. Some of them scratched the earth with the tridents while others rummaged the fire-pit. Trishulanand held the trident and balanced it as if he would hit someone but did not.

Iranian soldiers started ransacking the hermits' articles lying here and there just as children begin to catch the worms, insects and frogs and play with them, when it rains. Hindustani sepoys wanted to protest which they brought up to their lips but turned despondent and silent. Baba began to shout and Iranians became busy in enjoying the humour.

When Trishulanand saw that he could not bring harm to any Iranian soldier by his flaming eyes, he lifted his tridents and was about to strike a blow at an Iranian soldier when the latter saved himself by a swing of his body to one side. Immediately, one of the hermits engaged him in a duel. Then the Iranian soldiers drew their swords and started waving the same as children kill the worms and frogs after playing with them for a while during the rainy season. Hindustani soldiers did not partake in that bloodshed but could not intercede either. Trishulanand wanted to bring out his sword from inside the tent but could not get to it. He was killed by an Iranian sword. Other hermits were also killed, while fighting for their lives.

Mohanlal and his companions heard the commotion from a distance and were about to come back when they saw the Iranian and Hindustani sepoys going at a fast pace. Iranian soldiers were well aware that if Nadir Shah came to know about their mischief and hullabaloo made by them, he would order them to be killed.

Mohanlal was stupified by what he saw at Baba's place. He had witnessed bloodshed and corpses in many a battle earlier also, but what he saw near the scattered tridents and the fire-pits made his heart sink.

A voice echoed in the innermost recesses of his heart, 'Baba said that he would finish off Nadir Shah, but why was he killed that way?'

Even so, he tightened more firmly the knot of the ash in his cloth.

—❋—

34

With the passage of time, terror of Mohanlal's ghost receded from (the minds of Roni and Tota. The talk about his having been killed and then turning into a ghost and being watched at Agra and Delhi also subsided. Roni resumed work with her earlier gusto. Her passion was to collect butter, sell it and collect money and to this she concentrated all her energies. Tota felt that Roni's affection towards him had risen like a tide and ebbed; lately, her affection had made him shed his fear of her; now, he was awed by her again.

Roni was unable to collect as much money as she wished to.

All of them slept in a big room. Even otherwise, there were neither enough cots, beds and clothing nor so many rooms as to provide for their sleeping separately. Above all, it was extremely cold. A long straw mattress was spread lengthwise, on which was laid out a longish cotton-cloth bed and on this bed someone occupied a corner while another lay at the other, wrapped in the thick, rough clothes. With the fall of evening, a lamp was lit; after finishing the chores in the thatched verandah occupied by the cattle, the fireside warmth was absorbed for a while by all of them before they went in to relax themselves. That night, Roni was unable to sleep.

'That life of hers, her body—would everything lie wasting away? There were many people who possessed good utensils, good clothes, silver and gold ornaments. They were lucky indeed. God had ordained all that for them. Would destiny not smile on her at all? Has Fate willed me to grind, thrash corn, cook, and tend buffalo? Who has deciphered the writ of Destiny or is Destiny a mere device to console oneself?' Roni thought to herself.

'The old man has a son — a mere lad! Would I be married to him? Impossible....never. If he had been a girl and I were a man, I would marry him probably....Would not do so even then. He appears to be as cold as an image of clay. He eats – eats and eats and does nothing else. Tota! Well, Tota has some guts. But why does he feel so suppressed and despondent all the time? Why does he not talk in a manly manner? He behaves in such a way as if he is my servant. He does not utter a single thing smartly. Who else would I look upto? Even if I have someone, would he turn the tide of my destiny? I know Tota closely. I should awaken his yearnings for love. I would fail to be my own self as Roni if I do not arouse his love. But why rush it through? Should manage it by and by, but wherefore this slowness? Money can't be collected gradually! Many persons have gathered wealth, riches, ornaments and all types of finery. Have they come to possess these by and by! Fine, some have saved it from farming but look, how many have large fields and wells, for that matter? Others indulge in highway robbery — seizing an opportunity, they pounce on others. They are no longer poor and their homes are warm and comfortable. Well! I should now seek love in Tota,' Roni made up her mind though a little vaguely. She was still weighing the pros and cons to alter her decision when sleep overcame her.

Having finished the morning chores, Tota observed a mellowed gentleness in Roni's demeanour and behaviour towards him. 'Previous evening she was a different person and today she is a changed woman' — Tota was absorbed in trying to figure out her conduct and dialogue. Roni mistook that Tota was trying to distance himself. When evening arrived, she found a chance too talk to him.

'I should marry you off, brother-in-law.'

Oh no! Wherefore?

'I should pass my life like this only!'

'Why, one who comes to your home and hearth — will she not bring in her own luck?'

'One more burden will be added!'

'Supposing no burden is added.'

'How is it possible, sister-in-law?'

Roni smiled and her smile seemed to answer his query. He was well aware of Roni's idiosyncrasies. He surmised, 'Whether beneath her smile lay an unerring, lasting feeling of love or this effusiveness would vanish with the smile itself?'

'In the same manner as is enjoined by the custom', she could barely suppress her smile as she craned back her neck. Tota's body pulsated with passion but he did not lose his self-control. He said, 'When we have saved something, we can think of all such things.' Woman's innate nature was aroused in Roni.

'I am also saying the same thing but our present state of living is a pointer that if we have enough to make both ends meet, we should thank our stars.'

'Should I enlist myself into Badan Singh's army.'

'Are our neighbours who are wallowing in their wealth and riches and take airs in eating delicious sweets, working in the army? Perchance by your joining the army, misfortune may befall us.'

'Do you think one born of a Jatni has frights of war?'

'I wonder, when would wisdom dawn on you? I am not talking about your fears; I am talking about my own. But for you, who is there to take care of me?'

'And for me, you are the only dear one, all that matters in life, sister-in-law.'

'The one who has no anklets and bangles to adorn her feet or wrists!'

'What can we do? We work so hard, yet are able to save so little.'

'What about that neighbour of ours, who has neither farm nor cattle! How has he amassed all that wealth?'

'He rarely takes part in military exploits. His name is retained in records but his exploits by night on Agra-Delhi road are quite different.'

'Are you a nincompoop?'

'There is enough scope for money there but that profession is no good'.

'You are wasting away your youth by sweating out here. The whole day I spend by the side of grinding-stones day in and day out. Will happiness continue to elude us? You are somewhat coward!'

'I am not a chicken-hearted person, sister-in-law but I think members of noble families should refrain from such misdemeanour which is beyond the pale of decency and decorum. Don't you agree?'

Tota's tone could not convey the force, implied in his language.

Roni remonstrated, 'Who are those that call themselves belonging to noble families? I learn, the Moghul Emperor at Delhi has thousands of women in his harem, who bedeck themselves with jewellery worth lakhs and crores of rupees. All these wallow in wealth alongwith their maids and servants. When the Emperor founded his kingdom at Delhi, you think, he bought it from someone? How did Badan Singh lay the foundation of his kingdom? Did he get it from his father? How did he expand it?'

Tota feebly responded, 'It is all a matter of destiny!' Roni added, 'You may also turn the tide of your luck, try a little.'

Roni's smile thrilled Tota to the core. She turned herself a little. Tota heard her muffled tone, 'We shall be united for ever; you should not continue to waste your energies like this.'

Tota made up his mind, and said, 'You are quite right, almost everyone has been forced to indulge in that nefarious activity; those who don't engage themselves thus are either starving or have turned themselves into monks.'

Tota busied himself thenceforth in learning the tricks of the trade and in working out the 'plans' which had attracted countless, if not all, men living around Delhi, Agra and the neighbourhood.

—✵—

35

The populace of Delhi was at its wits' end like a person who has a shrunken head, a large chest and a belly larger than that — a person shivering in face of crisis with fear of being swept off his feet, relapsing into inaction and lack of direction. With the spread of news about the outcome of Karnal battle, the wealthy traders and money-lenders had fled Delhi but turned homewards again when Nadir Shah had ensconsed himself in the fort at Delhi, as if nothing eventful had happened. With business resumed, Delhi regained its lifestyle.

The palace again witnessed the unending series of merrymaking, the mehfils and majlises.[82]

Muhammad Shah deluded himself by concluding that Nadir Shah had been made to forget everything else. Nadir, however, set his eyes prying beyond the melodious ringing

82. Majlis – Assembly for a special purpose.

sounds of mehfil and the commotion of majlis, looking for the royal treasure. He had unearthed some but was hopefully and assiduously engaged in discovering the remaining. Noorbai's music was quite enthralling but he had managed not to engross himself therein; he did not wish to be enticed into Muhammad Shah's dicey tricks. He had made up his mind to take her along to Iran on his homeward journey.

Muhammad Shah had come to know that Nadir Shah had an eye on the treasure but there was no untoward incident which would prompt him to defy the latter, if at all he could muster the courage and strength to do so. He thought that if Nadir Shah was determined to acquire the treasure, he would have made lot of hullabaloo but he had done nothing like that as yet to give rise to any such apprehension. Muhammad Shah was fully convinced that Noorbai and other angelic damsels were making Nadir Shah drink deep at the fountain of music and love so as to make him lose his self-control and this understanding did not permit Muhammad Shah's dark thoughts and cloud his faint and dismaying doubts.

The tidings reached the 'harem'[83] which lodged the angelic beauties, that Dewan-e-khas[84] would witness festivities and merrymaking and their dancing and singing would feature therein.

The 'harem' was in commotion long before the hour of festivities arrived at Dewan-e-khas. Everyone vied with each other in doing neat and pretty parting and pleating of hair, choosing out the thinnest colourful clothes, selecting the jewellery, sprinkling aromatic oil and in how best to present herself and the curves of her sinuous supple body. The ones who were not to go to Iran were assiduous in trying to bring in shades and hues of rainbow but others whose fate ordained them to go,

83. Harem – op. cit. 33, p. 74.
84. Dewan-e-khas – Place for holding royal court or special audience.

looked lost at times as their wavering glances showed.

They bemused that Iran which had all the exciting gardens with flowers and haunting music of singing birds and for which any poetic expression in Ghazals and Rubaiyats or language would not approximate, with its specialities would certainly surpass India to some extent. Added to all this, they would find cool comfort in the shade and shadow of the magnificent charming Shah of Iran, which eclipsed and veiled the glory of the Emperor of Delhi. Besides, they would be rewarded regularly with highly valuable jewellery which would match with their costumes — jewellery made of diamonds, pearls, gems to match their brocade dresses. Among such damsels was Noorbai whose face, despite all pretty jewellery and embellishments could not hide the dampened enthusiasm and pallor.

Noorbai took out, from her jewel-box, the bracelets and the necklace given by Saadat Khan, put them on for a while and put aside, knitted her brows and then placed them in the box as they were before.

The hour of festivities arrived at night. Dewan-e-khas was spruced up to look a palace of pleasure. Seated on the throne called 'Takht-e-Taaus', Nadir Shah and Muhammad Shah drowned themselves in raptures of joy while watching the supple movement of bodies, the glistening and winking eyes and listening to melodious cadence and the tidal waves of music and dance by the danseuses. It was the same 'Takht-e-Taaus', from which Shahjehan and Aurangjeb had wielded the sceptre and the sway of ruling the empire according to their will and well laid-down tradition.

Noorbai also sang and lived upto standards of dance performance but she put her heart into that to an extent as was necessary for her to rise above the performance of the accompanying dancers.

As Nadir Shah watched the wavy, dancing movements of

their bodies, his estimation of their performance declined. His keen eyes gazed continually and observed the intricate engraving and craftsmanship of 'Takht-e-Taaus' and then penetrated beyond them in reckoning the value of the diamonds and jewels studded thereon. He pondered.' 'Wherefrom these diamonds and jewels were secured? Whatever might have been the source, surely Shahjehan would have obtained them free of cost according to his sweet will. How nice would it be to take 'Takht-e-Taaus' to Iran? It would add to the splendour of Iran. Wind wafts away the fragrance of rose and the melodious song of a nightingale but what about 'Takht-e-Taaus?' 'It is not swayed or carried away by the wind.' He thought within himself and murmured 'Hm' a bit loudly, which astonished the inebriated and indulgent Muhammad Shah. A lightning thought flashed in the mind of Nadir Shah. He imagined himself to be carrying the 'Takht-e-Taaus' while Muhammad Shah appeared to be sticking to one of its legs in a bid to prevent him from doing so. The flash of thought soon dissolved itself. Noorbai's singing and dancing were in full swing. Nadir Shah changed his 'Hm' to the applause of 'Wah....Wah'[85] but it was most inopportune.

The accompanists eyed one another and displayed a sense of disbelief. Noorbai was stupefied. Muhammad Shah checked the derisive laughter and mingled his 'Wah-Wah' to the echo of Nadir Shah's applause. Nadir Shah wished to talk business and put an end to music. He found out the opportune moment to conclude the same.

He exclaimed, 'Noorbai, your performance has been excellent!' Said Noorbai, 'Today, I have not done anything like that'.

Muhammad Shah intervened, 'That song about Kanhaiya has still to be sung, Shah. With certain indifference, Nadir Shah said, 'Which Kanhaiya song?'

'The one which is full of such emotional love and tenderness,

85. Wah...Wah – A form of address - an exclamation of joy and admiration.

Noorbai performs it very well' Muhammad Shah informed him.

Nadir Shah stretched his limbs and yawned ceaselessly. Noorbai got the message. Noorbai herself did not wish to sing that song. Muhammad Shah stared at Nadir Shah.

Nadir Shah maintained his cool and announced, 'Noor! You are, indeed, the light of life. You would get Four Thousand Rupees every month besides all comforts and luxuries.'

Noorbai got the message that she would have to meet her end in some palace of Iran, while watching in imprisoned state the luxuries and comforts heaped upon her. She bent her head fully and instantly in order to hide her pent-up emotions and performed the thanks-giving round of song and dance.

Mehfil was dispersed and every one returned to lodgings. On 'Takht-e-Taaus' remained seated only Muhammad Shah and Nadir Shah. Their personal security guards stood at a distance. Muhammad Shah's heartbeat increased. He eyed the dagger hanging from Nadir Shah's waist and took no notice of his own bejewelled dagger. Nadir Shah's eyes turned away in other direction. Nadir Shah turned back and entreated him, 'My Lord, I have to make a submission.'

The choice of words was excellent and the melodious intonation pleasing to the ears but Muhammad Shah's heartbeat rose in anticipating what was to follow.

'At your command!'

Nadir Shah spoke obdurately, 'Your courtesans are unworthy of themselves.'

'Indeed they are!'

'They have not conveyed properly the import of my statement.' 'May be, they could not follow it, out of fear.'

'This is why I am taking liberty to talk to you in privacy. I have to return to Iran now. There some people are likely to rise in revolt, I have to suppress them.'

'This is quite easy for you.'

'Thereafter I shall come back here to enjoy your hospitality.'

'I shall always look forward to that hour.'

'Help me in arranging my departure.'

'I have to take back a lot of goods....er and.'

'Your arrangements are in perfect order so as to leave no scope for error therein.'

'Noorbai will accompany me besides several thousands others.' 'There is no gainsaying that.'

'But my Lord, whatever losses have been incurred by Iran and myself in coming to India, make me giddy in making an estimation of the same.'

'Gains and losses are part of every man's life. My only regret is that you have not been looked after well in India.'

'I have been looked after very well but this cannot make up for my losses. I have been made to suffer a loss amounting to thirty crore rupees. Didn't your courtesans tell you all this? If your borders were well protected, the Pathans of the border and outlaws from Afghanistan who had settled close to the borders would not have shot up trouble for me. A loss of more than thirty crores has been inflicted upon me.'

The Moghul Empire is facing great crisis in these times.'

'I don't see any sign of it. One can't find in the entire world such a great exhibition of diamonds and jewels, such comfort and luxury, cheap foodgrains, and populace endowed with good clothing.'

Muhammad Shah groped for a suitable reply.

Observing his silence, Nadir Shah reminded him of his persistent demand. He made a final announcement of it, so to say, 'My Lord, you shall have to manage. Today, I am forced to open up on this, shedding all consideration of public appearance. I hope I shall not be called upon to repeat myself.'

Dewan-e-khas which was humming with life for a few moments back appeared to be quite deserted and swept by gusty winds.

Nadir Shah again stooped to make entreaties and departed from Dewan-e-khas in a spirit of supplication.

—✵—

36

Noorbai put aside the costume-jewellery which she had worn at the festive occasion. Left to herself, she stood before a mirror and heaved a sigh which gave rise to a few more. Eyes welled up with tears. Eyelashes shed the collyrium applied in eyes. Sitting on her bed, she began to cry and sob. Meanwhile, a maidservant came in. Noorbai covered her face; the maid paused, wavered a little and came closer to her. Noorbai continued to weep. The maid tried to console her. A little later, Noorbai's sobbing ceased and she lay on her bed. The maid began to massage her legs.

Noorbai asked her in an undertone, 'Would you help me a little?'

Pat came from the maid's reply, 'At your service, even at grave risk to my life.'

'Would you like to go to Iran?'

'I don't wish to go but how can I help it either way? Wherever you go, I should accompany you.'

'And if I do not wish to go.'

'Is it possible?'

'It can be made possible.'

Noorbai sat up in bed and said, 'I don't wish to go. I am determined that even if I have to lose my life, I would not go to Iran. Will you help me in winning my freedom? I shall reward you, of course.'

The bond-maid waved her palms over Nootrbai's head, seeking blessing of God and added: 'I won't flinch to lay down my life for your sake. Who does not yearn for freedom? Whatever you call upon me to do, I will perform only too willingly and blindly with head upside down even if I may have to lose my life-breath in your service. Excited as she was, Noorbai hugged the maid and rose on her feet. She looked around to reassure herself that no one was nearby. She brought a knife, opened the box and took out the bracelets and the necklace presented to her by Saadat Khan. With a quick glance at them, she cut them into such pieces that each had one precious stone sticking to it.

She said, 'They are priceless! Work out the plan to escape by dodging watch-women, eunuchs and soldiers.'

Many a barrier barring freedom loomed large and clearly before the maid's mind; how would she elude others, how would she demolish the barriers with the help of ornaments —these nagging thoughts overwhelmed her. Noorbai sensed it instantly.

'Wherefore? What's the matter?' Noorbai asked her.

'Nothing! By the by, it struck me as to how many wretched, abominable fellows we would have to face before making our escape.'

Pointing towards the jewels and diamonds, Noorbai added, 'You would be carrying with you the remedies for such fellows.'

The maid mustered her courage but no sooner had she worked out her escape-plan than it seemed to be breaking up.

The maid said, 'The Iranian guards are extremely alert. They may make out my Persian expression but how would I follow their talks?'

Noorbai persuaded her, 'After all, people would be going in and coming out of the fort.'

The maid interrupted, 'Yes, in daytime!'

Noorbai conjured up the vision, 'People would be going out on urgent business even at night.'

'Should like to try', the maid added as she gave expression to her indecision in flattering words.

Noorbai replied in a hoarse but suppressed tone, 'Let me try it myself! May be, I am killed! Nothing worse than that would befall me. Name the guards to come by first; you would know them surely.'

The maid's voice regained its unfaltering tone; she clenched her fists and said, 'My lady, do not bother yourself. I shall accomplish a lot. When a woman comes into her own, she can achieve every thing.'

Noorbai was enthused, I shall die for your sake, and give you so much that you would be overjoyed and become a happy person for all your life. Tell me all about the guards now.'

The maid recounted one by one, 'At first you would come by Negro women, then Negro eunuchs and after that Emperor's indolent attendants, most of whom are Jats and Rajputs followed by Iranians and Turanis.'

Noorbai said, 'This list, though small, is ominously long enough but we too possess, in our hearts, a lot of strength and courage, isn't it?'

The maid supported her, "And you know all about 'harem'. God only knows, how many lads disguise themselves as ladies in veil and gown to come in and go out of harem; nobody questions a lad here and a lad there."

Both of them revised the plan and worked it out again immediately.

—✵—

37

The night descended with absolute silence. 'Keep awake .....Be on the alert'- the calls of the guards were dying out slowly, mingling with languor of pervading sleep. It was past midnight and as the chill and cold of the wintry night became more intense and enervating, negro women and eunuchs were induced to sleep in their apparel and clothes at their posts as usual, leaving the call of duty and security to the alertness of Iranians. The bits of gold also stood them in good stead. The maid and Noorbai cautiously came out disguised as men. Carefully and with bated breath, Noorbai made her way out with little bags tucked in her waist.

There was stony silence in the guard room of the indolent Iranians, broken intermittently by the snores. They stood in the dark corner to plan further their escape route. Mohan's guardroom lay a little away. He was also dozing although he was not asleep as yet. His ears caught the rustle of clothes; he became alert and rubbing his eyes, started staring; he spotted two moving shadows. Seizing the sword, he began to wipe out shadows of doubt from his mind. A few moments flitted by. Both of them were whispering something to each other, seemingly in consultation to ward off impediment in their plans; or, it seemed as if they had forgot to reckon some snag in their plan or were going to risk their life in order to fight their way out.

Noorbai broke the silence, 'We have reached this point, now what to do?'

The maid replied, 'From here onwards, Iranians are standing guards. Let us return, we shall try to do it in daytime.'

The vision of daybreak and the slipping away of that chance to freedom sent a chill through Noorbai's body. When they saw someone heading towards them with a naked sword, they, somehow, managed to suppress their scream with their hand.

Mohanlal faced them now. Gasping in fear, the maid gurgled up the words,

'Protect us, save us; you must be a Rajput or a Jat.'

Coming closer a little in order to size up the situation, Mohanlal uttered softly, 'Of course, I am a Jat. Who are you? Oh! The lads who managed lo get into the palace.'

'Yes sir!' the maid answered.

'No, sir!' Noorbai interjected.

Mohanlal tried to figure out with a closer look.

He said, 'Come here in the light.'

They stepped out two paces in a manner as if they were made of clay. The dead of night was broken intermittently by the snores of sleeping guards and rustle of leaves wafted and swept across by the gusty wind. Both of them were shivering in awesome fear.

Mohanlal said, 'You are not lads, you are ladies. What's the matter?'

The maid knelt before him; Mohanlal withdrew and stepped back. Noorbai folded her hands. Her eyes seemed to be praying for something. Mohan came very close to them, again withdrew and said, 'I think I can recognize you.'

The maid was on her feet again. She replied, 'We are stricken by fate and adversity.'

Mohan disclosed his identity in whispers, and added, 'I have seen you earlier, either in Sardar Saadat Khan's encampment or....'

'You are right, sir!'

Mohan was perplexed for a moment. Noorbai told a lie: 'I do recognize you having seen you several times, my gentle and valiant knight!'

The maid replied in a flash: 'Protect us, noble gentleman! Protect us, we are the persecuted ones.'

Mohan beckoned them towards his post, seated them in a corner and continued his words in the same vein:

'I recognized you very well. Had been there some one else on guard-duty, God knows, what would have befallen you.'

The maid thought, 'I had sounded and won over the commander of the indolent guards in advance. Even if Mohan was not awake, there would be no hurdle in making an escape....' But thereafter Mohan intervened, 'You intended to go to Iran; now what's this all about?'

Noorbai replied quickly "My corpse would go to Iran. I wish to escape from here.'

'Where will you go?'

'First, let me get out from here and then I would go anywhere. Well! I have my hearth and home in Delhi but I won't go home as I will be caught there. I should like to go to some faraway land.'

'Where?'

'Wherever the Emperor of Nadir Shah cannot trace me out. Would I not get a little space for me in any place of pilgrimage for Hindus.'

'And this maid?'

The maid said, 'Anywhere with her and in her company.'

'Nay,.......or, as we may think and decide upon later. Meanwhile, please save us in our present predicament. I shall reward you profusely, so much so that you would live happily ever after without having to work.'

Mohanlal maintained silence. Noorbai begged in a soft tone.

'Besides you would receive the reward of this virtuous action in helping out two helpless women.'

Mohanlal still kept quiet. Noorbai added with a renewed, keen impatience, 'Here is your reward I have with me. I am ready to give some in advance, diamonds and pearls.'

Mohanlal was somewhat shocked and exclaimed : 'What!'

Noorbai responded, 'You would be rewarded to your satisfaction - the price for saving and reaching us safely outside the fort.'

Mohanlal said, 'I don't wish to receive any reward. We do not accept any price in return for saving the life or honour of ladies. I was pondering as to how to manage your escape safely.'

The maid urged him, 'Please think it out quickly.'

Mohan drily remonstrated, 'Keep quiet for a while.'

After a few moments, Mohan said 'By no means can you manage to escape at night. Iranian soldiers being alert will certainly humiliate if not kill us.'

It brought shivers to both ladies. Noorbai felt and ran her fingers over his rugged wrist and urged him, 'What is to be done now?'

Mohan felt as if some snake had crept over him.

He was going to use rude language but exercised restraint. Both of them thought that he was working out some plan for escape. Far away, they could hear the dreamy calls of 'keep awake..... keep vigil and remain alert.'

Mohanlal disclosed his resolve, 'I shall manage your exit in day time.'

Noorbai asked in a desperate tone, 'In what manner?'

The maid answered, 'Impossible!'

Mohan replied, 'I shall disclose that you are my brothers. We shall thus manage to get out under some pretext.' Noorbai, held his wrist and added, 'At daybreak, they would look for us and those who know us well would arrive here. We shall be killed, no doubt but you would lose your life without a purpose.'

'Oh yes, of course! 'You are right,' said Mohanlal surprised at his own lack of understanding. He said, 'We shall set out before dawn, that is, the time when the soldiers go away to wash themselves and the commanders are still asleep. It is three hours from now. We shall be questioned a little at the main gate. That will be the opportune time to run away easily. Once we are out of the fort, by god's grace, we shall reach a safe place.'

Eyeing the prospect for freedom, Noorbai asked him sympathetically, 'How will you carry your personal effects?'

As Mohanlal drew his arms inside his clothes, Noorbai's fingers slid to his knees.

Mohanlal responded, 'I don't need to carry anything. It will more than suffice if I have a blanket to cover and a sword to protect myself, with God overhead.'

Noorbai gladly reassured him, 'It's all right with us whether you wish to receive your reward now or after our safe passage outside. God knows, how many things it will fetch.'

At that moment, a soldier sleeping in the open balcony of the upper room coughed and repeating the name of god Rama two three times, he resumed his sleep.

When he started snoring again, Mohanlal told Noorbai, 'I am not going to do this good deed for any reward as I have already told you. Now shut up and wait for the dawn.'

Noorbai thought, 'He will risk his life for the sake of love if not for any reward. Whatever may happen, whoever it is, it will be far better to be with him than going to Iran with Nadir Shah. If this was not the result of her escape, it would still be better because the world outside Delhi was so large — there being the kingdoms of Brij, Kashi and Hindu Rajas. Noorbai turned to sleep for comfort even in that terrifying situation. Half asleep as she was, she thought she was resting her head on the shoulders of the soldier but in fact it was placed on the maid's shoulder. The maid did not get a wink of sleep. Mohan was, of course, alert and attentive.

Noorbai was awake much before dawn and said in a low, sleepy tone, 'Forgive me! Your shoulders must be aching with the weight of my head.'

Mohanlal listened to this conversation. The maid said, 'I am your maid. Why should my shoulders ache?' Noorbai regained her conscious self. Mohan's illusion vanished and he was instantly asleep.

After a short while, the cock began his crowing. Mohanlal was awakened and he stood up. Tying up sword in his waist, and wrapping himself in the blanket, Mohanlal beckoned them to follow. Both of them were ready to move. Their heart beat faster and they felt out of breath. Mohanlal held his only metal-mug in his hand. He had a jar made of metal, which he gave to the maid. Both of them followed Mohanlal. He was chanting

86. Radha Krishna – The two names of god Krishna and his devoted beloved Radha are chanted together by Hindus, especially in North India as part of daily prayers

'Radha Krishna....Radha Krishna.[86] He knew that to walk away quickly would invite questioning and their arrest. Overawed, stupefied and absorbing the severe cold, both of them followed their repetitive sounds of Radha Krishna. A few soldiers were also going to and fro for morning ablution. No one questioned or interrogated them. Iranian soldiers kept a strict vigil at the main gate. The sentry stopped them with the question,

'Who are you? Where are you going?'

'Mohanlal and his brethren the soldiers employed on contract.' He replied unhesitatingly and stood there. Iranian soldiers came a little closer, saw the mug and jar and stepped back. He said, 'Go and come back together quickly.'

'Surely...... surely.' Mohanlal replied and all three of them went out of the main gate.

Noorbai's teeth made grinding sound in the biting cold. By sunrise, they had gone quite far from the town. Very few people had come out on the roads. The City Police Chief's sepoys were dozing still or were in deep sleep after the rounds of vigil at night. Before sunrise, three of them had left the town far behind and stood behind a grove of trees. Mohan was the first to break the silence with the word: 'Now?'

The maid responded first, 'I shall go to a relative of mine in a village at some distance from here and thereafter somewhere else.'

Noorbai began to open the small packet which was tucked in her waist.

Mohan asked Noorbai 'What about you?'

Her face reflected her crimson complexion resulting from the strenuous exercise of the morning and the rays of the sun added to the blooming beauty and rosy hue of her face.

Noorbai opened the bundle and gave the maid all that it contained — some gold and a few large-sized pearls.

Noorbai's eyes glistened with tears. With a trembling voice, she said, I shall follow you wherever you go. Won't you go to Bharatpur? It is a large state.'

Mohan retorted a little rudely,

'Who told you?' But as he observed her tears, his tone softened, 'No, I won't go to Bharatpur. I shall go to Mathura-Vrindavan.'

'I shall also follow suit. I have no one here, nothing to look forward to.'

Mohanlal began to ponder. A little later, Mohan and Noorbai headed in one direction while the maid turned towards another with the jar on her head.

Making their way by avoiding large groups of people or even one or two persons walking by themselves, both of them walked at a brisk pace which made Noorbai perspire profusely. After a short while, Noorbai sat under the shade of a tree at a lonely spot.

Her parched throat could manage to gurgle up words 'Water — water!' Mohan turned back and mused: 'Was it the same voice which he had listened in Saadat Khan's camp near Mathura?'

'I shall fetch it in an instant,' said Mohan, and went in one direction and came back with a tumbler of water. Noorbai gulped water holding it in the palms of hands. She said, 'I can walk no farther. Where shall we get shelter?'

Mohan replied, 'In some place, in a village where Jats live when evening sets in.'

Noorbai entreated. 'Buy a bullock cart please, or take it on hire. I can't walk any more.'

'Buy a cart 'Mohan was amazed. 'By the time, we hire a bullock-cart, someone pursuing us will arrive here.'

Noorbai was thrilled as if renewed with energy; she rose and spoke softly,

'Let's walk slowly.' Mohanlal started walking at a slow pace. He said, 'I am thinking how I shall introduce you when we reach some village.'

Noorbai did not hesitate to suggest, 'I shall pass for a Jatni and you should also introduce me as one belonging to your inner apartments.'

Mohan who was already perspiring, then sweated profusely. He saw Noorbai with a side-glance. Noorbai's face did not betray any sign of love or attachment as she knitted her eyebrows and pursed her lips.

Mohan exclaimed, 'What about your accent and dialect?'

Noorbai pacified him as if she had found a solution, 'I know how to speak Brij dialect as I learnt it from the songs of Soordas and Nand Das.'

As she uttered the names of Nand Das and Soordas, Noorbai's voice faltered and tears welled up in her eyes, which Mohan could not take notice...

Noorbai asked him haltingly, 'May I ask the name of my saviour!'

Mohan told his name and added, 'Didn't I speak out my name in the presence of Iranian guards?'

As they trudged forward, Noorbai responded, 'I was not in my senses then.'

Back in Delhi, as the day advanced, a search was launched one after the other to trace Noorbai, her maid and Mohan — first it was a covert search, followed by a declared one. Muhammad Shah received the news around noon while it reached the ears of Nadir Shah in the afternoon. To Muhammad Shah, it was not a good augury as he had lost a support.

Nadir Shah muttered in desperation that he would save an expense of four thousand rupees per month. But from that day onwards, Nadir Shah relentlessly pestered Muhammad Shah with demands and desires to be fulfilled.

The search for Noorbai, her maid and Mohan was given up after a while. A more intensive search would have further spread the scandal that both women had eloped with an ordinary sepoy.

—❋—

38

A handful of Nadir Shah's soldiers arrived in the grain market of Delhi. Foodgrain shops belonged to Hindus, a fact known to Iranian soldiers. Hindu residents of Delhi and near about had come to know that Nadir Shah's soldiers had massacred Hindu hermits but nobody was aware of the circumstance in which they were killed. Hindus were, of course, embittered but Muslims too were alienated by killers of hermits and mendicants.

An Iranian soldier enquired casually at a foodgrain shop, 'At what rates are you selling, grocer?' It hurt the shopkeeper; even so, he told him the rates.

The soldier gnashed his teeth and exclaimed, 'Hindustan produces so much of foodgrains; even then you are selling at much high rates.'

'Look for some other shop.'

'An ill-mannered man! Why don't you sell it cheaper?'

'As we buy, so do we sell.'

'Give grain at fair rates; wretched fellow, you have quoted the double of prevailing rate.'

'Go away from here! What a fine buyer you are! Like a blind man claiming to be blessed with joys of eyesight by being named as such.'

The soldier could not make out the import of the proverb but could sense that he was speaking ill of him. The soldier knitted his brows in anger and throwing some coins in the shop, spread a sheet of cloth seemingly to receive foodgrains. The shopkeeper threw away the coins on the road.

He said, 'Look for some other shop. This is strictly in line with the royal writ.'

The sepoys could see through the insolent behaviour of the shopkeeper as he threw their coins. Some went up the shop and started beating the shopkeeper while others collected grain without paying any thing. The neighbouring shopkeepers gathered there. In hullabaloo a few Muslims who also came on the scene, supported the shopkeeper. Iranian soldiers beat them up and others as well. All this led to' the convergence of a good crowd. Iranians drew and brandished their swords, killing some Hindus and Muslims and injuring a few others. A posse of Iranian soldiers arrived at the scene followed by a large number of Hindu and Muslim citizens of Delhi. A pitched fighting ensued. Barring a handful of Iranian soldiers who could flee the scene, the rest were done to death. All the shops were closed without delay and a general strike was resorted to. A rumour floated fast that Nadir Shah had been killed.

Wherever people ran into Iranian soldiers they fought them. Hindustani Muslims had developed contempt for the Uzbek, Turkish and Iraqi soldiers besides the Kazilbashies sporting red caps — who altogether constituted Nadir Shah's army. They assessed the situation that they could free Delhi and the territories constituting its empire from those aliens.

Nadir Shah received these tidings. 'My Lord, the Emperor, all the sepoys stationed outside the walls of the fort have been killed.'

'Wherefore?'

'Because they were Iranian soldiers.'

'What was their fault?'

'Nothing! They wanted to buy grain which was not given to them. The market was closed and all of them were killed.'

'I shall have it enquired into. Who is behind this mischief?'

'Both Hindus and Muslims! A few Moghul nobles and commanders have also joined hands.'

'Well? Let me find out!'

'And the rumour that the Emperor had also been killed is current in the air.'

'What..., What!'

'This very news has been spread!'

'All right! That Nadir Shah is fully alive and kicking will be brought home to the people of this accursed city.'

And thereafter Nadir Shah ordered a general massacre.

He cautioned, 'None should be spared — neither Hindus or Muslims. Whatever will our soldier lay hands on will be his and his alone.'

Even so, what followed in Delhi surpassed the tortures of hell.

As long as the menfolk of Delhi could manage to save and protect themselves, they fought valiantly from within their houses but how could they stand up against a well-trained army and its superior weapons?

The men died fighting and were immersed into the flames of the burning houses. The women immolated by throwing themselves into wells or the flames inside the houses. Almost all streets and localities witnessed such ghastly scenes and were swamped with corpses.

Muhammad Shah received the news of this cruel, ghastly massacre. It was probably for the first time in life that Muhammad Shah wept on hearing such news. He rushed and appeared before Nadir Shah in supplication. It was five hours since the commission of massacre. Nadir Shah's animal instinct having been satisfied, the command for bloodshed was withdrawn by him. Nadir Shah's soldiers had shed blood and looted the property to their heart's content. Peace returned but Delhi was turned into one big burning cremation ground.

Nadir Shah raised the scale of his demands. The Emperor apprehended that after the devastation of town, it would be the turn of palace.

Nadir Shah wrested the tribute to the tune of seventy crore rupees.

He liked immensely the delicate engraving of diamonds, jewels and pearls in the royal throne, 'Takht-e-Taaus'. In his estimation Muhammad Shah did not deserve to be seated on the throne, 'Takht-e-Taaus' nor was the palace within the fort his proper abode. However, the day arrived when Nadir Shah set out for Iran restoring to Muhammad Shah, his Empire and the palace shorn of 'Takht-e-Taaus', with the looted property to the tune of about one billion rupees. Besides, he took along four thousand beautiful maids who were gifted to him by Muhammad Shah. But all of them fled the custody of Nadir Shah and never returned to Muhammad Shah's palace. Muhammad Shah acquired new ones. 'Takht-e-Taaus' bore no living legs; else, it would have also freed itself from the custody.

Delhi's dynastic rule already nearing its end, was then extinguished altogether. The area around Delhi and Agra witnessed highway robbery, dacoity, loot and extortion in an increasing number.

Jat farmers, however, were busy cultivating their fields. But they were robbed and persecuted so much that they also started indulging in robbing and looting others. The remaining citizenry who fled Delhi were not spared from the looting while those living in the countryside and villages were also deprived of their property by marauders.

The Maratha ambassador accompanied by his retinue had returned to Jaipur. He did not march towards the Deccan. He resolved to undertake a pilgrimage to the holy 'Brij' and turned towards Bharatpur and Agra.

—✵—

39

In the first part of journey, the foremost problem for Mohanlal posed itself in the shape of Noorbai's clothes. Lady's apparel which showed beneath the man's dress worn by Noorbai seemed to be out of the ordinary for members of the public. Summer had already set in. The gentleman's dress had been packed into a bundle but a woman's dress could have landed them easily into trouble in the ordinary course.

A number of people of Delhi and its neighbourhood were on the run. As the area around Delhi had been depopulated they did not attract attention at all. But this phenomenon of large-scale migration had reduced the supplies of ration, etc., considerably. They had to go without food on the first night which they spent in a ruined hut in a terrified, wearied and hungry state. But the deep slumber overcame and put to rest their appetite too.

At daybreak, they again set out. After trudging some distance, it became well-nigh impossible for Noorbai to proceed any further. She nearly collapsed and seated herself under a bushy shade and began to stroke the blisters in her feet.

She pondered, 'If she were to be killed, it made no difference whether she was in India or Iran.'

Mohan gazed at her wilted, downcast face with tears welling up and mused that the most delicate woman should also face the unforeseen troubles and pains in order to attain freedom. But that woman being a prostitute was paying for her sins. Bemoaning herself, Noorbai stretched her body on the dusty ground to get some rest and laid aside the bundle. Mohan's compassion was aroused.

'How comfortably she had been living! What a pretty and frail creature she is! I should help her.' Mohan resolved and placed the bundle beneath her head. Mohan said, 'Keep lying here for a while, I am going to look around for some food!'

Noorbai replied haltingly and with a choked voice, 'I have thrust upon you my burdensome troubles. When you are away in search of food if something untoward befalls me, I shall be ruined. I shall meet my death groaning and moaning in pain; else, someone may turn up and seize me causing my death, which will bring to nought all your efforts to save and protect me.'

Mohan assured her, 'No, there is no one around this place. I'll be back very soon. Take water from this tumbler if you need to. I shall get you something to eat.'

Noorbai sat up suppressing her hopeful breath. She reached for the girdle packet tucked in her waist and said, 'I have some gold and jewellery — take some, it will stand you in good stead.'

Mohan raised and knitted his brow but calmed himself watching her helpless, wretched state. He said, 'Who would accept gold and jewellery here? I have some silver and copper coins — they will do for the present.'

Noorbai reclined and rested on the bundle and entreated, 'Please rest a while.'

Mohan, hungry as he was, did not relish her pleading but he felt his mind prompting him to accede to it — it was likely that she would sleep and then he could go away.

Noorbai could not sleep and asked for some water. Mohan filled her palm with water; Noorbai turned her side. Mohan rose from his seat. Noorbai implored mildly, 'Please do not go!' Mohan emphatically replied 'No' and went away. Noorbai seated herself camouflaged in bushes moving a little away from where she was resting, so that no one could observe her there.

Two-three hours later, Mohan returned and did not find Noorbai at the spot where he had left her. Mohan had got enough food from a householder who lived nearby disguised as a hermit. He had enough to eat to his heart's content and also brought some for her. He found both Noorbai and her bundle missing from that spot.

Mohan sat under the shade of a shrubbery and was immersed in penitent thoughts, 'I allowed this helpless woman to die! If I had taken her along, it would have meant no harm. However helpless she might be, she was a fugitive who had taken refuge with me. I have wronged her; I sinned against her.' His choked throat could gurgle up only the words. 'O, Lord Krishna, my Lord.'

A voice pierced through the bush : 'Have come back? Is it you?'

Enthused, Mohan replied 'Yes.....' and turned towards the bush. Noorbai came out to him almost jumping with the bundle in her arms. Both seated themselves under the shade of a tree.

Mohan resumed enthusiastically, 'I have brought food for you.'

Noorbai sensed a lot of sweetness in Mohan's voice and her eyes glistened in gratitude. 'I would eat, of course, but let us save some thing —it will stand us in good stead when need arises — I know how much effort on your part has yielded this food for us.'

Mohan spread before her the frugal, plain food with the exclamation 'Yes'. Noorbai's appetite was satisfied with a little food. She gulped water by holding her palms together. After resting for a while, they took up lodgings with the same householder-turned-hermit from whom Mohan had fetched food earlier. The householder became restive in their company, but they set out again after procuring some food. It seemed, the hermit's imminent trouble was warded off.

Noorbai regained some strength. She pondered that the 'sepoy" was not all that impolite.

—✻—

40

'Your share in the booty came to only two and a half rupees'. Roni expressed her resentment while receiving money from Tota.

Tota tried to explain, 'Our gang is rather small and therefore, assaults smaller victims. We shall combine with a senior commander, which will give us bigger tasks and greater share in the booty.'

'You came back quite late in the night, went through all the trouble !! And in return, you received only two and a half rupees.!!'

'Isn't it enough? It is worth two months' supply of butter-oil, after all!'

'It won't fetch gold.'

'We shall possess that too some day.'

'Such a way of life would not have made Badan Singh's forefathers chiefs of their clan.'

'Badan Singh discovered somewhere an unaccounted treasure trove.'

'I am referring to Badan Singh's forefathers.'

'Who knows?'

'Better start digging up ruins; may be, you also strike up something.'

'Such ruins are not waiting to be excavated by me, at my doorstep. Besides, a hard day's labour and nightly work of digging up — how long can they go on together?'

Observing him to be sullen, Roni switched over to patting him,

'Yes, I talked about digging up ruins just by the way. Why don't you discover and join a senior Sardar's band.'

'I am already on the lookout.'

'Doesn't matter; today you got two and a half rupees; some day, you may receive two hundred and fifty rupees. Hard work can yield everything!' The use of the words 'hard work' recalled to Tota's mind the scenes of Fatehpur Sikri hut — his fields and harvested crop, grazing of buffaloes amidst bushy trees and of day's hard work in that village; his mind compared all these with the labour he had put in to get two and a half rupees.

Tota said, 'Sweating it out is quite different! This is robbery indeed!'

Roni observed that Tota was not enthused by her encouraging words.

She swung her neck to allow loosely falling hair to be adjusted by her nimble fingers, drew her veil longer in front of her, slightly turned her body and faced him with a smile playing on her lips and eyes full of affection.

Tota's depressing thoughts were dispelled.

Roni said, 'Do not keep awake longer through the nights.'

Tota laughed and said, 'When will I get time for digging up the ruins?'

Eyeing him with quick, side glance and a ringing laughter, Roni added, 'Oh! Oh! My advice touched and hurt you very much!'

Tota turned his eyes on all sides to see if someone was observing them. 'I wish to adorn you with a lot of gold but to accomplish it, I shall have to spend days together and, at times, nights away from you. But you will adorn yourself with plenty of gold one day.'

'My neighbours would not look upon my gold ornaments with favour.'

'It may not find favour with the neighbours. But I would like it very much.'

'We shall buy two buffaloes, first of all, milch ones.'

'Yes....Yes, of course.'

'And then, we shall grow sugarcane; yes, sugarcane.'

'You laugh at all this; sugarcane can be grown, of course.'

'Yes....Yes, we shall buy oxen first.'

'Then it will unduly delay our buying of gold.'

Tota was relishing this prank. Roni's closely set bright teeth as white as pearl shone beneath her laughter.

Roni said, 'May you live long! We shall accomplish everything.'

Someone else was also alive the other day, Tota imagined as Mohan's face appeared before his mind's eye.

Her laughter seemed to play on her lips for a while.

'Will you go out tonight also?' Tota, it seemed, paid no heed to these words as the faint smile seemed to vanish from her lips.

Roni asked the second question,

'Why are you so depressed?'

'I am not depressed in any manner.'

'What thought are you absorbed in?'

'It's nothing. I wonder as to which gang I should join.'

'You have a whole day before you to think of it. Even if you don't go out tonight, it will not matter at all. You have a whole night to weigh it.'

'Yes, yes....' He wanted to say something more but they heard someone coming and dispersed to attend to their daily chores. The old man arrived there.

The old man told Tota, 'You come back quite late at night these days. You thought all had gone to sleep; I was awake. Even otherwise, I get disturbed sleep. Where do you go these days and keep late hours?'

Tota replied unhesitatingly, 'I go about in the village for exchange of visits.'

'Well, Tota I have gone through and suffered for ages. This conduct does not behove a Jat hailing from a good pedigree of Jats. Whatever one earns from the sweat and toil is something which lasts longer than any other earning.'

'Well, what wrong have I committed?'

'O, Tota, you are not the only one to have taken to this work. You should take care lest you should face disappointment later.'

Tota mused, 'If you were not old, you would do the same thing.' He said, 'Yes, of course, I would have worked hard.'

—✻—

41

Mohan could not choose to travel on the wide and open royal roads. He was making his way through narrow paths, walkways which connect distant villages lying en route. The route and villages — all were unfamiliar. Despite frequent enquiries, they tended to go astray, losing their way to Mathura though, he thought, he was going in the right direction, towards Bharatpur. They had to pass through the rugged wild and the forest most of the way, where they, for a few moments, ran into persons fleeing and hiding on the way, but the wild lonely way seemed to stretch far and wide and covered greater expanse than ever.

Noorbai's face seemed wilted and dry and her eyes more deeply ensconced. They ate frugal food and got only roasted gram and grains at times. They carried sufficient food and ration to last them for some time. Noorbai was prompted by sores in her feet, dust-laden hair and parched lips to think that if she had chosen to go to Iran, surely, she would not have fallen a prey to some python.

The village towards which they were plodding their weary way was still far off but evening was farther than that. They sat beneath the shade of a tree to have some respite. Mohan ruminated as to how long it would take to get rid of her.

They spotted some people carrying goods on donkeys. As they came nearer, both of them noticed that there were two men and three women—an old woman and two young ladies.

Of the two men, one was a young man. They were all dressed in tattered turbans, torn tunic and pyjamas. Their dirty dresses were printed in dotted and colourful designs. Mohan suspected that they were either Meenas[87] or Kanjars.[88] All of them carried long sticks but Mohan could feel safe with his sword.

The wayfarers tethered their donkeys beneath the tree and approached Mohan as they shook off the dirt and dust from their bodies. The women seated themselves beside Noorbai.

'Where are you going?' One of them asked Mohan.

'And you....?' Mohan asked him. They told each other, villages located in opposite directions, as their destination.

The wayfarers took out their earthen smoke — pipe and tobacco and lighted the same with a flint. The smoke-pipe was offered to Mohan.

Mohan told them, 'I don't smoke.'

'Which caste do you belong to?'

'We are Jats. And you?'

'Kanjars.'

Mohan thought that he had already made out the same. Noorbai did not wish to know who Kanjars were.

The old woman asked Noorbai, "Are you 'his' wife?"

'Yes......Yes' Noorbai replied. The old woman smiled. Noorbai was wearing costly clothes which showed through and revealed their true character despite the dirt and disorder resulting from sweat and dust.

The old woman said, 'You seem to come from a noble family; you are not a Jatni. Have you run away with him from Delhi?'

Noorbai replied with some hesitation, 'It is not so'.

Both the Kanjar women had a feel of her clothes, touching them unabashedly and said, 'It is silk'....

---

87. Meenas – One of the tribes in India, mainly residing in parts of Gujarat, M.P. and Rajasthan States.
88. Kanjars – One of the semi-nomadic tribes of India reported to be indulging in minor crimes like theft, highway robbery besides selling small wares for the society.

Noorbai drew aside her clothes. Both of them burst into laughter and one started running in circles while the other began to do somersaults.

One of the men said, 'Give them something, only then you can get rid of them.'

Mohan stood up and remarked,

'Don't tease us. We are going our way and you go yours.'

A Kanjar woman came dancing her way to Mohan and was about to hold his arm when Mohan withdrew himself. Two Kanjar women closed in upon Noorbai as if they were bent upon tormenting her.

Both the Kanjars were laughing and smoking at the same time.

Mohan challenged them, 'Hold them back' One of the Kanjars said, 'She had fallen in love with you. She is doting on you already. Give her something — then alone, you can get rid of them.'

Mohan could not hit upon any way out. He drew his sword from its sheath. The Kanjar woman withdrew but her face betrayed no sign of fear. Noorbai went and stood close to Mohan after she managed to get away from those old and young women.

One of the Kanjars said with ease, 'We are not robbers; at least, we shall not rob you. But the village to which you are going is a robbers' home. We too have some goods and personal effects. Our large encampment is located at about four-five kms. from here in the midst of jungle. We are going there after selling some merchandise.'

'What merchandise do you sell?'

'Clothes of men and women. Take some for this girl — your bride or a kidnapped one who will invite trouble with the dress she is wearing now.'

'I shall buy her some clothes.'

'Will you give the silk dress in return.'

'You can take it'.

Kanjars brought out some rough clothes — a colourful spotted wrapper and a skirt from the bundle carried by the donkeys. Noorbai accepted them readily and with pleasure.

Noorbai moved towards some cover to change her dress. All the three Kanjar women ran after her. Mohan swiftly moved to that spot.

He rebuked Kanjar women, 'Go away from here.'

Both the women joined their husbands. Noorbai hid the packets and small bundles tucked in her waist. While she was changing, Noorbai's eyes betraying her fear for an instant met those of Mohan. A smile expressive of her gratitude played on Noorbai's lips. Mohan turned back. Having changed her clothes, Noorbai joined him under the tree. Mohan exchanged Noorbai's valuable clothes for the rough and thick clothes. They were still sulking. Mohan gave them a rupee along with the clothes. Then they seemed to be satisfied.

Noorbai asked Mohan, 'Do they have needle and thread? I should like to stitch my torn clothes.'

Kanjars were about to leave after giving needle and thread when one of them said,

'What about the price of needle and thread?'

Mohan paid that too. While leaving, the old woman told Noorbai, 'If you stay for the night in that village, someone will forcibly make you his mistress in his house and your man with the sword will be slain.'

Mohan and Noorbai also set out after the Kanjars had left. Noorbai was unable to move her footsteps. Looking all around, Mohan was walking firmly and carefully. That village was still far off.

'If you pardon my saying so, we should not stay in that village for the night.' Noorbai said apprehensively.

'Where do we stay then? There must be some good people also in that village.'

'Whatever you think proper — I am apprehending something. Times are bad enough.'

'If there are a few Jat families in the village, we shall not be put to trouble.'

'If there are no Jats there then...?'

'May be, there is none. We forgot to ask Kanjars about it. If we don't go to that village, we shall be forced to stay somewhere in the jungle.'

'Even otherwise, this jungle is all right for me. When you are in my company, I entertain no fears of the forest — indeed it is a good augury for me.'

Mohanlal quickly looked at Noorbai's face but found no sign of love. Of course, having sensed her fears, Mohan had to give in.

They halted at a lonely spot by a waterway, which formed a sizeable waterhole.

Noorbai took out small bundles from her waist, stitched a long pouch with needle and thread and filled the same with jewels diamonds and gold jewellery.

Mohan could not resist remarking, 'You must be feeling weighed down by this burden of yours.'

'It is not so. As it is, I am carrying it for quite some distance.' Noorbai replied and tied the pouch firmly.

By the time they finished their food, darkness of the evening had already spread all around. They sat under a tree with their heads resting against it. Mohan had only a blanket to serve as a bedding while Noorbai carried a few clothes for men's wear. It was a cold wintry night.

Noorbai said, 'You better lie and rest. I shall keep awake. You are very much tired.'

Mohan replied, 'Being a soldier, I am used to all this. I am not sleepy at all. I shall also snatch a nap when I feel like. Then you should keep vigil; I should sleep in the second half of night.'

Lying at some distance, Noorbai was continually alarmed out of sheer fright. She slid slowly towards him and came quite close. As Mohan was about to move away, Noorbai suddenly held him by his knees. She said, 'Frightened as I am, I am unable to sleep. If I keep holding your feet, I can keep cool and will not lose heart; or, if you ask me, I shall remain awake through the night.'

Mohan told her without any demur, 'Lie down as you please'.

Noorbai reclined with her head resting close to his thigh. While asleep, she made his knee her pillow. Mohanlal covered Noorbai with the blanket, a part of which he used to cover himself too. In his sitting posture, he dozed off and snatched a nap in the small hours of the night. He forgot to wake up Noorbai. When she arose, she stretched her legs and asked him, 'You sat through the night! Why didn't you wake me up? Kept shivering in the cold.'

Mohan, indolent with a sleepless night, said, 'Did not remember at all.'

Noorbai looked up in surprise. Mohan felt, her tone betrayed more of her helplessness than surprise.

'God knows how many occasions like this would come by us.'

'Let it be any number; at least, I shall keep vigil for half the night. We have to reach many a destination.'

'We have little fear of your identity being discovered now, hence, we shall take to neat and wide roads and look for a large village.'

'We don't know when we shall arrive at Mathura.'

'Where do you intend to go from Mathura?'

'I shall live there tucked away in a nook, under your care and shelter.'

'How much care and refuge can a mere sepoy provide?'

'Until now, sky has been the only limit for shade and shadow.'

'It is only Kanhaiya whose blessed shadow surpasses all.'

'No arguments on that score now! But I think I have nothing to repay your kindness with. If you permit, I shall make an offering in obeisance at your feet.'

'Please don't mention it.'

'Did I say what offering I was going to make?'

Mohan was pleased but he could not follow clearly her intentions.

He said, 'Perhaps we may have to stay in one or two villages en route and thereafter we shall face impediments of sorts.'

'What sort of impediments?'

'How to conduct ourselves as husband and wife?'

'You might face such a hurdle; I don't have any. If someone were to ask me, I would disclose and also conduct myself accordingly. We go about our business playfully even in the face of calamity', he added.

'If we have to stay longer at any place, you should not look like a dumb-driven person. Maybe, people will become suspicious about us.'

'I won't forget that at all!'

The smile playing on her parched lips appeared to be charming and unique. How trusting she was, in him! How innocuous was her spirit! All this, seemingly, showed through that smile, Mohan felt.

Noorbai, scantily clad as she was, had slept on the dusty ground, his knee serving as a pillow! The blanket alone could not provide adequate protection to her body. He said, 'We shall procure a bedspread and clothings to cover our bodies at night. You are already covered by dust.'

'I have enough money; you may buy whatever you wish to' Noorbai added.

Mohan said, 'Money can fetch anything one wishes to have in big towns but here it is best kept tied safely in the girdle. I have a few rupees and coins which will see us through.'

—✻—

42

Exploring their way while bypassing royal roads at the same time, they covered good distance in the direction of Mathura which was far off. Mohan and Noorbai had left Delhi far behind. Mohan had saved some coins after buying a bedding and some clothes besides incurring expenses on food. Noorbai appeared to be a half-blossomed rose-bud tucked in dry leaves by some unseen hand.

By evening, they had arrived in a village. There was a prosperous Jat farmer known as Chintaman. Both of them landed at his house. It was the sweltering heat of a summer afternoon. Hot winds were blowing all over. Their faces were reddened by the heat. Chintaman enquired about their caste and pedigree and offered them drinking water. He gazed at her closely from top to bottom. Noorbai withdrew a little, feeling shy. 'Is she Chaudharin'[89] Chintaman asked.

'Yes, Sir' Mohan told him spontaneously. Noorbai turned her back on him.

'Where are you coming from?'

'We are runaways from Delhi.'

'Are you permanent residents of Delhi town?'

'No! We hail from Hissar but used to work in Delhi. We were robbed there and so ran away.'

'What were you doing in Delhi?'

'We sold milk and curd; we possessed buffaloes, which were slaughtered. It is lucky that we could manage to save ourselves.'

'You had your children there?'

'No; yes, we had! They were killed.'

Noorbai tied firmly her dress with a flash and jerk and bent her head towards her knees.

'Your children were grown up?'

89.Chaudharin — op. cit. 9, p. 45.

'Yes, one was grown up and the other was still young. Please don't remind us, Chaudhary!'

'Ram — Ram. These aliens have brought havoc by killings in our country. This is why...this is why ....' He could not complete his speech as Noorbai heaved a deep sigh, which could be heard at some distance also.

Chintaman consoled her, 'Do not grieve too much. God will bless you with more children.'

Noorbai seemed to withdraw a little more; Mohan turned away his face. Chintaman completed his speech, 'This is why we pick on, one by one, to do away with them.'

Mohan faced Chintaman and eyed him with a questioning glance. Chintaman smiled with pride and added, 'How long would you stay here?'

Mohan replied, 'Until we earn and save some money.'

'What work would you like to do?'

'Whatever we may secure—wage work or ploughing of the fields.'

'My fields have been in shambles. I had a sizeable farm, of which a very small portion I could manage to secure for myself. I have kept away my harvest in a hiding where you may work on wages. But this will last only a few days. What will you do thereafter?'

'We shall seek and find some work at Mathura and Vrindavan.'

'How about a paid job?'

'Whatever we may get.'

'Monks, hermits, vagrants and loitering beggars throng that place.'

'You would like to accept a paid job even as a Jat! In whose service?'

'We shall see'.

'What did she do earlier?'

'She used to milk cows, buffaloes.'

Noorbai was almost shaken.

Chintaman said, 'You should better live here in our village. We have quite a few families of our caste here. Both of you would get work on wages with some one or the other. I have my own buffaloes. Chaudharin is not keeping well; she could milk the buffaloes.'

Mohan told him firmly, 'She also remains unwell. Since she lost children, she has become crazy.'

Noorbai began to scratch the ground with her nails, by sticking out her hand. Chintaman observed that her fair fingers were extremely delicate — more delicate than the udders of the buffalo. He thought, 'How did she milk buffalo with these fingers?' He exclaimed, 'She can't probably milk even a goat, it seems to me' and burst into laughter.

'No, it is not like this! She used to do all types of chores except fetching water, which I used to do.' Chintaman said, 'Of course my wife, Chaudharin, too does not fetch water. We have a young lad who does this.'

'She did not cook food for she was not trained in that.' Mohan added with a view to make clear the routine of work for future. 'I used to cook food, myself.'

'She will learn all sorts of cooking in our kitchen. Her fingers are as delicate as thread; despite this, she will learn all that.' Chintaman added with hope for a brightening future.

Noorbai could hardly suppress her chuckle by mustering up coughing. Mohan said, 'She would do the sweeping and collecting of animal dung.'

Chintaman intervened, 'She would make dung-cakes!'

Mohan completed his sentence, 'Yes, as long as we remain here. Thereafter, we shall go and live happily in Brij area.'

Chintaman addressed Mohan as Chaudhary, a respectful appellation, for the first time, 'I shall assign you such work as well, make you prosperous and your Chaudharin will not be required to make cow-dung, nor will you be made to wait upon someone as a domestic servant.'

'What work?' Mohan queried.

'I shall tell you,' said Chaudhary with an air of wisdom and sagacity.

'Today you must be tired. Take food and go to sleep.'

Mohan entreated him, 'Please, Chaudhary, give us a small room and one or two utensils for cooking.'

'Yes, of course!' Chintaman assured him of all help.

—✻—

43

In the evening, Mohan was cooking food in a small room and Noorbai was seated with her back resting against a wall.

Noorbai broke silence after a while, 'You saved the situation today very well.'

Mohan responded, 'Whatever struck my mind, I poured out. Don't address me respectfully all the time with 'Aap', call me 'Tum'.

Noorbai was thrilled to the core and her heart throbbed with emotion.

'Why?'

'Because no wife addresses her husband like this.'

'What! Not even a resident of Delhi.'

'Not a resident of Delhi but one who comes from Hissar. One who is used to collecting refuse and dung and making dung-cakes.'

'And one who knows how to milk buffaloes! You were marvellous indeed! I have not even seen anyone milking a buffalo nor do I know how to make dung-cakes.'

'Your fingers would have created a wrong impression in the mind of that Chaudhary. I had casually told him of your skill in milking the cow.'

'How could I conceal my fingers? And how long? Why didn't you say something else?'

'Nursing a child? Well, this is possible only for a woman who has borne children and then we don't take up such a job in our family.'

Noorbai chuckled and hid her face into her hands. She, then, peered through her large eyes and fingers.

'You had laughed even at that moment but Chaudhary could not make out anything.'

Noorbai suppressed her laughter and said, 'Presuming that he had understood, how could you manage the whole thing?'

Still engrossed in preparing food, Mohan replied, 'I would have said that apart from being unwell, you were a little cynical too.'

Noorbai could not help laughing while she continued facing him or turning her face intermittently.

Mohan had finished cooking. Both of them started eating separately but continued talking at the same time.

'When it comes to fetching water for Chaudhary, what will you do?'

'I would not fetch water in any case.'

'Oh yes! You haven't done it before — I have told him already. Even so, you can put a small pitcher on your head. An empty vessel you carried on your head the other day alternating the same with that maid.'

'An empty vessel is quite different.'

'The filled one would not be all that heavy.'

'But why should I offer drinking water touched by me to Chaudhary and Chaudharin.'

'Yes, it certainly is a handicap but we Jats are not blockheads.'

'May be, Jats are not like that but I do think like that. Knowing fully well my identity, if they drink water touched by me I would not mind.'

Mohan kept mum. Noorbai too maintained silence for a while.

With bowed head, Noorbai asked, 'You don't take water even though you know my identity!'

Mohan said, 'Don't address me with a respectful 'Aap' (thou); otherwise, the cat will be out of the bag.'

For a few moments again, they did not speak. Mohan replied while taking water, 'I shall certainly take drinking water henceforth.'

Noorbai was thrilled and her face turned crimson. She felt a lump in her throat. She wanted to say something but her vocal chords seemed to fail her. She gulped some water and began to chew a morsel of food. Chewing a mouthful of food, she added, 'Well, then, I shall be presumptuous to consider myself a Jatni.'

Noorbai felt as if the barrier between her and Mohan had broken down. Roni's face flashed in Mohan's mind and vanished in a moment. While in conversation with Saadat Khan, which language and choice of words would Noorbai be expressing similar emotions in? And in what style to the Emperor? And then whoever it might be? Penitence overcame him. What had she told Nadir Shah? The previous night travel in her company and the day journey thereafter followed by Noorbai's suffering — all that flashed in his mind. Raising his head, he looked at Noorbai — there she was, a coy, helpless and frail woman robed in rough, dirty and worn-out clothes taking thick bread made by him on a brass plate. She was smiling but Mohan looked quite sombre. Mohan pondered, 'I haven't accomplished my task fully as yet'.

Mohan said, 'You don't look like a Chaudharin!' Noorbai replied in a serious tone, 'I have seen Jat women too in the meantime — they are very pretty indeed! I am nowhere near them in beauty and don't count myself among them'.

Noorbai suppressed her heaving sigh. Mohan replied, 'Those who see you can alone make any observation in this respect. Jat women are not so weak. A few among them are such as can take on buffaloes by the horns.'

Mohan felt proud of it but he was reminded of the shrewish, ugly face of Roni at the same time.

Mohan's remark, 'Those who see you can alone make any observation' seemed to Noorbai to be suffused with honey. She said, 'I shall become stout now so as to be able to milk buffaloes at least.'

She finished her meal in good humour and laughter. Mohan also kept aside the brass plate and smiled without being conscious about its cause.

Noorbai washed her plate quickly. As Mohan was about to lift his own for washing, Noorbai held his arm. She said, 'Let me wash it.'

Mohan asked, 'Why?'

Noorbai took the plate from his hand with the remark, 'Even now, you ask why' and began washing the same.

'What are you doing? It is not good on your part' said Mohan in an undertone.

Noorbai responded, 'You don't understand how happy I am today.'

Mohan became conscious of the invisible chasm that separated both of them. He could not resist uttering, 'You seem to be a whimsical woman'.

Noorbai burst into laughter which sounded like the rhythmical tap of hand on 'Tabla'[90] accompanying Sarangi.[91]

Noorbai, still washing the plate, replied, 'If you had said it in the presence of that Chaudhary, it would have made me laugh all the more.'

It appeared to Mohan that he should not have uttered all that.

90. Tabla – op. cit. 6, p. 30.
91. Sarangi – op. cit. 61, p. 90.

Mohan suggested, 'Let's proceed towards Brij area hurriedly. If we spend two months here, we shall be in the thick of rainy season, which will make travelling rather tortuous.'

'Set out as and when you wish to. If we reach Mathura quickly, we shall be able to overcome lack of money.'

'How come?'

'I have, in my possession, diamonds and jewels worth several lacs of rupees. Please keep them in your custody and exchange some for rupees at Mathura'.

'At Mathura, I am not familiar with anyone who can give us money in exchange for diamonds.'

'Then let's go to Agra. There live many a jeweller and dealer in diamonds.'

'I have resided at Agra but there too, I am not acquainted with any jeweller.'

'I am also not familiar with anyone there nor shall I go to market but you will meet one big dealer or the other if you look out for one.'

"I'll see!'

'Please take these diamonds, pearls and gold here and now. I am unable to carry this burden any further.'

Mohanlal was taken aback. He said, 'I shall not take them. Please keep them with you.'

Noorbai insisted, 'You will have to accept them.'

Mohanlal added with pride, 'I shall not hide them nor will I keep them with me at any cost.'

She spoke in a tremulous voice, 'Don't you regard them as yours. I belong to my own Kanhaiya; I am under your care and charge.'

'Certainly!' Mohan responded firmly, then felt benumbed instantly. He said in an undertone, 'Who you are devoted to is my master too. In whose remembrance you left Delhi, I am also devoted to the same 'spirit'. For his sake, I have taken to your company. Now that both of us are together, it does not matter who keeps the diamonds and gold.'

Whatever Noorbai could make out from this conversation, that thrilled her to the core. Wiping the tears in her eyes, she said, 'I am indeed very happy today. What I could never secure, I have found today. Whenever you need, take it from me. Of course, it does not matter. I am reminded of one thing — we shall be able to sell gold in Agra easily but diamonds and pearls will fetch good price at Bharatpur. Rajas pay handsomely for them.'

The mention of Bharatpur annoyed him slightly. He replied drily and spontaneously, 'I won't go to Bharatpur at all.'

Noorbai agreed with him instantly. She said, 'It is all right. Agra will be a better place. I had said all that by the way.'

Mohan said in a normal tone.

'We shall not take to straight road that lies via Mathura. We shall take to paths crossing villages, however avoiding them or bypassing them as we go along. I shall earn as much wages on the way as would enable us to feed ourselves until we reach Agra.'

Noorbai tried to arouse laughter in Mohan by saying, 'I shall also seek some wages by making dung-cakes.'

Mohan was also in a good humoured mood and added, 'By milking buffaloes too.'

She responded, 'Also by taking on the buffaloes, catching and twisting their horns.'

At that moment, they heard a commotion of people gathering outside the house. Both of them lent their ears closely to it but could not make out what it was all about.

Mohan said, 'Let me go out and see.'

Noorbai said, 'Meanwhile, I shall go and sit with the wife of Chaudhary. Mohan turned towards the outer portion of the house while Noorbai made for the inner quarters. Noorbai touched Chaudharin's feet in obeisance.

Chaudharin was past her middle-age by then. She blessed Noorbai, 'May you bathe in milk, bear plenty of children and be blessed with several grand-children.'

Noorbai accepted the blessings with bowed head. Chaudharin lovingly touched and felt through her head first, then her forehead, face and finally her chin and remarked, 'You are extremely pretty, daughter-in-law but why are you so frail-looking?'

'God has bestowed me such a body and physique!'

'How do you say that? Look, God has not made Jats as weak as you are.'

Chaudharin patted her back and sized up her physique and frame. She spoke, 'Your cheeks are chubby but body is nothing but bones. What! Does he not give you enough food to eat, that damned fellow? I shall deal with him. You may take plenty of milk and milk butter here with us.'

'Yes please, I will....'

'And look here, I won't let you touch cow-dung at all; for, my husband told me that you would make dung-cakes. You should fetch water, isn't it? When you walk to well with a brass-pitcher clean and shining, you would look like Radha playfully dancing her way from Gokul to this place.'

While Noorbai was filled with pleasure and passion on hearing about Radha and her charming dances, she felt thorny pebbles pricking her on being told to fetch water from a well.

Noorbai said, 'Yes, Madam, but I have never been to a well for drawing water.'

Chaudharin was taken aback, 'What, you never drew water from a well and have borne two children already.' Chaudharin made no secret of her surprise.

'Yes please', said Noorbai and kept quiet. She started cursing that moment when she thought of sitting by the side of Chaudharin.

Chaudharin questioned her in order to know her background and family history.

'Children! Were both of them boys? Oh God.'

Noorbai wanted to evade the question by coughing and mumbling but it seemed, Chaudharin was bent upon doing in-depth study of her family history.

Noorbai spoke softly, 'They were boys!'

'Ram.... Ram, where's your parent's place?' asked Chaudharin.

'Hissar', she replied.

Third question followed, 'Your father's name?'

'Ram Singh', Noorbai replied without giving any thought.

Fourth question, 'What is your ancestral line?'

The reply was not forthcoming. Noorbai was silent; coughing failed her. Chaudharin began to ponder.

After a moment, she asked, 'You don't know your pedigree, daughter.'

'I forgot', Noorbai replied without thinking.

Chaudharin who had turned herself a researcher of her family history exclaimed, 'What a mistake and why? Speak out the truth, daughter-in-law. How long have you been with this Chaudhary?'

'From the beginning!' Noorbai replied firmly.

'Did you go round the sacred fire with him?' Chaudharin did not give up and asked.

Noorbai preferred to keep quiet taking it as a question connected with family history and lineage. Chaudharin laughed and added, 'I could make out. You belong to some other caste. Chaudhary has taken you as a mistress. Isn't it like this? Tell me, my little lass, tell me the truth.'

Noorbai was compelled to say, 'Yes, please; it is so.'

'And the children? You bore them to this Chaudhary or to your former husband.'

Noorbai said, in a hushed tone, 'I bore them to him.'

'Why are you feeling coy and shy? I may die as well for the sake of your coy beauty! Let me know if Dhareecha[92] has been performed for your union or not?'

Noorbai had never heard this word before but she could make out that Bhanwar and Dhareecha are akin in meaning. She was speechless when the word Bhanwar[93] was mentioned. Now she could only utter, 'It was not performed.'

'Oh God! Dhareecha also did not take place. You have not been accepted in our caste as yet. When the customary ceremony is performed, we shall be able to take water from your hands.'

Noorbai's intelligence helped her, 'This is why, I said I would not draw water.'

Chaudharin remonstrated, 'Why did not you tell me all this. I would not have asked you so many questions. But I could make a guess even at that time that there was something fishy. All right, you would make dung-cakes. As for work, everyone has to do something or the other. Noorbai found redemption. She inhaled a breath expressive of her relief and said, 'I shall make dung-cakes and do all domestic chores except cooking.'

'But for goodness sake, please don't touch my vessels of water until the customary ceremonies are over. I shall arrange them all here'.

Noorbai got further relief. She said, 'All right, Madam!'

Apparently with a view to atone for all those questions, Chaudharin patted, again, Noorbai's head, back, face and shoulders. She continued, 'How gentle and innocent is she! How pretty like a puppet! Work hard and eat well.'

Chaudharin did not mention milk and butter this time.

The commotion outside was louder. 'What's this, Mother', Noorbai asked by changing the topic of conversation. She told

92. Dhareecha – A union between man and woman outside wedlock but sanctified and accepted by society after performance of this ceremony.
93. Bhanwar – Hindu custom-going round the sacred fire seven times before being declared husband and wife by the priest.

her, 'This concerns men. Why should we interrupt and how are we concerned in all this?'

Noorbai touched her feet with folded hands and went to her small room.

Mohanlal also came inside after a short while. He was upset a little while Noorbai was full of good humour.

Noorbai asked, 'What's the matter?'

Mohanlal told her, 'A large crowd has gathered outside. All of them are 'Sepoys'. They are from different places — some from far-off places, others from elsewhere. They are about to mount an assault somewhere.'

'These are the times of clashes and skirmishes. Even in the city of Delhi, fighting and bloodshed are a daily affair. Where are they heading to?'

'Wherever they may get a large-sized, potential victim.'

'Is it?'

'Will they go far?'

'I did not ask that but I can make a guess all right. Chaudhary asked me to accompany but I refused point-blank.'

'Well done! He had stopped short of telling you about it in the evening. He said that you were tired then.'

Yes, he forgot all about it. I told him that even if I were to starve and die, I would not be able to do it.'

'He must be angry with you.'

'God damn him!'

'My foot! but he did not give vent to his anger. We shall stay here for a few days only.'

'Whatever you deem fit; otherwise, there is no danger in living in such a place where safety takes care of itself.'

'I would rather keep off such safety, I would prefer to work for wages.'

Both of them smiled. Noorbai related to him briefly her conversation with Chaudharin.

Noorbai said, 'You (Aap) did something marvellous by the remark about children.'

'Again, you have used the word Aap', Mohan interrupted her, 'It will let out all the secret. Address me with 'Tum' (you); do not commit this mistake again.'

'Never again,' assured Noorbai; 'sheer habit made me helpless.' 'Yes I will bear in mind! People will enquire about my family lineage on the parents' side, please tell me what to say.'

Mohan told parents' lineage of Roni, which flashed many a picture of the past in his eyes.

Mohan told her in a wearied tone, 'Go to sleep. I am feeling sleepy.'

Noorbai went to sleep - a sweet one at that but Mohan could not sleep for a long time. Roni was a shrew but he was married to her; she was from a good family; could he not soften her heart, somehow. How I got irritated over trivial matters! But she left home and hearth! She went away with Tota to Bharatpur! The wretch, the unfortunate! Turning sides for long, Mohan could regain sleep in the small hours of the night and got up late in the morning. Noorbai was up quite early. When Mohan returned after morning ablutions, he saw Chintaman carrying an injured person inside the house. He asked him no question at that moment.

—❋—

44

Tota having been out of Bharatpur for two days was back a little before evening. The old man was drawing a pull at hookah.[94] The boys had not returned after grazing the cattle.

On seeing Tota, the old man glanced at his clothes to espy the packet tucked beneath the uplifted dress. But he did not notice the packet. However, he thought that Tota must have hidden something in girdle. He drew deep draught at the smoke-pipe and exhaled the smoke between himself and Tota.

94. Hookah – A long wooden pipe attached to a water level below, meant for smoking tobacco placed in an earthen pan placed on the wooden pipe.

Inside the house, Roni was lying on the cot in the shade of the verandah. She had used one end of her saree as a pillow, which rendered her head bare. She was resting and relaxing her limbs in anticipation of the work that awaited her one or two hours thence. She looked back on hearing the sound of footsteps. Her shoulder was also made bare by then. Tota came there. Roni covered herself leisurely and stretching her limbs, stood up.

Tota's face was dry and sad. Roni welcomed her with the words, 'Brother, I felt tired waiting for you. Where did you spend all these days?'

Tota said, 'I shall tell you every thing. Let me have some water first, Sister!'

Roni brought a tumbler full of water immediately. Tota washed his face and hands and started drinking water. Roni began to alternately look at his face and the door expectantly. 'Why don't you have something to eat', She asked.

Tota replied with a wearied look and smile. 'You should have offered that before, Sister!' Roni said fondly, 'Well – Well! You asked for water first, which I brought instantly. I have some leftover from mid-day meal; shall I bring the same?'

'No, not now; I shall eat after resting a while. I should eat only hot food in the evening,' Tota said.

Roni said, 'Yes, of course; this little food will be taken by the lads. You should take piping hot food.'

Roni gazed at Tota expectantly and sized him up. Tota started relating to her, 'This time, I could not lay my hands on anything.'

'What'! Roni was amazed. Her smile deserted her; she got a shock but she was not angry at all.

Tota went on, 'Two-three days slipped by without any action. Then ensued the fighting with swords and guns. Both sides, some people sustained injuries and some others were killed. They had to withdraw; we too had to follow suit. This time we had to manage on our own resources.'

Seeing him safe and sound, Roni expressed sympathy, 'It was great that God saved you. Did you sustain an injury?'

Tota replied, 'No, I didn't but even if I did, would 1 turn my back on fighting. I would go for it again. In fact, I did not act wisely and with required understanding. We did not find out, in advance, as to who they were, what weapons they possessed and pounced upon them just like that.'

'Who were they?'

'Maratha! They were heading towards Mathura via Jaipur and Agra, by a tortuous route.'

'We learn Marathas themselves indulge in such nefarious acts.'

'Come on, Sister, do you think you know all the ins and outs, as in scriptures, about the whole world.'

'Just by the way during casual talks we also learn about men's affairs. Even so, you should have snatched something from them. After all, they would be carrying something or the other with them.'

'What can they carry! Fellows munch dry gram and onions to go with it!'

'What, have they found their way here to carry on with their robbery and loot? How strong were they? Must be a large group.'

'No, it is learnt that they have come here on a pilgrimage.'

'They should not have been provoked into fighting.'

'Well, yes...anyway, all is over and there is nothing else to it now.'

'You may take care of them some other time. Should I massage your forehead a little!'

'The old man is pulling at 'hookah' in a hubble-bubble. If he turns up here, what would he see?'

'What will he say? Am I his maidservant or a slave girl, or that lad of his has wedded me already?'

'In fact, he has cherished a desire to do so.'

'What a wishful thinker! Would he like to marry me even if I don't like the idea? I don't abuse others but have I forgot abusive language? We would get another place to stay if we wish to change. May God bless you a long life.'

Tota lay on the cot. He felt as if his weariness had vanished. Roni sat by his side and began to massage his head. Tota closed his eyes. He spoke with his eyes still closed, 'No, we do not have to pick quarrel here. We may come to possess enough money, after some time, besides cattle — buffaloes, oxen, agricultural fields, trees and every thing else. We shall, then, set up a hut and home for ourselves.'

Tota did not open his eyes. However, he looked at Roni with half-shut eyelids and side glances. Roni's face betrayed no sign of smile or cheer. Her eyes were fixed at the door with hesitant, anxious looks as if she was trying to lend her ears to any faint sound of footsteps and, in turn, apprehending some one's arrival there. Tota closed his eyes and after a few moments, he again looked at her with half-open eyelids and side glance. Roni's mood and posture were just the same as before.

Tota said, 'Bhauji, the day I see you adorned fully in gold and the house filled with foodgrains, buffaloes and cows, I shall consider it some achievement on my part.'

Roni's hand loosened its grip and thereby released the pressure.

She said, 'Everything will be accomplished; if it is not, we shall see to it. Keep lying at ease and if you are feeling sleepy, go to sleep. You have become very talkative lately.'

Tota, with his eyes still closed, quickly replied, 'As if you do not abuse and shout yourself hoarse unnecessarily'. Roni burst into laughter, Tota opened his eyes. Roni intervened again.

'May I utter a few gathering from memory? Then you would lessen chattering.'

'I am not sleepy. Even otherwise, I have shaken off weariness by your discourse.' Roni looked towards the door. Assuming an air of seriousness, she rose from her seat and said, 'Whoever has filled his belly with talks and talks?'

Tota urged, 'Sit down, Sister, where are you going? I like your sitting and talking to me.'

Roni asked with a smile, 'Would you take me on a pilgrimage?'

Tota agreed with her enthusiastically, 'It is not asking for something unattainable. Whenever you like to go to Mathura, Vrindavan, Gokul or Barsanna, we may set out for the same.'

Roni gave a shrug to her shoulders and said, '1 am not going there just like that. One needs to have clothes and some ornaments for a pilgrimage. You think I would proceed without having these things? What a man you are!'

Tota's ardour received further fillip — 'I would belie my name Tota Ram, if I do not procure all this within a fortnight.'

Roni replied in a tone suffused with and borne on her smile, 'But look here, do not push yourself too far into the enemies so as to receive injuries.'

Tota got up from the cot in a manner as if lightning had charged his entire body. Roni glanced at the door and moved towards a room with a smile on her lips, which was followed by the words, 'Let me go and bake the evening loaves. Cattle must be wending their way back.'

Gazing at her, Tota headed towards the outer apartments.

—❋—

45

Mohanlal's curiosity was aroused many a time to know as to who was the wounded person but Chintaman slept off the day so long that he could not meet him. By evening when they met, Chintaman himself raised the topic.

'During last night's sweep, we ran into a Maratha squadron. In the course of fighting, a few got killed and injured but Marathas sustained greater losses.'

'Which squadron was this?'

'I am not aware, who was commanding it? It was coming from Jaipur side.'

'How strong was it?'

'No one counted; they outnumbered us but could not face the Jats. They had to withdraw and flee the ground.'

'Did you lay hands on some booty?'

'We could not get any but we have tied up and brought one of the commanders with us. As he was wounded, they left him behind.'

'Marathas do not conduct themselves like that.'

'How do you know that? Well, they do it.'

'I have heard about it; I had something to do with Marathas in Delhi.'

'It is quite possible that they did not do it on purpose; we also wanted to leave him behind taking him to be dead, but he was discovered to be alive. Now that we have brought him, we shall release him only after receiving tribute and compensation from the commander of that squadron.'

Mohan's curiosity was spurred. He asked, 'Is he seriously wounded?' Chintaman replied, 'Not seriously; as much as, at times, an ox who runs amuck injures us while we are at work in the fields.'

'How is he now? Is he unconscious?'

'No, he is not. He was; he took water and has also eaten something.'

Mohan kept quiet. Chintaman looked at him for a moment with an air of impartiality and said, 'Do you wish to see him?' Mohan mustered the word 'yes' upto his lips but uttered, 'I don't have any special desire for it.'

Chintaman was confident that having been in contact with Marathas, he would possibly be knowing something about that squadron, and the designation and position of that injured person. He said, 'See him; it may be that you had met him in

Delhi. If he is discovered to be an acquaintance, it will augur well for us. Come, I shall take you there. There is some daylight still.'

Mohan accompanied him. When they reached close to the room where the wounded man was lodged, Chintaman mischievously told him, 'I shall not come with you inside the room. If he is known to you already, he will not open up in my presence. Go inside alone.'

Chintaman turned to move towards outside-the-house. Mohan somewhat impatiently went inside the room.

Mohan could not make out anything inside the room for a few moments. He could hear only the groans. When his eyes could see clearly, he saw the wounded man lying with his side and face turned towards the opposite direction. Mohan moved in the same direction so as to face him from the front side of the wounded, and was a little away from the door.

The wounded Maratha was wearing a turban. His mouth was half-open. Hearing Mohan's footsteps, he opened his eyes and asked for 'water'. The tumbler was kept nearby. There stood, in the room in a corner, a pitcher of water. He fetched water in another tumbler, poured it into the one lying near the wounded and said, 'drink!'

The wounded person seated himself resting on his elbow. It appeared that he was wounded in one of his thighs. The wounded uncovered his face. He lifted the tumbler to take it to his lips for drinking while fixing his eyes on Mohan at the same time. The wounded person did not take water. His hand shook with a jerk, loosened its grip and the tumbler tumbled to the ground. A little water was spilt from it but it was not overturned.

The wounded person could muster in an undertone, 'What?'

Mohan's eyes could not see clearly. He came close to the wounded person. On seeing him, he uttered the word 'What' a bit loudly. Mohan recognised the wounded person — he was Shubrati. Shubrati had already recognised Mohan.

For a moment, both kept looking at each other. Mohan seated himself. He lifted Shubrati's tumbler and took it close to his lips.

He urged him, 'Take it.'

Shubrati moaned and kept quiet for a few moments. He spoke in a tremulous voice without taking water 'Were you also there in last night's raid? Since when did you start this activity?'

Mohan replied a little loudly, 'I was not among them.'

Shubrati questioned him, 'How are you here then?'

Mohan said, 'I'll tell you, first take water.'

Shubrati drank water but did not lie again. He moaned.

Mohan insisted, 'Do not sit, lie down.'

He managed to help Shubrati lie again. Shubrati's eyes welled up with tears. Wiping his tears and clearing his throat, Shubrati said, 'If you were not there in last night's clash, how did you come here?'

Mohan softly entreated, 'Have a little patience, my brother. I'll tell you every thing.'

Both of them were silent for a while.

Mohanlal broke the silence, 'Where are you hurt? Are you wounded seriously? Which weapon caused the injury?'

Shubrati related, 'It does not appear to be serious. I have sustained deeper injuries earlier but it is more painful as the body has bled.'

'Has it been bandaged?'

'I feel so, well then, whatever might be the kind of bandage.'

'I shall bandage again and apply some medicine also.'

'I need a cot more than the medicine. This hard ground seems to be striking blows on me.'

'I'll bring it just now.'

'Wait a bit. Whose house is this, where am I lying? Where am I?'

'You are not far from Mathura but far from Agra. You are now in a Jat Chaudhary's house. Whatever he is, you will get to know by and by.'

'Who brought me here?'

'The same, the same Chaudhary brought you.'

'The poor fellows behaved gentlemanly, even though they found me lying injured. When I am well, I shall offer my respect to them.'

Mohan dissented with a wry grimace. Shubrati looked askance at him. Mohan maintained silence. He was about to leave for fetching the cot.

Shubrati asked him, 'Where are you going?'

Mohan told him, 'To fetch the cot.'

'Keep sitting. Let's see after a short while. I am overwhelmed with emotion on seeing you. It appears I have regained my household, children, etc., here and now.' Shubrati said.

After a moment later, Shubrati asked, 'Did you go home or not? The members of family are all right?' Mohan replied, 'Let me first bring a cot; then I'll talk about something' and left.

Coming out of the room, he saw Chintaman moving away towards the outer door with an air of indifference.

Mohanlal told him, 'A cot is needed.'

'Is he a commander? You discovered him to be an old, familiar face?'

Mohan replied, 'He is an acquaintance but not a nobleman.'

Chintaman put the second question, 'Is he not a Maratha?'

Mohanlal replied in the affirmative and requested for a cot again.'

Scratching his head, Chintaman said, 'We have few cots but since you are repeatedly asking for it, I shall arrange it from somewhere. Please come with me.'

Chintaman took him outside and procured a cot. Mohan arrived with the cot on his back.

On reaching the house, Chintaman told Mohan, 'You are offering him a cot and it shows this sepoy must be some important man, if not a commander or nobleman.'

Mohan resented the remark and burst forth. 'He has a big heart though he is not a rich fellow.'

Chintaman could not gauge the resentment of Mohan. Absorbed in thought, he asked, 'Who is the commander of that Maratha squadron, you must be knowing?'

His innate pride and self-respect prompted him to say, 'Poona-based Baji Rao Peshwa's ambassador, who resides at the court of Delhi Emperor, is the commander of this squadron.'

Chintaman said, 'Then he will have to pay penalty to us.' Mohan's anguish and pride cooled down.

Mohan said, 'We have to see to it that he gets well first.'

Chintaman tried to persuade 'Surely — surely, take this cot and let him lie at ease. He will be properly treated. We'll give him milk also.'

'All right', said Mohan and went inside with the cot. He laid Shubrati on the cot with care.

The evening was closing in. Chintaman's buffaloes and cows had come back. Shubrati wished that Mohan should sit by his side. Mohanlal said, 'Let me arrange milk and some food and then I'll come and sit by you.'

Mohan went away.

—❋—

46

Mohan busied himself into making preparation for cooking while Noorbai went and fetched some milk from Chaudharin. Noorbai said, 'First heat up the milk.'

Mohanlal extracted some cinders from the hearth and put them for boiling the milk. Noorbai sat beside him but at a distance and taking a little cover for herself.

She said, 'Chaudharin was telling me that the wounded commander is a friend of yours.'

'He is not a commander but, of course, a friend of mine. How did Chaudharin come to know of it?'

'I do not know, Chaudhary must have told her.'

'We worked in the same squadron earlier, in Maratha squadron.'

'But how did you land in Delhi fort?'

'I have been a wanderer. I have been in Poona too. This sepoy hails from Poona.'

The very name of Poona flashed back several pictures of Shubrati's house, his children and the puppet tucked on the thatched ceiling. Mohan's face was lit up wilh smile which endeared Noorbai and made her smile too. Mohan gauged her smile with a blank look.

Noorbai asked him, 'Which caste and community does your friend belong to?'

Mohan said, 'To none. He is a Mussalman, Mussalman.'

'Yes! In Maratha army there are, like here, people of all sorts — those from Kannauj, Jats, Marathas, Rajputs. 1 do not know what others.'

'Don't take the trouble then. 1 shall try to do the cooking.'

'First you should learn how to cook; otherwise, pulses will remain half-cooked or more boiled than necessary or the bread half-baked, unbaked and sticky.'

'Well! I am not as worthless as that', Noorbai exclaimed.

'The less said the better! Have you ever cooked before?' Mohan asked.

'Haven't cooked myself but have watched others do it.'

'I have watched others dance and sing; thus you can presume that I can do the same,' interjected Mohan.

On hearing this, Noorbai's smile vanished into airy nothing and her face became wan. She felt hurt. She could think of nothing and bowed her head. Mohanlal observed this and was penitent about his own remarks. He did not wish to hurt the feelings of Noorbai. He said, 'Come on! Why are you sad, you will see so much of dance and music in Brij area that you will get bored, Gopis do please Lord Krishna by their devoted dancing and singing.'

Noorbai raised her face. Her eyes had lost lustre and the forced smile had withered.

With a view to making her laugh, Mohan said, 'Aren't you a Chaudharin? Chaudharin as you are, you must laugh and smile like a Chaudharin as you were doing just now.'

Noorbai's face wore crimson hue. She burst into laughter and stood up.

As she laughed, she said in her resonant voice, 'I shall give such a unique musical performance before my Kanhaiya as I have never done before. I feel like reciting some stanza just now.'

Mohan turned serious. He said, 'O, dear, keep silent. Talk in undertones. Chaudhary and his wife are hell-bent on eavesdropping even by standing close to the wail.'

'I am not afraid of anyone', Noorbai said, as she slumped with a thud and added, 'Chaudhary Saheb, I shall not be taught by that Chaudharin how to cook. I shall learn it from you. If I am unable to become proficient in a day or so, chop off my fingers. Cooking good food is the first and foremost duty of a woman.'

'Well, well, you will learn it quickly, I agree. Come, cook the food and serve it to my friend.'

'I won't go in his presence.'

'Why?'

'Why — What, let it be clear that I won't go in his presence. Even if 1 were forced to do so, I won't talk to him.'

After a moment, she said, 'Bring it to me, 1 shall at least boil the pulses. You would eat — won't you?'

Mohan replied, 'How can a sepoy object to this? Water and pulses are alike for him!'

Noorbai considered it a hollow, meaningless remark but she did not go deep into the meaning.

Noorbai said, 'Chaudhary saheb, it is Chaudharin who will have an upper hand in kitchen — her writ will run in kitchen matters.'

Mohan thought, 'The matter had crossed limits.' He said in under-tones, 'Not now, we shall see later on. Don't hasten it?'

Noorbai took care of the milk. Mohan said after a while, 'I could never think that I would ever see my friend Shubrati.'

Noorbai maintained silence. Mohan said, 'Chintaman would release him only after he recovers penalty.'

Noorbai exclaimed in surprise, 'Penalty! What wrong has he committed so as to be called upon to pay the penalty?'

Mohan told her, 'His only fault is that the wretched fellow has fallen into the hands of Chaudhary's band. The penalty is for saving him or for surviving on his own.'

'How much is to be paid?'

'I don't know!'

'Who will pay?'

'The Commander of Maratha squadron, or Peshwa of Poona or his kinsmen'.

'Kinsmen! Who lives here, among his kinsmen?' 'Anyway, let's see.'

'Mohan began to serve food in his brass plate.'

'Serve in my plate and offer the same', Noorbai offered.

'I shall offer in my own and then wash that.'

Noorbai looked askance at him as Mohan could judge from her looks. He smiled 'This plate too is yours.'

Noorbai looked up wistfully and a smile played upon her partly glistening set of teeth.

That smile seemed to reveal her feelings — 'Yes it is, certainly; everything is mine.....' Mohan hinted to her to be quiet. Lifting the plate, he said, as he was leaving, 'You should take food.'

'Yes', Noorbai uttered as she pursed her lips. Perhaps Mohan's ears could catch the same. He mused, 'The smile is very sweet.'

Noorbai stood at the door and kept on looking at him. Shubrati's small room was dark. After a short while, Chintaman lighted a lamp and took it to that room.

—❋—

47

Shubrati began to take food. Mohanlal sat there. Chintaman in a spirit of hospitality fetched, sequentially water, pickle, salt or chilly to go with the food. When Shubrati had his fill, Chintaman said, 'Milk must be ready by now. Why don't you bring and give it to him.' Shubrati did not know that Mohan had not taken meals.

He said, 'Sit down for a while. There is no hurry for milk.' Chintaman interjected, 'Oh no! Drink it just now' and called aloud, 'O, Chaudharin, bring milk here.'

Chintaman's wife called upon Noorbai in a low pitch, 'O, What are you doing there, sitting inside? Take milk there, they are asking for it.'

Noorbai coughed and stood at the threshold holding a miik-pan in her hands. Chintaman's wife commanded in the same vein, 'Why don't you go in, why are you standing there at the door?'

All of them listened to this dialogue from inside that room. Chintaman repeated the instructions while peering in the same direction.

Noorbai was dumb founded. Mohan made a dash and carried the milk. Shubrati replied gratefully, 'Is your family here with you?'

'Yes.....Yes, it is so'.

She is a little unwell. Mohan was silent. Shubrati drank milk slowly.

Chintaman said, 'By God's grace, he will be all right very soon and would be able to join his squadron.'

'Isn't it, Mohan?'

Mohan assented, 'Yes, Yes.'

Chintaman remarked, 'His commander would not be aware, at all, about his whereabouts. What is your name, please?'

Mohanlal replied instantly, 'Ramarao; he is a Maratha.'

Shubrati moved his eyeballs while still taking milk.

Chintaman intervened, 'Maratha, he is, of course. His face reflects too well that he hails from a high-class family.'

Shubrati finished milk and as he lay, he said, 'I do not belong to a high family, I am a poor soldier. Marathas from noble families are few and far between.'

Chaudharin coughed vigorously in the courtyard as if she was calling Chintaman for dinner.

Chintaman said, 'Wait a while, I am coming. I shall take meals a little later.'

Then unhesitatingly and without shyness, he told Shubrati, 'There is no question here about any one being poor or rich. Last night your squadron ran into us just by the way. We sustained heavy losses.'

'I was not in the forefront but I know that much that our squadron was attacked first and then, in return, we mounted the assault.'

'It is wrong, it is a lie. We were going to attend to our business when Maratha squadron provoked us?'

'First salve was fired from your side.'

'Was any one hurt?'

'I don't know about that.'

'A few of our men were killed and wounded. Who will support their family and children?'

'It is all a matter of fate. How are we to blame in all this?'

'Our clan assembly has determined that Maratha squad is to blame and you will have to pay the compensation for our losses.'

With a moan, Shubrati became quiet. Mohan said, 'Let him become all right and then you may talk to him.'

Chintaman objected. 'Then what shall we talk? Taking advantage of loneliness, he will slip away quietly. Would you pay us the compensation, then?'

Mohan was about to answer in the affirmative. He managed to bring up assent to his lips but suppressed the same. With bowed head and keeping silence, he began to pick small straws with his fingers, lying on the floor of the closet.

Chintaman continued in the same vein, 'Wherever your commander has gone — Mathura or Viindaban — send the message that we shall release him on receiving a sum of rupees one thousand.'

Then he added in an undertone, 'Yes, we assure you firmly that as long as you are here, you will face no problem and will leave here in an absolutely fit condition and disposition.'

Shubrati asked, 'Who will carry the message?'

Chintaman replied with an effort to sweeten his voice, 'Do not worry about this? We'll find someone or the other. Otherwise, this friend of yours, Mohan will do it. He knows every one.

'Isn't it, Mohanlal.' Mohan nodded his assent but did not utter a word.

With an air of craftiness, he spoke firmly. 'You must bear this in mind that if Maratha squadron plans to free you forcibly, we shall prove our mettle and then we shall not be held responsible to save his life. We care a fig even for Delhi Emperor and Peshwa of Poona is of no consequence to us.'

Chaudharin again coughed. Mohanlal entreated him, 'Chaudhary, go and eat your food. We shall not transgress your limits.'

Chaudhary replied in a contented tone, 'Well, I know all that. A straightforward and frank person as I am, I do not like to bandy words with craft and cunningness nor do I like to listen to such talks. It would be better if you go tomorrow, Chaudhary. You must be knowing all members of Maratha squadron and we have none else for this job. Your wife Chaudharin will remain here in all comfort until then. We are all here. She won't be alone.'

Mohan got exasperated to the hilt but chose to be quiet. The veins in his forehead swelled as he continued to cough for a few moments and nodded his head. Chintaman went out.

From the courtyard, Chintaman called out, 'Chaudharin is waiting for you with the food already served in plate, come and eat, Mohan.'

Mohan replied from inside the closet, 'Coming'. Mohanlal sat there immersed in worrying thought and Shubrati breathing slowly and making little sound, alternately looked at him and the thatched ceiling.

Shubrati said, 'No one can go against what is ordained by fate. I have faith that I shall recover completely. Thereafter even if I am not released, I shall work for them on wages then...'

He became quiet. The picture of Shubrati's children, laughing and playing, flashed in Mohan's eyes, and peals of laughter in the midst of coughing echoed in his ears from the courtyard in Poona.

Mohan remarked as he straightened his head, 'You will recover and get freedom too.'

'Even if 1 don't, it doesn't matter. One should think of the possibility of death before one gets enlisted in the army. Both the sepoy and the family should anticipate all this. I fought in several battles. If I had died, what would have befallen? For a few days, the members of the family would have mourned and wept for me and then life would go on as ever. They would presume Shub.... Ramarao to be dead, that is all.'

'No, please, Ramarao would recover and go back home.'

'What, would he be set free so cheaply?'

'However costly, but he will be freed certainly.'

Shubrati began to smile as if some ointment was being applied to his wounds and said, 'All right, now you should take your meal; poor Chaudharin is waiting for you. Food must be cold by now. I thought that you had taken your meals already.' Mohan stood up. His face was crestfallen but his eyes glistened with vitality. Shubrati added as he grinned, 'Better go smiling; otherwise, you will pick quarrel there.'

Mohan smiled and Shubrati also wished for the same. He said, 'My formula, it seems, had worked. Did you try it?'

Mohan was reminded of the puppet tucked on the thatched ceiling and he burst into laughter. Shubrati said, 'It is not a prescription, it is a panacea. This is why neither her voice nor even her coughing could be heard.'

Mohan went out trying to resist laughter. He carried the brass plate with him. He found Noorbai standing at the door of his room. She spoke sweetly, 'Food has turned quite cold, but there are some embers still left in the stove. Please heat it up and eat.'

'Have you finished?'

'I'm going to take now, I wasn't hungry.'

'Now, it seems, you are feeling hungry.'

'Yes.....Yes I am very very hungry.'

'Why did you keep on waiting?'

'I wasn't sitting at all; you found me standing, isn't it?'

I didn't realise that you were so immature... why did you starve yourself?'

'It isn't so. If you delay very much, I won't wait for you.'

Noorbai took Shubrati's plate with leftover of food, from his hand. She said, 'This is my job.'

While Noorbai was washing the plate, Mohan warmed the loaves. Noorbai gave him the plate.

Mohan expressed his surprise over his own foolishness.

'I committed the folly of not serving you bread before going.'

She said, 'Excellent! Couldn't I pick it up myself. Tell me, if I could take it or not.'

'Of course, you would! Pick it up now.' Mohan said but unintentionally, his hand reached for the loaves and he picked up a few to serve Noorbai.

Noorbai said with a piercing smile, 'Why should I make haste?'

Mohan smiled and served food in Noorbai's plate.

The earthen lamp lighted the room dimly. Both of them were eating food quietly. Intermittently, Mohan stared intently at the door, as if he was trying to grope and penetrate some mystery. Noorbai also gazed at him with side glances and vacant looks. Having finished meal, Noorbai was preparing to go to bed. It seemed, Mohan wished to convey something to her but was unable to do so. Noorbai lay down and closed her eyes. For some time there was pin-drop silence.

Noorbai spoke from her sleeping posture. 'Why are you sitting? Go to bed. You are tired of day's hard work.'

Mohan said, 'I am not tired as much.'

Having sat in the company of a friend, all his weariness had gone away.

Noorbai opened her eyes, looked at him for a moment and then closed them again. After some time, Mohan coughed and asked in an undertone, 'Are you asleep?'

Noorbai did not respond. Mohan repeated the question a little loudly. 'Not at all', replied Noorbai and sat up.

Mohan's eyes reflected his shyness which yearned to see a smile on Noorbai's lips. Mohan's eyes skipping her, peered through crevices of the door in the darkness of the courtyard. He could not see anything there. The earthen lamp in Shubrati's room flickered dimly from one direction.

Noorbai began to gauge the extent and limits of Mohan's shyness, which sent waves of rising emotions in her heart.

Observing Mohan's silence, Noorbai opened the conversation, 'I had dozed off but was not asleep as such.'

Noorbai did not have a wink of sleep and Mohan believed her. 'You too would have worked hard in daytime.' 'I swept the cow-dung — a little here and there and learnt how to make dung-cakes. I fetched water for myself, what else — and did nothing else.'

'You waited long for me.'

'That has whetted my appetite! I ate to my fill—in fact so much—that?'

'Sleep overcame you soon!'

'I did not sleep at all but merely dozed off.'

'You must be sleepy now! Are you feeling sleepy.'

'Not now! I can keep awake the whole night.'

'Then let us talk.'

'I too am yearning for it. I am very talkative but you talk much less.'

'I wish to have a long chat tonight — the village — womenfolk must have talked to you when you went to the platform of the well to draw water.'

'They whispered among themselves first and then....

'What were they whispering?'

'Who is she, where does she come from, how has she come here and so on?'

'And... so on... What does that mean?'

'Come to think of it — if they had abused me, should I sing praise of that too.'

'Yes, of course!'

'Would you like it?'

'Ladies won't abuse without cause.'

'They were saying, 1 am rather rustic and unmannerly.'

'Well, let me tell you what they must have said.'

'All right, tell me.'

'They must have said, some angel has come down from heaven.'

Noorbai burst into laughter. Her pearl-like shining and pretty teeth added grace and charm to the peals of her laughter.

Mohan looked at the flickering, dim light of the earthen lamp and guessed how long it would last and give light.

Noorbai's peals of laughter ceased. She gave a jerk to her neck; a lock of hair slipped on her cheeks reaching her ear. Noorbai's large, intoxicating and passionate eyes opened, for once; the eyelashes touched the eyebrows and then dropped again. She ogled at Mohan with slanted glance. Her lips wore a prominently pointed smile. Noorbai said, 'It seems, you were listening to all the conversation going on at the platform of the well.'

Mohan breathed deeply and said, 'Then let me know what they were gossiping about. Tell me the truth.'

They said, 'She is very lean and thin, how can she do chores? And I can't recall what else?'

'And that you are extremely fair and your eyes are like those of a doe....'

'Go on speaking, go on, and say whatever you like. I am going to close my ears.'

'All right, what did they say after all that whisper?'

'They had asked me questions.'

'What questions?'

Noorbai turned back her neck but Mohan could watch her smile coupled with the lock of flowing hair playing on her smiling face.

'One of them enquired about the well-being of my parents' family; another asked me about my age. Others remarked that the age is quite apparent; yet another asked how long back did 1 get married to Chaudhary by going around the sacred fire?'

I said nothing and all of them burst into laughter. One of them, thereafter, started teasing me by her loose talk. They enquired about children. What you had conveyed to Chaudhary, I repeated all that One of them was rather rude and indecent.

She asked, 'Chaudhary must be loving you intensely; this is why, your fingers are as soft as the cotton wool and almost without vitality of life.'

"If I were at the water platform, I would have remarked, 'Not like cotton but as soft and smooth as silk'?"

'And if you were in my shoes, what you would say to that lady in reply to her query.'

'What query?'

'You want me to repeat that too.'

'I am telling the truth that I don't recall what question you are alluding to. You have talked about many a question.'

'Hm, — Yes, — Well I am forced to say — didn't she ask that Chaudhary must be deeply in love with you?'

'What did you say to that?'

'Come on! I am asking you if you were there at the well in my situation, what reply would you have given?

Could you keep quiet as I did?'

'I could not keep quiet, of course!'

'Then what would you say?'

'Whatever would have dawned upon me'...

'What would have dawned upon you?'

'I am not at the platform of well, presently.'

'Well, did you wake me up to force me to relate everything, in hyperbole, on my own?'

'Where was the sleep? You had only dozed off.'

'For my sake, tell me, on oath, what reply you would have given to that question?'

'All right, tell me, did you really doze off.'

'Do not parry, come out. I am not going to be dissuaded. Take it that I am in a state of trance and then'...

'I am going to tell you.'

Mohan laughed at first and then became sober suddenly.

He said, 'What can I say? Even my heart has come to realize now.'

Noorbai added as she smiled, 'You may not disclose; my heart also knows it that I am infatuated with my Lord Krishna.'

Noorbai turned her neck a little and faced Mohan. She looked at Mohan wide-eyed. Her eyes did not reflect any passion. They welled up with tears which trickled down her cheeks. Her lips quivered with fearful gasping for breath. Noorbai made an effort to suppress it. Her lips quivered and shrank continually. Mohan observed, in her tears and on her lips, something which shook him completely.

He exclaimed suddenly, 'What's this, Noor....'

Noorbai suppressed her tears and pointing to him with finger not to speak, she could manage to say, 'Silence.....silence.'

Mohan restrained himself. Noorbai too calmed herself. Once more, she gave Mohan a cool look and began to gaze towards the door. The courtyard was not visible from that distance.

After a few moments, Noorbai spoke tenderly but with vigour, 'I have buried my past and my former self—the Noorbai of yesterday. She has disappeared for ever. Never recall her name. Now she belongs to her own Kanhaiya as his Gopi. Give her any name you like — Roopa (the beautiful one) or Kurupa (the ugly one), whatever you like best.'

'Neither Roopa, nor Kurupa but Saroopa, Saroopa Chaudharin, isn't it?' Mohan said with bowed head.

Noorbai turned her neck and said, 'I have no right. Whatever you give me, I shall accept and tie it in the anchal[95] of my saree.[96] After a moment, she said, 'I have got every thing', and tied a knot in her saree.

Mohan was silent for a while appearing as if he wanted to say something but found himself unable to. Noorbai came face to face with him again. Mohan raised his head again. As he looked at her, he felt as if he had washed his face in the

95. Anchal – Saree's portion used to cover head or allowed to fall.

96. Saree – The long flowing sheet of cloth worn and wrapped round the body by Indian woman by tradition.

Ganges water. Noorbai's smile played on her face as if moonlight suddenly shone and filtered through the clouds. She said, 'What thoughts are engaging your mind, Chaudhary saheb. What's there to say now? Are you composing some poem or reciting some devotional song?'

Mohan replied, 'Whatever I wish to say, I do not have courage to express.'

'Lack of courage on the part of a chivalrous person when faced with a lean frail lady! May be, some one will accept it, but I can't swallow, it', said Noorbai and added 'Swear by me and tell me everything, whatsoever good or bad comes to your mind, without hiding anything. Tell me just now.'

Mohan replied, 'That Shubrati is a close friend of mine I have already told you. He had saved my life. He has small children living at Poona. Chintaman and his gang want a ransom of one thousand rupees for his release. He will not budge without taking the money. Neither he nor I have got any money. I am in a quandary what to do — please help me.'

Noorbai said, 'Is that all or there is something else to it? Tell me the truth.'

Mohan replied enthusiastically, 'There is nothing else, I am telling you the truth. There is nothing else but is it something insignificant?'

Giving vent to her mock regret by ogling obliquely and artfully, Noorbai said, 'My grievance is why did you fight shy? Whatever I have is not mine-all that is yours. I go about carrying this burden tied on my waist. You said, you would not touch it. I tell you, it pricks me like a thorn in the flesh. Take it here and now and keep everything with you', she reached for the girdle packet.

Mohan replied spontaneously, 'Don't give all of it! Don't do it and take my advice in this matter.'

A smiling Noorbai interrupted him, 'At your command, sir; at your command, Chaudhary saheb!'

He said, "Well Saroopa, please don't repeat 'at your command!' Listen to me! I shall try to strike a deal with Chintaman for a lower sum but give me something which, by selling, can fetch me one thousand rupees. Whatever is saved will stand us in good stead. I shall not carry all or most of it on my person, because I have to take off my clothes, at times, which may expose it to view. If anyone gets an inkling, we won't be able to protect either this or our own person. It will remain intact and tucked safe beneath several clothes."

Noorbai said, 'Well now that you are going to Agra, take with you as much as can fetch enough coins to remain in our possession so that you are not obliged to work on wages;' and added, 'I may not have to make dung-cakes.'

Mohanlal conceded. Noorbai took out bits of ornaments and carrying, in her palm, near the earthen lamp a few large pearls and a piece of gold, she beckoned to Mohan to come. As Noorbai stretched her hand to hand over pearls and gold to Mohan, her face reflected such an aura and halo in the light of the earthen lamp that had she gazed at the mirror, she would have discovered her graceful looks and features in such glory and distinction at that moment as she would never have watched in the past. Mohan took possession of the small heap of ornaments without looking into her eyes.

Mohan remarked, 'The earthen lamp has little oil to keep it going. Let me go and convey to Shubrati that I shall set out, at daybreak, to arrange for ransom money which will induce him to sleep without anxiety.'

'And would you relate the whole story to him?'

'No, I won't tell him; in any case, not now.'

'If he asked how you would arrange, what would be your reply!'

'I have been roaming from place to place, and can't I find any pretext? From Delhi to Ujjain, Poona and God knows how many other places.'

'All right, go! Now I am going to sleep joyfully and completely relaxed.'

'Joyfully or in deep meditation?'

'Why should I meditate now? I have been bestowed with all I wished. I shall have a sound sleep now. You would come back quite late?'

Stretching her limbs, Noorbai went back to bed while Mohan made his way to the courtyard. He saw a shadow moving quickly towards Chintaman's room. It gave him a little jolt; then, ignoring it, he went into Shubrati's room. He was not asleep as yet.

Going close to him, Mohan said in an undertone, 'Here walls too have ears. Someone was trying to hear our conversation just a few moments back.'

'Between you and Chaudharin?'

'Yes.'

"Were you talking confidentially with her?'

'Yes, of course.'

'Well, then it appears, Chaudharin has chased you and this had made you come to me?'

'Listen to me, I am going early in the morning and will be back within two-three days. By that time, you would have recovered and then you will regain your freedom. We'll also accompany you.'

'How will you arrange so much money.'

'How are you concerned?'

'The commander cannot dig out and muster so much money; besides, he would not have gone towards Agra — must have gone to Mathura.'

'I say, you should be interested in fruits, not in the trees.'

'I am afraid you might get lost or something might happen to you. How will Chaudharin manage to live here?'

'She has cheerfully, asked me to go away.'

'Well, she is far ahead of you.'

'Surely! I shall be anxious about your well-being.'

'Now that we are trapped in this hole, we should not be frightened of the blows inflicted by others. Of course you may go but come back quickly. Don't worry about me. I'll manage to get food and water, meanwhile.'

'Chaudharin will supply you everything. There is, of course, Chaudharin, the wife of Chintaman also. Hence you may call her by the name of Saroopa.'

'It is a good name indeed; besides, she is not quarrelsome.'

Roni's face flashed before his eyes for an instant.

Mohan said, 'I am going now.' Standing at the door, he said loudly, 'Ram ... Ram ... goodbye brother Ram ... Ram.' Shubrati replied rather in a weak voice, 'Ram ... Ram' Mohan made his way through the dark courtyard but did not see anything ominous. When he reached his room, he saw that the flickering light of earthen lamp was about to die out.

While lying in bed, he asked her, 'Are you asleep?'

Getting no response, he repeated the question. There was still no response.

Noorbai was fast asleep.

—✵—

48

Before dawn, Mohan prepared a few loaves for himself, Noorbai and Shubrati. Explaining to Noorbai in detail how to take care of Shubrati's meals and comfort, Mohan set out in the direction of Agra with loaves tied in a cloth for himself.

Day was breaking. Blended with yellow the rosy hue splashed through the morning sky. Oblique, slanting sunrays glimmered and moment to moment transformed the surroundings. A cool and light breeze seemed to be fondly patting the sleepy dust. The drone of the beetle was slowly dying out. In the nests, the young ones of sparrow chirped with beaks half-open, soliciting to fill them with mouthfuls of morning helpings. The birds flapped their wings as they chirped and clamoured to fly out from the nests. Wafted and fondled by soft, light-wind, margose flowers dropped from the branches and added fragrance to dust.

Noorbai felt the knots of the small bundles of gold, pearls and diamonds in the girdle of her long skirt and tied them firmly. She tucked her colourful blouse neatly and covered herself with the flowing 'Chunri', the long sheet of wrapper cloth. Sticking her face out at the door she looked towards the courtyard. It seemed lively and lifelike, sunlight itself was peeping through the window. Drawing her veil, she picked up the pitcher and a rope lying in the corner of the courtyard and went out. Chintaman had already gone out for the morning ablutions.

As she went out, her attention was diverted to the eastern direction. There was no movement on the road yet. She slowly lifted her veil. Managing her veil with two fingers as she looked wide-eyed at the yellowish, pink hue of the horizon in the east as she moved towards the well. She balanced the brass pitcher with her soft lotus-petal like fingers. She recalled a quartet of Omar Khayyam[97] which can be summarised as follows :

'When the Goddess of Dawn sent her
first, beauteous, golden orb of light,
I listened to the call from the wine-bar
echo, 'Arise, arise, my dear young ones,
fill the cup, do not delay anymore,
lest the nectar of life should run
dry rendering the cup empty.'

She began to hum the quartet. Her feet slowed down as if they were trying to keep in tune with the humming song. Memories of her past life flashed in her mind's eye — the bedecked, enthralling spot where the musical instruments,

97. Omar Khayyam (1071-1123) – The famous Persian Poet whose romantic rubaiyats (quartets) have earned him a world-wide fame.

sarangi, tamboora and cymbals were played vigorously and in harmony, where Emperor, saturated with intoxicating liquors leant his head intermittently and exclaimed, 'Well done — well done' Noorbai was filled with remorse. At the same time, the remark, heard by her previous night 'What can I express, my heart cherishes better my feelings' echoed in her ears. How in a simple, straightforward manner Mohan had conveyed his feelings, left its impress and drew her attention. She heard someone's voice from one direction, "O lady! You have come out so early! Has 'he' gone in that direction — which is why you are looking in that direction so wistfully?"

Noorbai drew the veil and turned away her neck. An old woman was going to draw water. Noorbai addressed her. 'It is not too early, mother. Day has started breaking already.'

They found themselves in each other's company and arrived at the well. Noorbai entreated the old woman, 'Maaji! May I help you draw water?'

The old woman said, 'I may give away my life! What a sweet voice she has! My daughter, your hands are so tender that the rope will peel off your palm. I shall fill my pitcher, I have been drawing water for years. Give it to me. I shall draw yours too.'

As she said this, she began to snatch the pitcher from Noorbai. Noorbai was adamant on not bothering her. The old lady said, 'You are reaching the prime of your youth while I have already slid past the same. But my bones are so strong that I can push to floor two or four ladies of your constitution and frame'. The old woman did not give in. She pushed Noorbai's pitcher into the well and after drawing it from the well, put it on the platform.

'Take it and if you need to fill again, draw water yourself from the well.'

Noorbai knelt and touched the knees of the old woman to express her gratitude and started moving away with the pitcher.

Overwhelmed, the old woman blessed her joyfully, 'May you be blessed with sons and milk of life; may your lap always carry a child.'

Apprehensive of other women's arrival there, Noorbai returned with the pitcher on her head. The sun's first rays were filtering into the house. The droplets of water hung on the pitcher reflected and seemed to absorb those rays.

There was no one in the courtyard. Noorbai went into her room with the pitcher. A little later, Chintaman came into the courtyard. His wife came to the door of her room. She asked, 'Did you come across those people?'

Chintaman replied, 'Yes I did. I have settled everything with them. They have also followed him.'

His wife said, 'Now, get the cow milked. As long as he is here with us, we'll have to nurse him.'

Chintaman pointed towards Noorbai's room and asked, 'Hasn't she come back?' She said, 'She has not come yet.' Chintaman went back to his room. Noorbai had overheard this dialogue. Then they started talking in a low tone in their room. Noorbai tried eaves-dropping but failed to make out the conversation.

Chintaman said, 'I wished to convey to Ramarao that my men have followed him. Let's see where Mohan goes and what he does, whether he returns with squad of his own.'

'This Maratha has received only a minor injury but the fall must be hurting him more. I wish to get rid of this troublesome creature after receiving ransom and then turn to some other business.'

'Do I have to go and serve him food and milk?'

'Mohan's wife is right here; if she were not here, it would be different.'

'Whether she is, his wife or someone else, I have a nagging doubt on that.'

'Could you dig out and discover something?'

'I have tried to do that just now, got nothing among clothes.'

'Whatever I could gather from last night's conversation it seems she has got some large-sized ornaments with her.'

'Where did they keep all that?'

'Be on the lookout for that.'

'Would like to figure out at bathing time.'

Then both of them busied themselves in their routine.

Noorbai was now preoccupied in her thought 'Who all had gone chasing? And after whom? Must be pursuing him only? Why? With what motive?' She was lost in worrying thoughts.

From Shubrati's room, a voice was heard - 'Water — - Water'.

Noorbai went with a tumbler full of water.

Shubrati said, 'Lady of the house, may you enjoy all happiness. It seems I can manage to walk. I wish to go out for toilet'.

Noorbai turned back and waved at him asking him to refrain from that. Shubrati observed that her hands were handsome and tender. He said, 'Sister, don't worry ! While I finish my wash, you may get me some milk'.

Noorbai did not dissuade him any further and went out. Shubrati came out limping with the help of a stick. Chintaman accosted him questioningly, 'O! What are you doing? Where are you going? The wound will open up again and remain unhealed.'

Shubrati reassured him, 'It is much better than before, Chaudhary Saheb!'

Chintaman escorted him to a nearby compound which was in ruins and himself stood guard at the edge. When he was back after the wash, Chintaman felt relieved. In a short while, milk was boiled. Noorbai offered it to Shubrati. Thereafter, she cleaned up the cow-dung and filth made by Chintaman's cattle and made dung-cakes. Then she fetched water for bath. Some women were bathing themselves at the well but she did not have bath there. She began to take bath behind a cot which served as a cover. Chaudharin was alert and on the lookout. Chaudharin began to converse with her so as to keep standing there. Noorbai had placed the pouch containing ornaments beneath her clothes. A sizeable portion of the pouch would be visible to Chaudharin while she was changing her clothes.

Chaudharin started talking so as to remain standing there.

Chaudharin said, 'My eyes are weakened and I can't see properly. While making loaves, tears trickle from my eyes. I would have to make loaves for that sepoy as well today.'

'I shall prepare for him. Your man told us that you did not know how to make them.'

'I'll make for him. After all, I am going to do it for myself.'

'You would make them half-baked. As it is, the poor fellow is not keeping well.'

'They won't be half-baked. May be, they will be burnt.'

'Don't worry, Maaji.'

'Then put on yonr clothes and go to your kitchen. I shall share work with you.'

'Won't you feel smoke in your eyes there?'

'Let's see. Now that you have finished your bath, I shall pick up your clothes. Put them on; then we'll go and see.'

But no sooner did Chaudharin advance than Noorbai collected her clothes. The apparel which covered the long, thin cloth-bag of jewellery had to be gathered properly before being picked up. While she was doing it, Chaudharin observed one end of the cloth-bag. Noorbai went into her room still wearing her wet dress. While changing her clothes, she tied the cloth bag to her waist. Chaudharin had observed enough to confirm her suspicion.

'You were in such a great haste! Hurried back to room even without changing the wet dress!'

Noorbai tried to allay her apprehension, 'Suppose Chaudhary or someone else had turned up there, he would have called me rustic and indecent'.

Chaudharin's plump face then reflected her cunning nature and a little anger too.

'There is still time for you to start cooking but my stove is already lit and burning.' Chaudharin thus gave vent to her non-cooperative attitude.

'Mother, you better go, I shall do everything. Don't worry at all,' assured Noorbai. Chaudharin went out. Noorbai washed her clothes at the well and fetched water. Thereafter, she began to try her hand at cooking. She began to cook with as much perseverance as she would have applied her talents in performing her dance beautifully and efficiently besides singing devotedly to achieve the nuances and beauty of the Raga (form and style) in which she was singing. Despite her attainments in creating beautiful form while performing dance and singing, the loaves made by her remained distorted in shape and size — some of them being half-baked and one or two partly and improperly heated. Water added to the pulses got separated on being heated, making porridge of the same in the process. Serving in the metal plate, she carried it to Shubrati.

He was asleep. Noorbai attempted to cough once or twice but he was not awakened thereby. Then she used the latch to knock at the door. Shubrati was awakened. She placed the plate in front of him and stood taking the door as a cover.

Shubrati, it seemed, was struggling to make morsels of the bread. He mused, 'She is such a great beauty that God himself seems to have given shape lo her body but she is just a novice at cooking! This appears to be the cause of quarrel between husband and wife. She would be conducting herself haughtily and Mohan would not be able to bear all this. A hungry man cannot satisfy his appetite merely by the beautiful features of his wife. She is a grown-up woman and I wonder what she had been doing all these years.'

Meanwhile, he lifted and put a morsel of half-baked loaf in his mouth. Shubrati vomitted and put it aside. He could not resist saying, 'Sister, you should devote yourself fully in the service of brother Mohan.'

Noorbai clasped a little more firmly one plank of the door.

'And do everything by putting heart into your work. Do not quarrel with him.'

Noorbai coughed a little as if to protest or to express her surprise. Shubrati thought she had fully understood or accepted the sermon with a bowed head and was conveying it by coughing.

He finished his meal, somehow, by grappling with the porridge of pulses and half baked loaves and added in a sermonising tone thus, 'Quarrelling spoils families, Sister! Please take it from me for ever'. Noorbai had to remain contented by suppressing her deep breath.

She came in to pick up the plate. Shubrati asked her to refrain from it but she did not. Shubrati pondered, he should not question too much or prevent her from doing things; it might be that she had a bee in her bonnet which would flare up to make her come down upon him heavily. Noorbai had taken away the plate.

—❋—

49

Mohanlal arrived in Agra by evening. He lodged himself in a temple. Tired as he was by the day's arduous journey, he was soon asleep after consuming the leftover of bread. He could not observe that a few other travellers had also come and occupied a corner of that temple and instead of going to sleep, they continued to whisper among themselves.

Mohanlal was up quite early in the morning. Having finished his toilet and wash, he came out and proceeded towards the Johari Bazar (Jewel Market). That he was being followed by some people, he was not aware of.

Since noon, the road leading to Johari Bazar was being washed by water. Every Tom, Dick and Harry could not pass through the road. Mohanlal was also questioned, 'Where are you going?'

'To Johari Bazar.'

'That is obvious. Which shop are you heading to?'

'In whichever I can clinch a deal.'

'What deal?'

'This will be conveyed to the jeweller alone.'

At that moment, those following him also arrived there. A group of five persons, they were also interrogated. They also replied on similar lines. The newcomers offered a solution to the interrogators, 'When we come back, we won't forget you. We shall give you your customary and rightful dues.'

The questioner asked, 'How long will you take to come back?'

Pat came the reply, 'We come back quite soon. We have only a little business to transact.' They had a word with Mohanlal also about the customary dues. All of them arrived in the market.

Mohanlal was not familiar with any one of them; neither did he wish to introduce himself to them nor did he seek their acquaintance. Even so, he asked, 'Why are the roads being washed?'

'This evening, the district governor will visit the market-place. This watering is with a view to cover and compact the dust.'

'Is Subedar's[98] body made from flowers?' Mohanlal could not help asking.

'Suppose some one from here will listen to this?'

'So what? He will not devour us. Has Subedar banned movement on the road?'

'O, brother! Here everyone is a Subedar; this is why you also agreed lo pay the customary dues.'

'You had agreed to pay, hence, I followed suit.'

'Otherwise — otherwise what would you do?'

98. Subedar – Provincial governor in Moghul times.

'I would return and lie in my own bed and would have come back some other time.'

'Which caste do you belong to?'

'Jat'!

'Hm! Whose shop are you going to?'

'How about you?'

'For a while, we shall loiter here and there and then whichever, shop appears to be a good one, we shall negotiate there'.

'I shall also roam about. I am not in a hurry. By evening, I wish to buy things. I should like to watch Subedar too while sitting in a shop, as to how he dresses himself, which conveyance he uses and what brings him here?'

They could make out that Mohan was a frustrated and sad person. They dispersed themselves. Mohanlal went to a shop after making a round of the place. There was no crowd there. The shopkeeper was chewing betel with his back resting against a pillow and the body relaxing on a mattress. A servant was pulling fan. The accounts-man was writing out accounts in the ledgers. As soon as Mohan stepped into the shop, the owner knitted his eyebrows and asked him as he kept relaxing on the pillow, 'Who are you? Why are you making a forcible entry into the shop?'

'I have come on business.'

His clothes did not betray any sign of business. His stout and robust physique could certainly be begging questions.

The accounts-man examined him and assessed that he was carrying no weapon. He became very courteous and asked, 'Which village do you belong to, Chaudhariji? You are a Chaudhary, isn't that so?'

Mohan replied, 'How are you concerned with my village? A Chaudhary I am, that is about all', and he set with a jerk of the knee. 'Give me some water and then I shall talk about business.'

The owner of the shop raised his head from the pillow and sizing up Mohan from head to toe looked at the accounts-man, who had risen from his seat to offer him water though unwillingly and perforce. But before he filled water in the tumbler he asked, 'You have got to do some business or not? What is the business?'

Mohan eyed the entire shop, and said, 'Business it is! I have brought some valuables.'

As their ears caught the words valuable, the faces of both the shopkeeper and the accounts-man assumed soft and sweet look of endearment. The accounts-man quickly offered Mohan water. In front of the shop, one of the group of five started moving up and down. Mohan did not observe them. He took out gold and pearls from his girdle-bag. Both the owner and accounts-man assessed their value. With a smiling face, he said, 'See, I had business. If I strike a deal, I'll sit; else, I shall look for another jeweller.'

'Why do you talk like that? Chaudhariji! We did not recognise you earlier. You have come to see us after how long, we do not recall. Where will you go away in this scorching heat without resting for a while? Where are you residing these days, Chaudhariji?'

'Today and tomorrow, I am right here in this shop but otherwise I am serving in the Maratha platoon which comes from Poona.'

'The one camping in Mathura?'

'Yes....Yes the same! It has arrived here recently.' The owner and Munim were assessing the valuables alternately and continued the conversation at the same time.

The accounts-man asked with a grin, 'Chaudhariji, you have received enough as your share.'

Mohan could not help indulging in an expression of pride, He said,

'Yes, I left behind a lot of it, businessman.'

'Now speak out Chaudhariji, what would you accept for them here?'

'Let me know the price which you would like to pay. Quote the price separately for pearls and gold.'

'Well, Chaudhariji, the pearls are worth twelve hundred rupees and gold rupees fifty. We want to enlist you as our customer; hence, we have assessed the maximum value. Even if we do not agree to a deal, we'll not let you go without a meal.'

It occurred to Mohan that he should give his consent but he stood up apparently to make a move.

The owner said, 'Come on, we'll not let you go just like that.'

The accounts-man said, 'We'll pay fourteen hundred for pearls and fifty live rupees for gold. We can't pay you more than that. Now whatever you wish, Chaudhariji, you may do!'

Mohan accepted the value without demur. That very moment, gold and silver coins were counted and put in a small pan. The jeweller gave him a long thin cloth-bag. Mohan tied the money in his girdle. The passers-by ohserved a part of these proceedings; others who did not see, made it out by adding imagination.

The jeweller offered him sweets and fried loaves to eat. After the meal was over, he was offered a place to lie and rest. He was able to see the procession taken out in honour of district governor. When the procession made its way back, the market swelled with crowd. Buying some food, he got lost in the crowd and returned to the place of his stay in the temple. He got back the weapons and articles he had left behind on the spot in the temple premises.

He was turning sides in anticipation of sleep. Lost and wallowing as he was in sweet dreams, he thought how important was money in life. It bought horses, elephants, cannons, swords and all that counts in one's possession! Whoever possesses wealth, can rule a state. With valuables in hand, the accounts-man and the shopkeeper were tempted! Otherwise, they would not have allowed him to enter, what to speak of making him sit.

He could listen to some whisper and movement a little away from the place he was lying. He tried to eavesdrop but could not. He ran his fingers on the cloth-bag and tied it more firmly. 'Hm! I am a sepoy and this money belongs to another person. Another person! Noorbai! She had told me that I could name her Roopa, Kurupa but should not call her by the name of Noorbai. Saroopa, Saroopa is a beautiful name....Yes, this money belongs to Saroopa....If I could also earn that much money by my sweat and toil! Where did Saroopa get all these pearls from?...Gold..... The pearls were shining.....Well it was a good show there.' All these scattered thoughts made Mohan fall asleep.

—✵—

50

The wavy clouds — aslant, slender and moving in several folds and moulds seemed to be saluting to and spreading red carpet for the goddess dawn, 'Usha' by the time Mohan had reached a little distance from Agra. Five men keeping an eye on him followed closely while maintaining a little distance. They came across a village at sunrise. After a wash, Mohan took a brief breakfast followed by some rest under the shade of a tree. Mohan had traversed a busy road so far. He had heard many an ancedote about highway robbery, loot and assault by Marathas. He decided to take to a less busy and much less crowded way. Laxity and weakness had crept into keeping of peace and order by administration even before Nadir Shah's campaigns so much so that the neighbourhood of Delhi also witnessed looting and highway robbery. After Nadir Shah's attack, disorder and maladministration was rampant in an area of 100 Kos[99] around Delhi.

The Ruler of Jaipur had bestowed upon Raja Badan Singh of Bharatpur, the title of 'Brijraj'.[100] He claimed and collected several titles and sub-titles of Kingship but preferred not to call himself 'Rajah'. Prosperous Jats living far and wide from Mathura and Agra raised their own fighting squadrons and became the chieftains of forts. These nobles accepted the titular headship of Raja Badan Singh but all of them were persevering to strengthen their position and power. None of them was willing to be subjugated by the other. At times, they fought among themselves. Having been tormented and looted by the Muslim marauders, they had also taken to the profession of plunder and booty.

The vassals of these chieftains had to toil by the sweat of the brow at farming and face all its attendant hazards — if they did not, they would starve; if the harvest was saved, whatever was leftover for them was only due to grace of God; else, they were doomed. Led by their chieftains, such fellows would stir, at leisure, for highway robbery; if fighting broke out, doubtlessly, it was their duty to take part therein. But they too were not amenable to discipline and control, be it that of their chieftain or of their own kind.

Robbery campaigns were not regulated by seasons or timings. This calling was not dependant on limitation of day or night. Wherever there was movement of carriages and passengers or overcrowding, it signified presence of goods which, if not escorted by an army detachment or army itself, gave them clue to embark upon their enterprise.

Mohan enquired in that village about the way leading to his destination, which would not be busy or crowded. He found

99. Kos – op. cit. 55, p. 122.
100. Brijraj — The king of Brij area i.e. neighbourhood around Mathura in an area of 100 kms. or so.

out the way but those who guided him also came to know about his destination. Leaving the shade of the tree, Mohan set out on his journey. It was nearing mid-day. There was still some nip in the air; Mohan thought, he should cover as much distance as he could and, then, after resting a while in the afternoon, he would be at home by evening, where a sweet smile and a melodious voice would receive him warmly besides the genial humour of his friend for whom he had undertaken that risk which seemed a trifle to him. At mid-day, Mohan came across a pool which was partly filled with water. Around this nullah, the place was desolate and full of trees in the thick of forest. Across the nullah, there lay a village but before one could reach the village, one had to go through an undulating slopy terrain. He looked around and stood still. At some distance behind, a few persons followed him. He felt relieved a little. He advanced. The path lay beneath the shadow of the trees. He carried a sword even though he was all alone. He arrived at the pool without fear and sat by the waterpool. Thirsty as he was, he kept sitting by the watery side for a short while for he was perspiring too. He had not rested fully when four-five persons came down towards the pool point and advanced apprehensively. With their beards covered, they could not be recognised. As they were about to advance, a loud call could be heard from behind - 'Stop!- Don't move forward.'

They turned around to look towards the source and direction of the call.

Mohan too stood still. From the same direction, a gang of ten-fifteen masked men arrived on the spot.

Mohan was one of those who are initially stupefied by an assault but do not weigh pros and cons before plunging themselves in a fierce battle in the next few moments. These four-five persons were also armed but the group of ten-fifteen had already drawn their swords, taking the group of four-five by surprise.

Mohan too had unsheathed his sword. He shouted, 'Be warned, we are far too many.' Then he started shouting at the top of his voice, 'Come on fellows! Run! Catch them! Hold them fast and kill them.'

Mohan began to brandish his sword then and there. One of the new arrivals, shrieked, 'Run ..... Run for life! It is a ghost! Oh! O! O, fellows, Hm!

The man who was shouting, turned back and ran for life.

His companions joined in shouting 'Hm! What's the matter? What's that!' and fled in the direction they came from. The man who had been shouting continued in the same vein, it is a ghost.... It's a ghost! My God! Oh Rama, my God!' until the cry faded.

Drawing back his sword, Mohan addressed the group of four-five persons, 'What's the matter? What's all this?'

None of them responded; instead, they headed fast towards the village. Mohan, then, suddenly recalled the custodial trust tied in his girdle. Thirsty and startled as he was, he gulped water quickly and ascended the bank of the nullah again. The village, a little distant still, was clearly visible but those who had gone ahead of him were not to be spotted there.

'Were all of them ghosts?' was the question which agitated his mind. He heaved a sigh and 'Hm' and made his way up to the village quickly by the uneven path above the pool of water. There was a temple in the proximity of the village, which had a few broken idols and a few idols were smeared with sanctified red powder. Mohan lay in the enclosed verandah as he was unable to proceed further on his journey. The path he had taken branched off from the royal road which lay behind. But this path seemed longer and circuitous. He thought that he would reach home late at night. Mohan was caught on the horns of dilemma, 'What to do'. When it was past afternoon and the evening was closing in, he was exasperated. He remonstrated himself, 'What an utterly worthless fellow I have proved by being indecisive.'

He was about to leave when he looked at the sun. He sneezed. He decided to halt there for the night and to set out quickly early before dawn so as to reach home by afternoon, if not by mid-day. In those moments, as in the previous night, when he was unable to sleep he was constantly reminded of the custody of the articles he held in trust; intermittently, he was also reminded of the day's experience — 'It was ghost! it was a ghost!! Were all of them Ghosts? What! Ghost in daytime! Where did they disappear?' He was unable to figure out. He left the temple-premises while there was some daylight still and sought a place to rest in the courtyard of a farmer.

—❋—

51

It was a little before noon. Roni was making preparations for cooking the mid-day meal when Tota arrived home. There was no one at home at that hour. Tota's face wore a despondent look. His lips were dry and parched and the body smeared with dust. He put away his arms in a closet, took off his clothes and seated himself in the closed varandah.

Roni managed to smile and with a bend at the waist entreated. 'A whole day and all night toiling like this! You must be very tired! Shall I bring you some water?'

Tota could muster to mutter 'Yes!' Roni brought a little jaggery and a tumbler full of water. Tota took the same alongwith water.

Roni continued in the same vein, 'I don't recall, how many times did I get up from sleep awaiting your arrival. Even a little stirring startled and woke me up. The old man too got up a few times. It was so hot that everyone slept outside in the open. I kept on thinking that if you knocked and tapped the latch, I would run to open the door and then give you the repast which is still there. I have kept away some butter-oil also for you. This morning, I mixed and put it back in the earthen jar. What else could I do? You seem to be fully exhausted and depressed too. Stretch yourself a little; meanwhile, I shall cook something for you. I was feeling quite lonely and lost in your absence, I don't know why?'

Tota was humming and nodding in agreement in between her remarks. Having finished his meal, he washed his face and placing a cot seated himself on it. Roni stood there and entreated, 'Lie down, I will be back right away after bolting the door.'

Tota stretched himself on the cot. Roni came back after bolting the door and began massaging his head, sitting by the head of the cot. She added, 'Close your eyes. I shall massage your head like I did the other day. Then I shall massage your arms, back and waist too?'

Tota looked askance and enquired, 'Would it not delay cooking and making of loaves?'

Roni satisfied his query, 'No, it won't. Already there are loaves of bread leftover from previous night. I need to make only a few warm ones.'

Tota looked intently at her. Roni craned her neck and smiled. Heaving her chest above the side planks of the cot, she pressed it against the same and added, 'You won't get to sleep by looking at me like this! Isn't it?'

Tota closed his eyes. His face did not betray any passionate response.

Roni bent over him a little more closely and began massaging Tota's head. Her exhaled breath touched and wafted softly over Tota's chin. Roni gazed at his face intently and enquired. 'Are you asleep already?'

'Not at all', Tota replied and opened his eyes. Roni espied something in his rosy glowing eyes.

Expressive and effusive in sympathy as she was, she winked and knitted her eyebrows and asked, 'You never felt so tired earlier?'

Tota uttered in a drawl, Bhauji[101]

101. Bhauji – Sister-in-law (Elder brother's wife).

Roni offered, 'Heat is too much for you. Let wavy motion of my 'Aanchal'[102] serve as a fan for you.'

With one hand resting close to Tota's ear, she put forth the other arm to stretch her 'Aanchal' in motion.

Tota said, 'It's not too hot for me; put both hands of yours on my head. It is very comforting thus'.

Roni loosened her 'Aanchal' but rather than waving the same, she pressed his head with both hands adding, 'I wish you would go on gazing at me but since your eyes are red by sleeplessness, you need to sleep immediately. Let me go on gazing at you.'

'I am having a severe headache. Even if I shut my eyes, it does not lessen my headache at all; instead, nerves of my temple seem to be splitting up.'

'Let me press and massage your temples.'

'Now the back of my head seems to be splitting.'

'Did you sustain some injury?'

'No, there is no injury.'

'You had to go through a lot of strain?'

'Yes indeed.'

Roni's aanchal had slipped and rested on one half of her chest. Tota turned away his face a little. Smiling, she said, 'Don't you feel interested in anything just now?'

'No nothing.'

'What's the matter, then?'

'What can I tell you?'

'You did not get any catch by this time. Isn't it the only thing weighing on you?'

'If it were the case, it was nothing. I have seen him with my own eyes!'

'Whom?'

'Mohan, my elder brother or may be, his ghost!'

'What!'

---

102. Aanchal – op. cit 95, p. 228.

Roni withdrew her hands with a jerk. She detached herself from the side beam of the cot. Her whole body was shaking as she stood aloof. She stood quietly for sometime. Tota was looking at her with his hands pressing his head. To Roni, the cot with Tota lying on it, the mud wall with the thatched roof seemed to be reeling and shaking. Roni made an effort to keep her calm and balance. She questioned him with a lump in her throat; 'Did you see him in daylight or at night? Or, in darkness? Or, in broad daylight? Where? At what distance from here and when?'

'Yesterday, in broad daylight, between Agra and Chintaman's village in a nullah.'

'You alone saw him?'

'No, I wasn't alone. Our entire gang accompanied us.'

'How did you see him? What was the sequence?'

'We saw some men making enquiries about the road to Chintaman's village at a spot where we were hiding ourselves. I thought, they were either spies working for an enemy or carriers of goods and merchandise. We followed them at some distance and made up our minds to settle scores with them near the pool of water beyond which lay the village where we had acquaintance. They had tied cloth around their heads, so had we; they were armed too but we had already drawn our swords. No sooner had we surrounded them and mounted an assault with a hoarse shout, than I found Mohan Bhaiyya standing at some distance. He wore no mask but was brandishing his sword which shimmered like lightning. I shrieked out of terror and fled the spot. My companions also ran for life and rested only after covering a distance of about three kilometres.'

'Your companions also saw him?'

'They did; but they did not recognise him.'

'And who were those, you set upon?'

'Didn't I tell you that they had tied cloth around their beard and thus were not recognisable. It was all over within a few moments.'

'Was it daytime or night?'

'Oh, Bhauji, it was broad daylight; didn't I tell you just now?'

'Did you see him again elsewhere?'

'No, he was not to be seen again.'

'Can one see a ghost in daytime too?'

'We have been told that ghosts are not to be seen in daytime, but these are the times of Kalyug.[103]

'You didn't turn back to have a look.'

'Who had the courage to turn and look back?'

Roni was immersed in thought. Her face wore a parched, grim look and her eyes lost their sparkle. Tota sat down.

'If one dies in the battlefield, one goes to heaven ....,' Roni uttered in a flattering voice, 'but he died in suffering, it seems.'

Tota said, 'I fail to understand what to do. I must stop going out. This time, if there is a clash again at night, even my dead-body may not be allowed to pass on way back.'

Trembling, Roni added in a tearful tone, 'I suggested that we might go on a pilgrimage'.

"Come what may, we must now go immediately to Mathura and Vrindavan. I have saved some rupees which will suffice. We shall have 'Darshan' in all large and well-known temples and will make some offerings in each one of them."

Tota lay himself and entreated his sister-in-law, 'Bhauji, please come near me, sit here and massage my hair as before. Now it will rid me of my headache.'

'No, no, not now,' Roni added softly, 'Some thing will emerge only on return from pilgrimage. Please do not go out for that kind of errand henceforth. Roni was about to leave with these words. Tota wished her to stay, 'Talk to me for a little while more! Bhauji.'

---

103. Kalyug – Modern era is called Kalyug in Hindu mythology. It is attendant with evils and sins of all kinds for sinners outnumber the faithful and law-abiders.

She said, 'No, I shall make loaves now' as she went out.

—⁕—

52

Mohan was back home in the scorching summer afternoon. He met Chintaman in the porch. Chintaman received him warmly as he looked at his dusty limbs perspiring in the heat, 'Returned rather early! Good! You must be quite thirsty; let me get you some water.'

Chintaman's eyes betrayed his mischievious nature though his tone expressed sympathy. Mohan could see through both.

Mohan said, 'I shall take it inside the house.'

Chintaman added, 'It will be quite humid inside. Cool yourself and dry up the sweat here in the draught of wind. I shall get you some water' and saying this, he went inside the house, 'Oh my dear, bring some water. Mohan Chaudhary is back.' Chintaman shouted from the courtyard and came back to the porch. He was anxious and impatient to talk to him. He asked, 'Where have you been, Chaudhary?'

Mohan said, 'I went to Mathura.'

'Did you meet Maratha commander?'

'Yes!'

'Did you accomplish your task?'

'Yes, sir!'

'Every thing was all right both ways.'

'Yes, as much as one could expect these days.'

'Did someone pursue you?'

'Apparently, yes.'

'Who were they?'

'Could not recognise them. But I could make out that their intentions were far from desirable.'

'Where did they shadow you?'

'I cannot recall the name of the village.'

Mohan's voice was dry and rough.

Chintaman intermittently looked towards the courtyard and hardly gazed into his eyes directly.

Chintaman's wife brought a tumbler full of water; she was followed by Noorbai who also brought some water. Chintaman said, 'Put down the tumbler and go.'

Both of them placed the tumblers and went back inside. Noorbai kept standing at the doorstep of her room, from where she could partly espy Mohan who was sitting at the platform outside the house.

Mohan washed his face and hands with water fetched by Chintaman's wife and gulped water from the tumbler brought by Noorbai; Noorbai could watch all this.

Chintaman told him, 'Ramarao's wounds are healing up fast. He has been looked after very well. He was given plenty of milk and butter-oil. He has started going out for toilet.'

Mohan replied enthusiastically 'It is good progress! I shall go and see him now.'

Chintaman asked him, 'Was Maratha commander angry? Did he say some thing?'

'Nothing! He said nothing in particular', Mohan replied.

Chintaman said, 'He knows every thing. Whatever is happening in the country, he is well aware of. Who tells that Marathas too are not honest in their dealings? They also behave the same way. Hence the Commander must have readily agreed to it!'

Mohan said, 'Yes... yes.'

Mohan's face did not reflect any ardour.

Chintaman assured him, 'Now wherever Ramarao wants to go, he is free to go, in a day or so, of course.'

Mohan agreed with him, 'I shall reach him at his destination; he would not know how to find his way back.'

Chintaman had no objection. He said, 'Please pay off the maintenance charges in a little while and then enjoy yourselves as you may wish to.'

Mohan nodded his assent and went into his room. Noorbai was standing. Mohan closed the door behind him. He took off his clothes, sat down and began to fan himself with one end of a piece of cloth.

Noorbai offered to do it with an effortless ease, 'Let me do it for you.'

Mohan told her 'no' and added, 'Hold on, tell me how you spent the days in my absence.'

Noorbai lifted her eyebrows—her eyeballs seemed to move in awe. She said, 'I would have run into trouble, the day you had left. I was bathing behind an improvised screen when Chaudharin arrived at the spot.'

'To see the statuesque beauty!'

'Oh why do you interrupt me like that; listen; I had put the girdle bag below the clothes. I did not wish to open the bag in her presence and hence took a lot of time in bathing, but she did not budge. Then, I wrapped it in the bundle of clothes and retreated into my room.'

'Well, if I had returned that very moment when you were in that state.'

'A naughty man! If you had come, Chaudharin would have beaten a hasty retreat.'

Noorbai began to laugh and added amidst her laughter. 'At first, it seemed to me that she had watched it all, but then I felt reassured. She came and stood at the doorstep to make her own assessment but in a corner spot, I carefully tucked and tied the pouch in my girdle without dropping any hint about it. She could not make out at all.'

Mohan asked her, 'You have kept it tied, still.'

She replied with sideways glance, 'Why don't you see it for yourself?'

'Well, I am carrying a bigger burden at my waist—gold and silver worth rupees fourteen hundred and fifty five.'

Noorbai said, 'Well' you got a good price. 'It is all right. Please take them all to a jeweller on time. My waist is already giving way under this burden.'

Mohan replied zestfully, 'Let me size up your burden and you may see mine!'

Mohan stood up. Noorbai hid her face between her knees and said, 'Examine it as it is.'

Mohan seated himself close to Noorbai and embraced and hugged Noorbai, moving her and clasping her close to his shoulder. Noorbai removed her head from between the knees and snuggled it close to his neck.

Mohan said in faltering tone, 'Are you happy.'

Noorbai replied in a quivering undertone, 'I could experience only in the recent past what could be termed as happiness.'

Noorbai's eyes were wet with tears which Mohan wiped with his rough fingers. Both of them were sitting in the same posture for some time.

Chintaman called him from outside, 'Are you taking meals?'

'Yes, I am coming after finishing my meal.'

Noorbai embraced his neck and nearly touching his ears with her lips, she said, 'Dispose off this apple of discord and then decide what is to be done next. My heart prompts me that we should not stay here any longer.'

'All right' Mohan whispered his assent. Both of them then separated themselves.

Mohan asked her in an undertone, 'Is there something to eat?'

She replied, 'Yes, I have something but it is half-baked and remains partly uncooked.'

Noorbai's face was writ large with real and unfeigned feeling of shyness which blended inextricably.

'I'll eat all the same. Hungry as I am, it will taste sweet.'

'The same which I have cooked?'

'Yes, yes, why not? How long shall I take the meal cooked by my own self?'

'I am going to light the fire and knead the flour. You may cook your own meal on return from toilet. Food cooked by me is rather insipid.'

Mohan held her chin up and gazed into her eyes. He said, 'I follow everything. A Hindu who nurses inferiority complex and wishes to raise his status in the eyes of people, gives impetus to attitude and feeling of untouchability. If he is able to demonstrate to others that he does not eat or take any drink touched by others, he thinks he has attained a high stature and become a man of status.'

Noorbai remonstrated, 'Do not say such things. It is quite flattering to me. Hindus have accepted, by custom, casteism and distinction between castes fon centuries.'

Mohan retorted in a firm tone, 'It is not so among us, Jats. We regard ourselves as inferior to none and, at the same time, do not indulge in hypocrisy about eating and drinking.'

Noorbai placed her hands on his shoulders and said, 'I accept defeat at your hands but earlier than this, you had not taken water touched by me.'

Mohan laughed, 'I am a simple farmer and you are a well-educated woman. I cannot win against you.'

She also laughed, 'My real study starts now'; she became serious suddenly and added, 'Come on, take it as it is, simple, rough and ready to eat; eat and then retire.'

Noorbai served the food; he began to munch the loaves. Half-baked and partly burnt up, they were as hard as wood, too. Mohan continued to chew and munch the loaves while Noorbai's joy and humour knew no bounds.

A smiling Noorbai said. 'These are the small, rounded pieces made of steel prepared by Saroopa.'

Mohan replied, 'They are sweetened by sugar all right. Playfully recalling the sweet memories of such delightful remarks, I went to sleep that night in Agra.'

'What about your passage both ways?'

'Don't ask me about what happened on the way. I shall tell you all about it on return; I had been plagued by the ghosts.'

'Ah, was it so?'

Mohan having finished his meal untied the girdle and the pouch and slowly took out the silver and gold coins. He said, 'Now I take change in coins worth rupees one thousand and you may keep the rest. Do not insist. I shall take it some other time and put it back in the pouch. I should not carry extra money there.'

Noorbai agreed. Mohan tooks change worth rupees one thousand to Shubrati. After exchange of greetings and pleasantries, Shubrati asked, 'Where did you get it from?'

Mohan put a finger on his mouth and asked him not to broach the subject by dropping hints thereto, 'We shall talk about it some other time. I have told Chintaman that a Maratha commander has given me this money at Mathura.'

Shubrati expressed his surprise, 'And he believed you!'

Mohan cautioned him, 'Keep silent now. He is concerned with getting money and is not interested in knowing its source or the mint where they were minted.'

Shubrati too replied in a low tone, 'Well! But no one would believe that a commander could spend one thousand rupees as ransom to get a poor sepoy released.'

They heard the footsteps of someone in the courtyard and became silent. Chintaman arrived there. He was quite happy.

He said, 'I am in no hurry but since you had mentioned, I thought we should finish this job and why leave it incomplete! Then both of us would retain goodwill for each other. Isn't it so, Rao Saheb?'

Shubrati nodded his head nonchalantly. Mohan opened the pouch and began to count the coins. Shubrati's face reflected sorrowful penitence. Chintaman began to count the coins attentively before accepting them. It took quite some time to count and assess the value of coins. Chintaman tied them all in a small bundle. His joy knew no bounds. He told Shubrati, 'Your wound is much better than before. What can I do? We can't get even sugar to mix with your milk. Food too is without delicacies and simple and for that matter, it may be as good as Mohan Chaudhari's wife should be able to prepare. She belongs to an upper class family and should know how to cook well. If it is not tasty enough, I would ask Chaudharin to prepare delicious dishes for you!'

Shubrati said, 'Yes, she belongs to a high family, of course, we are all poor. The housewife cooks well; you should not bother Chaudharin in this regard.'

Chintaman did not intend to extend his courtesy any further so as to turn it into solicitude. He went away after collecting all the money.

Shubrati's eyes welled up with tears. He said, 'You have taken a great risk for me. I can never repay your obligation.'

Mohan interrupted him, 'The same dialogue again!'

Both kept quiet for a while.

Mohan said, 'Discuss some thing else.'

'How was the food?'

'Excellent.'

'My teeth too have had the taste of some sample of that good food.'

'It seems you would start quarrelling on such trifles. After all, she is just a slip of a girl. As she could not bear all this, she picked up quarrel, which made you run away to indulge in loitering about leaving her to her ownself.'

'Yes.'

'I hold that you are to blame wholly. She appears to be a goddess.'

'Did she talk to you?'

'Have you gone crazy? She is as old as my sister but then she is younger brother's wife and since I am older than you, how could she talk to me? I did some explaining to her, of course.'

'What?'

'Come on, it was merely to tell her to keep peace at home. Go and rest now.'

'I am going now. We have to get ready to leave here as soon as possible. We shall hire a vehicle upto Mathura.'

'It will be very expensive.'

'Don't be anxious, I have it all.'

Shubrati said, 'Let me wish you well.'

'I can't say or judge as to what is to be done!'

Mohan lay in his room after withdrawing from the company of Shubrati. He was feeling very tired. Noorbai fanned at him with a piece of cloth. Sleep overcame him and he was asleep until evening. He did not remember to regale them with the story of the journey nor did he feel interested in doing so.

As the night closed in, Noorbai and Mohan busied themselves in cooking the evening meal. They wanted to prepare delicious and tasty dishes.

Mohan said, 'If he asks me, I shall tell him that every thing has been prepared by you alone.'

Noorbai laughed and said, 'Would he accept all this?'

'Why should he not? Would he not believe my statement?' He said with a feigned air of pride.

'Hm-Hm' She replied with a child-like innocence. 'He would believe all-truth and lies?'

'I shall speak nothing but the truth,' she replied.

'What a truthful person are you,!'

'All right, tell me what lies have I told my friend?'

'You went to Mathura and met a friend of yours.'

'Be silent... Keep mum. Don't talk about that.'

'All right, let it be. Tell me, when did I quarrel with you?' Noorbai interjected.

'Today itself, when I came back in the afternoon, did you not quarrel with me?'

'What kind of a person are you? You are much different from what you appear to be. I ask you with folded hands; tell me, when I fought with you?'

'Did he tell you all this?'

'He told me not to fight, for it ruins the family.'

'Oh! He would have said something in a lighter vein. Do you expect me to tell him that you are a great beauty lit up with a halo of peace around you.'

Mohan became serious suddenly. His effort to laugh it away left a sign or two of his laughter. Noorbai was joyous. Mohan was reminded of Roni—'I had told him about her'—Roni's shrewish nature and Noorbai's exquisite beauty full of joy and her calm nature flashed in his mind's eye at the same time and did not seem to vanish soon.

Mohan became more engrossed in cooking so as to ward off those thoughts.

'Does it behove you to indulge in such humorous pranks with your wife?'

Mohan concentrated on puffing up the fire in the hearth, alternately trying to reduce the intensity of the flame. He puffed air into the fire needlessly also.

Noorbai smiled and added, 'I could handle the hearth fire better than you.'

Mohan forced an apparent smile but could not bring himself to utter anything more. A question arose within, 'Would she also pick up a quarrel with me someday?' Then he observed a smile playing on the lips of Noorbai who gazed at him innocently he, then, found an answer to his own questioning. He tried to absorb the feeling, 'She does not possess the same gaze, the same ogling which she had delightfully dedicated to Saadat Khan.'

Mohan said, 'Shall we call and serve him food here?'

'Yes, you may. I shall sit in a corner and shall hear both of you converse. It will be quite interesting to listen to you both.'

Mohan ushered Shubrati into the room. He came limping a little. Happiness was writ on his face. He sat a little apart from the kitchen. Mohan served the food. Shubrati began to eat.

Mohan asked, 'How do you like the food?'

He replied, 'Very good, indeed! It is simply wonderfully delicious today.'

'She has cooked it all.'

'Is it so?'

'She cooks whatever she likes and whenever she is in a mood to.'

'It is upto you! If you make my sister happy, the happiness will spread in the entire household.'

'I had expressed my admiration of her talents the other day too.'

'Yes, you had remarked that she even surpasses me.'

'Of course, I did not remark that she indulges in quarrelling.'

Mohan suppressed his tongue as he remarked this jocularly.

Shubrati held up the morsel of food and became effusively humorous in saying, 'Even if you did not say anything that day, you had already told me at Poona that she was very quarrelsome and you had to leave home on account of this!'

Shubrati put the morsel in his mouth and having focussed attention towards the plate, did not observe that Mohan's face was rather put out. As he was about to gulp another morsel into his mouth, he added, 'This is why I had instructed your housewife not to pick up fight with you, but let me tell you candidly you are no less to blame in all this. You would have uttered some nonsense or mischievous remarks which prompted her to fly into temper—after all, she is a mere slip of a girl. And then you fled home!'

Shubrati observed that Mohan's face was crestfallen and in order to cheer him up, he added, 'That is why, I had given you that formula of the puppet. Did you or did you not tell your housewife about it?'

Mohan forced a smile on his lips and nodded his head to convey that he had not done that.

Shubrati added with a laugh, 'Shall I repeat the same formula.'

Mohan said, 'It is not required now.'

Shubrati replied amidst laughter, 'Even so, let me repeat it; it may stand you in good stead in future. Otherwise, repeating it is also quite beneficial to oneself. If I relate my formula now, the story will be recalled by her wherever she gets into the frenzy for a fight and then, surely, there will be no clash.'

Mohan hinted to him to refrain from telling that story but Shubrati retold the same amidst his own laughter. 'To remind everyone of my story the puppet is still tucked into the thatched ceiling of that hut?'

Noorbai was shaking with joyous laughter. She pressed some cloth into her mouth in order to control herself. Mohan was reminded of the laughing and coughing of Shubrati's wife and her slow withdrawal from the courtyard of the house, in which were lovingly mingled the peals of laughter from his children.

Shubrati finished his meal and quickly washed the leftovers from his plate. Mohan tried to stop him from doing this. He said, 'Why should I make the housewife wash leftovers from my plate? One day, she had taken it away in spite of my protest.'

'I felt rather uneasy about it. How good is she; How well disposed to others.' Shubrati said, as he was leaving, 'Go to sleep after the meal, tired as you must be after day's hard work. I shall also sleep for long hours. Do not come to see me.'

—✵—

53

Having finished the meals and chores in the kitchen, Mohan and Noorbai readied themselves to retire. It was quite warm inside the house but they had to tuck away safely the change of coins which they had saved after paying rupees one thousand. He did not wish to lie in the courtyard. It was quiet but dark in the courtyard. It took quite sometime to put the coins one by one in the pouch. Then they stretched themselves after putting out the lamp.

As soon as they were in bed, Noorbai questioned him, 'What quarrel did you disclose to this friend of yours, in Poona.'

'I don't recall how many things I related to him.'

'You had complained about a shrewish woman.'

'All this belongs to another age.'

'I am amazed that some woman used to quarrel with a person like you.'

'Yea,' Mohan uttered.

'What kind of woman is that! Where is she now?'

'Don't know.'

'Why didn't you try to find out?'

'It is no use.'

'All women quarrel but they reform themselves too.'

'Let us talk about something else.'

Noorbai kept quiet. After a little while, she said, 'If I come across her, I shall kneel and touch her feet to persuade and keep her, for ever, in good humour.'

Mohan said, 'I shall never go home'.

'Even if you don't go, I shall go there.'

'Don't ever do this, you will move about wasting yourself. These are the worst of times.'

'I mean you will accompany me when I go there.'

'Do you know where my home is?'

'In Fatehpur Sikri as you told me.'

'Not in Fatehpur Sikri, but outside it.'

'I don't know whether that thatched hut still exists or whatever happened to it. Give up this crazy idea. We shall go to Mathura-Vrindavan, where we shall see Krishna-Kanhaiya, besides enjoying musical instruments, flute tunes, jingling of cymbals, beating of drum, psalm singing and samples of colourful performances of songs and poetry.'

Noorbai's flight of imagination took her to the sanctum sanctorum of a large temple where the intermingling of emotional outburst of devotion to God, dedicated humility and musical performances were reflected in the coming together of people and meeting of their minds. Then her fancy turned to the so-called thatched hut of Mohan. It did not seem to be distasteful to live there with Mohan but her mind's eye was distracted again by the imaginary scenario of a sanctified performance of music and melody. She said, 'Yes we shall go to Kanhaiya's Puri.[104] Both of them kept quiet for a while.

She asked, 'Are you asleep already?' He replied with a lump in ihroat in a tone expressive of his feelings, 'Not yet, but I shall get to sleep soon, tired as I am.'

Noorbai said, 'Let me massage.'

Mohan said, 'No, no, sleep will overcome me otherwise too.'

Noorbai suddenly got up from her bed; she heard some footsteps outside and began to listen with rapt attention — she felt, some people gathered outside were conversing in whispers.' 'Who are they', 'why are they whispering' her mind seemed to ask her ownself. She felt disturbed and came closer to Mohan. Keeping her mouth close enough to Mohan's ear, she said, 'Listen! Outside there is some commotion, some imminent trouble outside.'

104. Puri – A religious place in Orissa State of India, where the temple dedicated to Lord Jagannath, one of four peeths or sanctified places, is situated.

Mohan was already asleep. His spontaneous response was 'yes.' Noorbai put one of her hands beneath his head, shook it a little and said, 'Wake up for a while.'

Mohan embraced her in his arms. He said, 'First of all, we have to go to Mathura-Vrindavan. Do you remember?'

Noorbai whispered in her ears, 'Talk of Mathura-Vrindavan later: first wake up and listen to me.' Mohan was awake by now. He reassured Noorbai, 'All weariness has vanished already; do not massage any more. How tender and pretty are your little palms.'

'Listen to me,' she said, A bunch of people are gathered outside and whispering to one another on something. They seem to be members of Chaudhary's gang.'

Mohan got up and both began to listen with ears close to the door. The commotion signifying the coming together of people had petered off but whispering, still continued. Both kept listening for a while and then started talking in low tone.

'Must be the robbers belonging to Chintaman's gang.'

'What has made them gather at this hour?'

'Must be going for some raid?'

'It was quite late in the night. Who will they assault at this hour? The road and path must be quite deserted now.'

'They may be planning some strategy for tomorrow.'

'Could they not do it during daytime? You told me that these days highway robbery and looting take place even in daytime and then who prevents them from holding consultations in daytime?'

'You are right. Let me go and see what it is all about.'

'I shall not let you go there. Let me listen to whatever is going on.'

'What nonsense? You would go out to listen to their talk. Suppose, someone would see you!'

'Don't get disturbed. There is a place for toilet adjacent to the door of inner verandah. It is close by. I shall stand there close to the wall and listen. If someone comes there, I shall sit to ease myself. No one will suspect me.'

'But what do we gain by listening to them?'

'I suspect that either they are talking about us or about your friend who has given them a chance to receive a sum of rupees one thousand so easily?'

'My intuition is that you should not go out.'

'Do not get disturbed or be anxious at all. You do not know as yet how many things a woman can accomplish.'

'If something happens to you, I shall come out; come what may.'

'You are unnecessarily giving vent to your anger, if they are conspiring against us, we shall be able to plan and devise our defence as much as we can.'

'How long will you keep standing there?'

'I'll be back in a short while; of course, I can keep standing the whole night without a wink.'

Mohan could not stop her.

Noorbai opened the door carefully, took stock of things in the courtyard and stood at the door sill for a while. It was all quiet in the courtyard and in Shubrati's closet. Then, very slowly and stealthily like a cat, she went up to the door of the inner verandah and stood close to and behind it. Outside, opposite the door, some men stood talking among themselves. Noorbai observed outlines of large shadows. With bated breath, she began to listen. She could make out in bits but most of it was not a audible.

... 'Don't let him go. We'll extract something more.'

'I ask you, why catch branches and leaves of the tree? Why don't we take hostage the one who has supplied gold, etc'?

'Break open just now and finish the job..'

'Chaudharin is merely guessing. If we don't get any thing we will be damned.'

'That lady would have a lot more in that girdle pouch.' 'Either these people have brought gold and jewels out of the booty looted from a Nawab or his kind during the course of Nadir Shah's marauding campaign against Delhi or this lady comes from a noble family and had run away with Mohanlal.'

'Her features and demeanour also betray such a past.'

'No, she is his wife, of course. Chaudharin has already enquired into this aspect.'

'But you said, Chaudharin had told you that they had not gone through any customary ceremonies to admit her as housewife. Now don't dilate upon it any longer Chaudhari.'

Thereafter, they began to talk in a low tone, which Noorbai could not make out. Finally, Chintaman's voice came loud and clear, 'I acknowledge that Mohan did obtain money at Agra by selling one of his own ornaments and I am inclined to agree that his wife possesses more ornaments but as long as they are under my care and shelter, no one can raise his arm against them.'

'Why, then, did Chaudharin make her own enquiries?'

'She did, for it is part of our task to spy and pry into matters, but it does not include throttling to death those who visit our household.'

'Well, we went to Agra, then, without any purpose and kept watch throughout! We acted as ghosts without any use. That other gang descended upon us and we had a hair breadth escape.'

'What did you possess, which they could snatch from you?'

'They had jumped into the fray with naked sword; they would have hacked our limbs first and then frisked our bodies. It was good that they too mistook us for ghosts and fled the scene.'

'They did not mistake you for ghosts. Instead they imagined Mohan to be an apparition.'

'We are unable to figure out your speech today, Chaudhari.'

Jat's speech and Jat's way of life is understood best by Jat only. As long as they are under the care of Chintaman Jat's household, no one can harm them even a bit, I swear by Baldeu.[105]

It was followed by an absolute silence for sometime and whispering thereafter. 'Outside the house, it is quite different'... Noorbai could make out Chintaman's voice.

Thereafter, for some time more conversation went on in whispers. Chintaman added in a louder tone, 'Draw a pull of tobacco at the earthen-pipe and then go to sleep.'

The earthen-pipe was readied and filled with tobacco again. All of them had smoke from the pipe and began to disperse. Noorbai withdrew into the room with the gait of a cat. She closed the room with utmost care and snuggled herself to Mohan who was sitting.

Noorbai said, 'You did not sleep at all! Kept sitting like this! You could have laid yourself, at least.'

'How could I lie? I was all set to tackle any untoward happening. You have been standing upright for long—must be feeling tired'... Mohan told her and added, 'See, how much you are perspiring.'

'What did you listen and make out in the meantime? Anything worthwhile for us?'

Whatever she had heard she related to him. Mohan exclaimed, 'How courageous of you!'

'I tiptoed like an ant and crawled back likewise.'

'It is I alone, who can visualise... my state of mind.'

'Let it be! Now tell me what is to be done!'

'There is danger for us tonight. I knew that Chintaman's conscience is still alive. We are safe until we are here in his household.'

'In my opinion, let us leave this place.'

105. Baldeu – Lord Krishna's brother and companion worshipped in his own right in Mathura region.

'Let us set out tomorrow but our friend will be put to trouble. Let's wait for a day or so.'

'He won't suffer. Make him lie in the cart. Both of us shall keep sitting through the journey. How long will it take to reach Mathura from here?'

'From here, Agra is more distant than Mathura. In fact, we had to trudge the distance at times losing the way, by a zigzag path, which bypassed the highways. If a straight line was drawn from Mathura towards Agra, we would have gone far ahead towards Agra by covering the distance we did. Now we shall return by a straight road. Leaving in the morning, we would arrive at Mathura by night time. Walking all the way, we would reach more quickly than by the cart.'

'We have not hired the bullock cart as yet?'

'I shall hire it early in the morning. If we find out that we'll arrive late in the night, at Mathura, we shall stay overnight in a village.'

'Would we come across big villages on the way?'

'Rarely; they must be in ruins but we shall certainly come across some habitation, don't you worry!'

Both kept quiet for a while; they listened with rapt attention to the footsteps— there was pin-drop silence. Some one asleep in the courtyard was snoring.

Noorbai entreated him, 'You should go to sleep. I shall keep awake through the night and will awaken you before dawn.'

Mohan protested, 'I can sleep no longer as sleep has deserted me just now. You better go to sleep and make my thigh your pillow. I shall keep fanning you,'

'Ha, well said!' she said, 'I can't have even a nap, to say nothing about sleep proper. If Chaudhary has told them not to trouble us, we should not take it to mean that his companions will not enter here stealthily. They have developed a suspicion. I thought I had dodged the eyes of that witch Chaudharin but now

I understand that I myself have been tricked. Having committed the mistake, once, I shall not repeat it now.'

Mohan embraced her and said, 'Then let us together keep vigil through the night sitting like this.'

'We shall keep talking intermittently. If some one watches us, he will make out that we are awake.'

'Start discussing something.'

'Such a discussion that may never end.'

'I too do not wish that it may end soon.'

'That talk about ghost, I could not follow.'

'You did not tell me all about it.'

'There was no sense in it —hence I did not tell you. They mistook me for a ghost and when I reached the upper end of the culvert and began to look for those five men, they had vanished. Then I thought them to be ghosts! I thought, terrible men here surpassed the ghosts. Now I can see that Chaudhary had sent his men after me and they got to know that I had not been to Mathura.'

'Where will you stay in Mathura-Vrindavan?'

'In any Dharamshala[106] or temple premises which have plenty of rooms to stay.'

'All right, let us start discussing something else.'

'First of all, you should untie the pouch from your waist and tie around mine, otherwise, it may invite some trouble for you.'

'Well thought! You may remove the coins from the waist and give them to me; I shall tuck them on my body for if there is any assault, it will be on me positively. I shall take it off and throw away.'

'It is quite burdensome and your waist would be breaking underneath.'

'Then let us exchange. This will be a good bargain. Even if we have to part with something, we shall save a lot more.'

106. Dharamshala – Literally a place to serve religion; colloquial for a building to stay at a religious or other place.

'Let it be as it is, let us reconcile to fate.'

Noorbai hugged him and said, 'Not to fate, surrender to one's own Kanhaiya.'

'Yes to Kanhaiya! Would you sing for Him? In cuckoo's cooing voice!'

'Surely, I could sing just now. But the villagers may rush towards us with sticks. They will discover that I am not Chaudharin but an impersonator.'

'I am your Chaudhary alone! Kanhaiya lives there where we are going to.'

'Kanhaiya is omnipresent —informing every particle and then you are the Kanhaiya who has enraptured my eyes!'

Noorbai rested her head on the wide chest of Mohan.

Mohan told her, in a rapturous tone —'Kanhaiya's Gopi[107] will have communion with real Lord Kanhaiya and thereafter touch waters of Yamuna before uniting with me.'

Her throat choked in emotion, she said, 'I had already been united. When I left that hell of a place and saw the light of freedom —that very moment. Now I have to apply sindur[108] to this earthen statue on its forehead.'

'When you would sing songs for me, what should I recite to you?'

'My song is sung by my throat and tongue, but yours suffuses your heart I shall sing only after listening to yours. My strings, musical notes and cymbals all are embedded within your heart.'

'You are well-read and I am a mere sepoy.'

'I have asked you not to mention it but you don't pay heed to it. If you utter it again, you would find me to be a most wicked person on earth. What I have read is a mere trash! Now it is revealed to me how great you are!'

---

107. Gopi – op. cit. 67, p. 93.
108. Sindur – Red paste applied in the parting of hair in the forehead running through hair backwards, symbolizing the married status of woman and her devotion to her husband.

'You are indeed a most beautiful woman to look at. I wish I would prove worthy to be a man of renown.'

'Be that as it may, lie down at ease. You are perspiring all over. I shall fan you, after wiping the sweat, to make you sleep; then you would be persuaded to say that you have become worthy of respect.'

'All right, you may also lie down.'

'The same obduracy again!'

Noorbai separated herself from him. Mohan was lying now. Noorbai wiped his sweat and began to fan with a cloth.'

Mohan spoke indistinctly, 'Come on, lie down.'

Mohan was asleep quickly. Noorbai placed her cheeks on his forehead and said, 'Sleep well; sleep deeply", as if Mohan was a small child.

While Mohan was fast asleep, Noorbai remained awake. It was before dawn that Noorbai woke him up.

Mohan could not help saying, 'Ah me! You did not sleep at all!'

Noorbai answered back 'How does it matter?'

—✻—

54

Mohan was able to hire a cart without any delay but they could start by the time the day had advanced into the forenoon. Mohan wanted to cook and take meals under the shadc of a tree, close to a well but the driver of the cart became obdurate putting forth one demand after another — firstly to arrange for one or two spare parts of the cart, then to take the oxen to water and finally to take breakfast and keep tiffin to eat on the way. It seemed to Mohan that the driver was delaying the departure deliberately but unable to figure out the reason for the same, no suspicion crept into his mind.

All three of them took their meals, carried some repast for the journey and set out. The cart was covered to provide shade and make Shubrati lie in the same. Noorbai seated herself facing backwards. Both of them began to converse. The driver seemed to be lost in his own fancy and thoughts.

Mohan said, 'These Nawabs, nobles and their henchmen have become haughty beyond limit. The roads are sprinkled with water before their procession passes the way as if we do not matter, as if we don't possess nose or breathing power.'

'Their nose is equal to twice the length of an arm while we can't claim to have one.'

'They indulge in such lawlessness and tyrannical acts beyond endurance that I wish I could collect excellent people with very good demeanour and determination so as to destroy them.'

'Many people are indulging in it.'

'Many people have taken to loot and robbery avidly—not that way.'

'Like Marathas?'

'Somewhat like them but far more effective in maintaining the honour of women and religion and in rising to the call of duty.'

Mohan's eyes and Shubrati's attention were rivetted towards Noorbai. The topic of conversation changed.

Shubrati opined, 'In these northern parts, one earth-shaking event comes following another.'

'An unfortunate but highly respected monk was killed alongwith his disciples by the sepoys of Nadir Shah!'

'What harsh times are we living in? Monks and mendicants are put to death. Nadir Shah will be condemned to hell after death.'

'And whatever has befallen Delhi, sends shivers in our bodies.'

'We had also heard about it.'

'The manner in which women were molested, indignities inflicted upon them and the way they embraced their death are quite nauseating to think about.'

'These hapless veiled women were also killed. I had also heard about it.'

The conversation, then, turned towards discussion on women. Mohan's eyes were directed towards Noorbai. She was reclining with stupor forced by sleep. Her head was drooping with sleep.

Shubrati said, 'If Baji Rao had clashed with Nadir Shah, the latter would have been beaten hollow and defeated.'

Mohan replied, 'His army was well-trained and tuned to battles, their weapons very sharp and brand new and discipline strict. Marathas are a divided house these days.'

'But a campaign stretching to twenty to twenty five kos and then a swift withdrawal after mounting an assault can be accomplished by Marathas alone. Men from Iran would have been overwhelmed by them, their mouths gaping in amazement.'

'Delhi army fought in the old style and hence suffered ignominous defeat in no time.'

'Who will inculcate a good style in Delhi army? The ill-mannered Emperor is preoccupied in merrymaking.'

'On the other hand are Baji Rao and his beloved Mastani!'

'This was nothing - it was like adding salt to a preparation of pulses. Here we can't get even a little pulse to go with the salt that we have. You must have watched and observed every thing at close quarters.'

'Yes, I did. Nadir Shah held thousands of women hostages to carry them along. All of them managed to escape from custody.'

The conversation again veered to discussion on women. This time, both of them eyed Noorbai and then turned away their gaze. She was sleeping with her head resting against the wooden planks of the cart. Seating himself, Shubrati said, 'I should like to sit now. Reclining in the wide and front portion of the cart, I shall manage to sit. You will sit next to me. This will provide enough space for the housewife to lie in.'

Mohan tried to dissuade him, but Shubrati did not budge. He said, 'Hale and hearty, as I am, I can even give a fight if an eventuality arises.' The cart-driver smiled and as he began to prod the oxen to move forward, his smile mingled into the refrain of 'Teck...Teck.'

Noorbai woke up, seemingly, with a jolt.

Mohan said, 'Brother Ramarao suggests that you may lie and stretch yourself.'

Noorbai declined the offer with the wave of the outstreched palm of her hand, which appeared to be a fully blossomed lotus waving its head about the wafting cool breeze.

Mohan entreated, 'Please lie down; you were awake through the last night.'

'Noorbai coughed to indicate her protest.'

Mohan laughed and added, 'If we persist and insist, she will fly into anger. Hence I won't say anything more.'

Shubrati remarked humorously, 'You are indeed mischievous, never felt tired of back-biting against her. It seems you were determined to quarrel at night and would like to start it here and now all over again. Sister, you may abuse him now and I would give him a thrashing.'

Noorbai began to laugh with her back towards him. Roni's dark, large eyes, face swollen with anger and her red lips expressive with words, flashed in Mohan's eyes.

Shubrati said, 'His sister-in-law, that is, your sister was also ill-tempered. I made a puppet with the head representing my own self and placed before her one day, telling her to give the same five strokes of her shoes morning and evening, whenever she flew into rage.'

Noorbai kept on laughing. Roni's image flashing in Mohan's eyes made his laughter vanish. Shubrati thought — Mohan was not relishing the joke. He tried to change the topic by saying, 'Let it be! I know that you would never fight. I shall now tell you the story of another type of battle.'

Baji Rao had made up his mind to mount an attack on Delhi. A handful of Muhammad Shah's whimsical commanders tried to repulse the attack, with the strength of ten thousand soldiers. Baji Rao chased them away after killing a sizeable number and seizing a number of elephants and horses.'

Shubrati related the story of that battle in vivid detail. Thereafter, he also narrated the sequence of events of that battle, wherein Mohan had saved his life. He held back his real name and identity. Mohan also described how his own life was saved. Both of them vied in showering their praise on and gratitude to each other. Having finished storytelling, when they rivetted their attention towards Noorbai, they found her fast asleep.

Mohan raised his voice slightly, 'Now listen to the tale of Krishna-Kanhaiya.' Apparently, he addressed these words to Shubrati but intended them to be heard by Noorbai. Noorbai was awakened.

Mohan said, 'Whatever may happen to this world, Krishna would go on playing his flute in the Brij area. Temples resound with the singing of psalms, dance numbers and ballets of Krishna Lila[109] staged by Gopis (female companions) devoted to the Lord. Even the gods yearn and pine to witness these ballets. Hindus and Muslims alike flock to witness them.'

Mohan's expression betrayed certain hypocrisy but his tone penetrated her heart like a drop of oil on flowing water.

Shubrati questioned, 'When do you go back home? To Fatehpur Sikri?'

His dilapidated house, Subedar's[110] Qanungo[111] escorted by a 'sepoy' and Roni — all flashed into his mind's eye for a moment and vanished. Mohan said, 'We shall stay in places of pilgrimage for the time being and then we'll decide on it what is to be done?'

The talks spilled over to the afternoon. The driver suggested, 'I would like to rest the oxen for a while.'

Mohan said, 'You had already delayed our departure until noon. Now you want to while away time here.'

---

109. Krishna Lila – Staging of the sequence of events in Lord Krishna's life in the form of dance or ballet.
110. Subedar – op. cit. 98, p. 240.
111. Qanungo – Government Revenue Official who supervised recovery of land revenue dues.

The driver insisted, 'Half an hour only. The well is nearby. We have some shade of the tree as well. Take some water or tiffin. Meanwhile the oxen will feed on two bundles of grass. We shall then set out again.'

The driver unhooked the cart and the oxen under the shade of a tree and began to put grass straw to oxen. Shubrati went and reclined against a tree. Mohan offered some water, first to him and then to Noorbai. Her back towards Shubrati, despite some anguish reflected in her eyes, Noorbai remonstrated Mohan with smile playing on her lips. 'You are indeed quite mischievous! Time and again, you represent me as a shrew! I should surely itch for a quarrel some day.'

With a bowed head, Mohan added in low tone, 'My honourable lady, please cool yourself just now with water —I'll take care of your temper later on too.'

Noorbai's pretty, glistening set of teeth seemed to adorn her smile. She prayed after taking water, 'Let's set out quickly from here. The gusty hot wind blowing now augurs well for the journey.'

After some respite, they resumed their journey.

The fact that the driver alone had the knowledge of the route leading to Mathura prompted them to refrain from saying anything harsh to him despite his casual and relaxed manner. They did not come across any village on the route they took. However, on both sides of the road, at intervals, they saw one or two huts or a small habitation which could hardly be termed as a village. But neither did they come across a traveller nor pass by a regular habitation. It was two hours before the evening. Mohan become impatient. He asked the driver, 'Does any village lie on the way or not?'

The driver said, 'Yes, it is a little away; over there! First we shall pass a small forest, then an open drain and beyond that lies a village.'

A small forest, then an open drain full of water and beyond them, a village! Mohan's mind was filled with apprehension, Are we about to arrive at the same spot where we were about to be waylaid the other day.' He carefully looked around and asked the driver the name of the village ahead. An hour before sunset, they came close to the forest area.

Mohan asked eagerly, "How far is the 'Nullah', the open drain."

'We shall reach there quite soon, say, in a few minutes. For us, the sun will set in the village itself.'

The cart was then making its way through the forest. Mohan wished they would cross it quickly. He urged the driver softly, to drive fast. He patted the oxen and twisted the tail but the pair of oxen trudged leisurely.

They were in the midst of a thick grove of trees, viz., gooseberry, capprice, acacia and flame of forest. That patch of road was full of potholes and hence the cart moved in a zig-zag manner producing a jarring sound.

It raised so much dust that the knotty branches of trees which touched the cart on its way also seemed to be disappearing in the thickness of dust The gusty, dust-laden wind struck against their faces. All three of them, barring the driver had covered their faces.

The cart was by then in the open space.

From behind the grove came a roaring voice, 'Stop the cart?'

The driver pulled up and halted the cart. The oxen, out of breath, were exhaling air through the nostrils. The dust-storm rising in the forefront was left behind. The driver spotted some masked men rushing from behind the bushes. Jumping out of the cart, he stood aside without betraying any sign of nervousness. With a bowed head, he began to count the masked men and to make out their profile in-as-much as he could see behind the masks. Mohan removed the cloth covering his face, Noorbai and Shubrati followed suit. The oncomers surrounded the vehicle.

Shubrati's hand reached for his sword but he loosened his grip instantly. The newcomers had already unsheathed their swords. Some of them were carrying long sticks.

Some among them shouted, 'Get down!' but they did not come out.

Mohan said, in a hoarse voice, 'Wherefore, Brother! What's the matter? We are poor Jat farmers. We are going on a pilgrimage. Please do not torment us.'

One of them shouted, 'Ah! Poor Jats! Our calling does not distinguish between castes. You belong to our caste. Hence, we have spared your heads of the blow from our sticks, nor have we slain you with our swords. Take out and put it here - what are you carrying on your person, tied in your waist?'

Noorbai uncovered her veil. She was stupefied. Shubrati's mind visualised helplessly a yearning. Had there been three of us, Maratha soldiers, they would have to put to death all of them. Dumbfounded as he was, he could only gnash his teeth.

Mohan said in suppressed hoarse tone, 'I have nothing in my girdle, I can swear by any one.'

The blows from the sticks came showering on the cart. The cloth covering of the cart meant to provide shade was torn into pieces and the supporting bamboos nearly broke up. The oxen became restive to break away, but were encircled by men who obstructed their movement. Inside the cart, all three of them bent their head. Two of the intruders dragged Mohan out of the cart.

Shubrati with a lump in his throat pitifully prayed, 'Please kill me and spare him'.

One of them shouted, 'Neither he nor that woman is going to be spared, nor you too, take them in custody.'

Mohan's hoarse voice was split when he spoke, 'Heretics! Demons! You are not Jats!'

Swords were raised on Mohan. Shubrati's eyes were closed as he moaned 'Ah!'

Noorbai stood inside the cart with her face uncovered. Her face was smeared with dust and sweat. Her hair too was spattered with dust. Her lips were parched and her eyes bloodshot. In a tremulous voice, she said, "Hold on! I have the ornaments here' and jumped out of the cart. While jumping, her long wrapper was entangled in the split bamboo plank and jacks of the cart and torn thereby. Her skirt was nearly upturned as she knelt a little and while doing so, the wrapper was torn a little wider. She tried to shake off the wrapper with a jerk in order to preserve her modesty and in doing so, the wrapper was separated from pleats of the skirt. Now she was left with only a blouse to cover her bare limbs above the waist. Her uplifted, pointed breasts heaved and fell with her panting breath. With great effort, she could muster to say, 'Here it is, tied in my waist. I shall take it out and throw off the same in a moment. Release my master. He has nothing on his person."

They raised neither swords nor sticks any more. A stupefied Noorbai said in a quivering voice, "I am going behind a tree to loosen my skirt so as to take out the girdle 'pouch'."

They started looking at one another.

A leader like person among them again growled in a loud tone, 'Yes, she must be planning to hide something, left to herself, there.'

'Take out here and now......otherwise........'

Mohan made an effort to rise but his shoulder received an instant blow.

His chest was shoved and hit by several legs. Mohan shrieked and trembled.

Noorbai's limbs heaved and swelled as if they had been activated to make sacrifice and penance as also to give up all she possessed willingly.

She stood erect and her chest heaved more intensely

Raising her snow white lotus like hands, she said in spontaneous sharpness and loudly, 'What are you doing? I am going to bare my limbs and will be stark naked in your presence. After all, you too would have mother and sister like me!'

The feet trampling Mohan's chest slowed down. Noorbai turned her back. In a moment, she pressed the string of the skirt between her teeth and loosened the same. She untied the large pouch strapped on the hips. Her bare back and body shimmered like an exquisite statue of the marble carved by the same architect and the sculptor who was engaged for building the edifice of the Taj Mahal; in the same posture, she knelt a little and untied the knot of the pouch, and taking out the same with one hand, she threw it towards them. Tightening again the skirt, she turned with her back towards them.

The sunrays, filtering through the quivering leaves converged on her dust-covered face, tight breasts and clenched fists. A lingering ray seemed to be reflected in her bloodshot, wide-open eyes and refracted thereby, giving the impression of being playfully absorbed in the capillaries of the eyes.

She commanded them in a harsh tone, 'Pick it up and release my master. He has been injured.'

The leader advanced and picked up the pouch. Leaving Mohan aside, the rest of them closed in upon the leader. The leader untied the knot of the pouch and spoke in a relaxed tone, 'You may go now. In the entire region now, no one will disturb or intercept your passage.'

Noorbai recognised the voice which was that of Chintaman. She clenched her teeth in sheer anger as she saw Mohanlal lying on the ground. She rushed to him and placed his head in her lap. She glanced around with vacant wild looks as if she was seeking some water.

The leader of the dacoits, Chintaman also observed this.

He disappeared in the thick of the forest having called upon his men to follow him. The driver faced the oxen. Shubrati came out from the cart and stood behind Noorbai. Mohan was unconscious still. He patted him on the head and gazed at the sky as if praying for and seeking some blessings. He looked at

Mohan again. Tears trickled from his eyes and fell on Mohan's cheeks while the rays of the sun also played on them. Tears had turned into grains of light before they trickled down the eyes.

Noorbai craned her neck backwards. Tears were streaming from Shubrati's eyes.

A sobbing Noorbai said, 'Elder brother, make him lie down in the cart.' Then she faced the cart driver and looked at him. The driver replied, 'I suspect, the oxen will bolt if I move away.' Overcome with grief, Shubrati commanded him. 'As if they are horses, not oxen; come here!' Noorbai prayed, 'Brother come on, give us a helping hand.' The driver patted his oxen and helped to carry Mohan. With some difficulty, the three of them were able to place Mohan on the cart. Noorbai nervously pulled at her wrapper sticking to the beam on which the cart was fixed. As half of it remained entwined therein, she used the rest of it to cover her body, however, leaving the head uncovered.

Shubrati said, 'You are my god-sister.' With her head bowed still, Noorbai could not help saying, 'Yes I am!' Her attention was focussed on Mohan. She put Mohan's head on her lap and began to rub it gently and anxiously. The cart was on its way again. It was twilight when the cart arrived at a nullah-bed across the forest. A little away from the nullah lay a village— desolate, yet partly inhabitated. They reached the village a little after dark. Mohan had regained a little consciousness before they reached there. He had received a serious injury, on his shoulder. His injury was compounded by the bashing received by his legs when he had been unconscious. As the cart came to a halt, Mohan spontaneously said, 'Where is she?'

Noorbai raising his forehead to her chest, replied 'Here I am!'

Shubrati said, 'Brother!'

Noorbai said, 'We have arrived in a village.'

'Now?' Mohan said in an undertone and asked for some water.

Noorbai replied, 'Yes it is a village!'

The driver unhooked the oxen. Shubrati got down. His wound was aching. Suppressing his moan, he said, 'Keep lying as you are. Meanwhile, we shall arrange some accommodation and water.'

The driver was familiar with the village which was rather small and deserted. Some houses, partly in ruins were lying open. Shubrati accompanied him limping.

Noorbai eagerly asked, 'How are you now?'

Mohan said, 'I was saved. There is a lot of pain in the shoulder. Are you not hurt yourself?'

She bent over Mohan and was overcome with hiccup. She could, somehow, muster a reply, 'You were saved by God so was I! Keep lying quietly.' She put her finger on his mouth so as not to allow him to speak.

After a short while, the driver accompanied by Shubrati brought some water. Behind him stood a middle-aged person carrying milk in a battered tumbler.

Noorbai had covered her chest with a piece of her wrapper. She retrieved the other portion from one of the split, shaggy beams supporting the cart and covered her abdomen. Mohan got down from the cart with a little support from Noorbai and Shubrati. Shubrati had secured a place for overnight stay in a dilapidated house. Shubrati and the driver lodged themselves in the porch which was open to the sky.

Mohan was made to lie in the courtyard. No lamp could be arranged for lighting. In that village, only two-three shepherds possessed a few goats whereby they were able to make both ends meet.

Shubrati said, 'Sister, what a good Samaritan this shepherd is! He was willing to give some milk after he came to know of our plight.'

Noorbai reached for her forehead so as to keep the veil in position but there was no piece of cloth left for that.

Noorbai addressed the shepherd, 'Brother, this world is sustaining itself on the good deeds of fellows like you.'

He said, 'Not so, Sister, we are too poor to carry our own burden. We have neither foodgrains to live on nor clothes on our body. We had a little milk which I have brought.'

He was wearing only a worn out, dirty 'dhoti.' In a tremulous voice, Noorbai said, 'Brother, we can't narrate our tale; we have been robbed. We have nothing to pay you for milk.' 'I don't want any payment; I have come to know everything. Such things happen in this neighbourhood off and on. You are bound for Mathura?'

'Yes brother!'

'It's not far off!'

'How long will it take to reach there?'

'By afternoon tomorrow!'

'God willing, when we are better off, we won't forget the favour done by you.'

She told Shubrati, 'Brother! You should eat something; I shall feed him with bread shredded into milk.'

Mohan replied in undertones, 'Give him some milk and keep some for yourself...'

Shubrati interrupted, 'Keep quiet and rest. Don't worry about us.'

Shubrati and the driver began to eat, sitting in a corner. Noorbai put the shredded bread mixed in milk before Mohan.

The shepherd said, 'I have some jaggery with me. Would you like to take it?'

'Excellent; brother! Excellent! Give it to us and if you have a lump of onion, bring that too, —I need it to serve as a medicine.'

Nodding in assent, the shepherd went away smiling. It seemed to Noorbai that behind that wan smiling was a god-like person.

The shepherd fetched some jaggery and a lump of onion. Noorbai mixed jaggery in milk. Mohan could not be seated properly. He rested against Noorbai's shoulder and began to eat with the hand which was not injured. Noorbai supported him with one hand and held the pan containing bread.

Shubrati and the driver went into the porch after the meal. Having finished eating, Mohan lay again. Noorbai, then, had her own meal, crushed the piece of onion and took out a piece of cloth from the leftover wrapper lor warming the crushed onion.

Mohan expressed his wish. 'A little for Ramarao's wound.'

Noorbai's 'no' welled up in her throat but she could not bring herself to give vent to it. Noorbai was on the horns of a dilemma.

Mohan repeated, 'Surely for the wounds of Ramarao.'

Noorbai gave a piece of onion to Ramarao and began to give warm massage to Mohan's wound. After a short while, Mohan said, 'Please tie and tuck in the onion on the wound and lie close to me —your ear touching mine?

Noorbai tore another piece of cloth from her wrappper in order to bandage the wound. Mohan saw that she had torn off the wrapper.

He exclaimed, 'What! What's this? You have torn off your wrapper.'

Noorbai bandaged the wound with the crushed onion.

Mohan said, 'Come and lie here.'

'Well! Brother is resting in the porch. If he happens to see me what will he say? He would take me to be a shameless woman.'

'I have to tell you something! Lie apart thereafter.'

'I am putting my ears close to your mouth without lying, tell me now!

'The thing tucked in the waist has got loosened. How to tighten it now!

'I shall tighten your dhoti.'

'It won't serve the purpose. Tighten the knot with one bit of my turban.'

'What about morning time? And Mathura is still far off. I shall improvise it for you.'

She untied the portion of wrapper covering her abdomen, from which she tore off two bits. She tightened Mohan's waist with all her strength.

Kissing Mohan's forehead with her mouth she said, 'Go to sleep, now.'

Mohan said, 'Place your head on my chest for a moment.'

Noorbai placed her head on his chest and her arm on his shoulder.

Mohan ran his hand on her back down to waist. He exclaimed, 'You are uncovered, what about the wrapper?'

'Hm' It is gone!'

'Where to?'

'To God's home.'

Noorbai briefly related to him the story how she had to throw away the pouch and tear off the wrapper.

Mohanlal began to sob loudly and weep. His sobs were heard in the porch. An anxious and nervous Shubrati shouted from there, 'What's the matter? Is your wound aching too much? Should I come over?'

Noorbai replied, 'I have bandaged the wound rather tightly. I am now loosening the knot.'

Noorbai loosened a portion of her leftover wrapper and wiping tears with it she said, 'Here it is, my wrapper!'

'Oh! What has become of you?'

'I have accomplished everything. If you go on weeping my heart will be broken and shattered. Whatever they could not bring about would be forced by your tears.'

'I won't weep any more, my... ' 'Whatever you wish to say, please do so in my ears.' Noorbai came closer to him and said, 'I wish I would sing a devotional song to lull my dear Kanhaiya to sleep. I would sing so melodiously that this house in ruins would be moved to keep rhythm with me and burst into dancing.'

Mohan maintained his poise and self-control and said, 'I would listen to you at Mathura or Vrindavan and at all other places all the time.'

—❋—

55

It was a little before dawn when they were ready to move. The driver said, 'What about my hire charges? I did not ask for it, because you were made to suffer. If you can't pay the charges, I'll go back from here.'

Shubrati suppressed his anger and questioned him as he rose from his scat, 'How shall we reach Mathura in that case?'

'Whatsoever may be your mode of journey, I shall not take you any lurther free of charges.'—The cart-driver replied.

'Yes', Shubrati flared up.

Noorbai said, 'Brother, we have a brass plate, a tumbler and a bedding. Can't we pay off his rental with all this?' She turned towards the cart-driver and addressed him, 'Brother, let us cover the distance while it is cool enough. I shall pay your hire charges.'

The driver was convinced that one who could throw away her pouch so easily would be able to pay off the charges as well. She would be, presumably, hiding something beneath her clothes. The driver agreed to proceed. Mohan was laid in the cart.

Noorbai seated herself with her back turned outwards and the leftover wrapper tucked on her chest. The cart resumed journey.

Mohan was relieved a bit of the aching of his wound but could hardly lift his injured arm. He was lying with his eyes closed. Noorbai was all alert. Shubrati was dozing off and on.

As the day advanced, his attention was turned to the bit of wrapper which was tied firmly round Mohan's waist. He asked in sympathy, 'Are you hurt in the waist as well?'

Noorbai looked around rather anxiously and asked Shubrati not to mention it. She replied, 'Yes he has some pain in the waist — perhaps due to injury.'

The driver turned back to have a look. Noorbai said, 'Drive on fast. Whatever may be your charges already settled, the value of our utensils will certainly exceed the same. We shall pay you immediately on arrival at Mathura. Reach us there quickly.'

The driver drove the cart fast. They reached Mathura in the afternoon. The first question that faced them was where they would stay, what they would eat?'

Shubrati suggested, 'I shall go and find out the location of Maratha cantonment. Let's go there. There will be no problem of boarding, etc'

The driver said, 'In Maratha cantonment! I shall not drive there my cart at any cost.'

Noorbai said, 'No, not to Maratha cantonment. Any inn or dharamshala will do.'

Shubrati was in rage. He told the driver. 'You were instrumental in getting us robbed. You drove the vehicle so slowly as if you had fixed an appointment to reach a particular place at a given time.'

The driver protested without fears, 'If it were so, I would have disappeared in the afternoon itself. If you are threatening me to take you to Maratha cantonment, you should know that there are a sizeable number of Jats there too. Having arrived here, you are now looking for some pretence not to pay.'

Mohan denied this and said, 'Drop us at some nearby dharamshala and take your full charges.'

Shubrati's anger was changed into indistinct murmuring. A dharamshala was traced. All of them got down there. They then, faced the question of payment looming large over their heads.

Noorbai took out both the brass plates and told the driver, 'Go and sell them in the market. Whatever may be your charges, you may take a bit extra and return the rest to us.'

The driver said, 'I am not so gullible as to go to market leaving behind my cart which you might, then, take to Maratha cantonment.'

Shubrati could not resist his anger this time and burst forth. "If Marathas turned towards this direction, you would bolt from here shouting 'oh...oh.' You would find yourself under the yoke in place of oxen and then you would... "

A duel seerned imminent between the two when the servant of a Panda[112] arrived there. He mediated. 'What's the matter... what is this?' the remark was heard. Noorbai was standing with her half-bare back towards them. She came face to face with them. She told the driver, 'Brother, we are in trouble. We have come on a pilgrimage. We don't wish to quarrel with anyone. Take these two brass plates. You would be able to recover your hire charges. We shall manage somehow.'

The Panda's servant could follow very well that it was a dispute about the hire charges. But he could not make out how such a beautiful woman and her two companions could be so poor. The servant offered, 'Let me pay the hire charges for you. Stay in dharamshala or at my place and repay the sum whenever you wish to.'

Noorbai was impressed. She mused, 'Well this is a place of pilgrimage! What a generous person he is!'

Panda's servant paid off the hire charges from his pocket. The driver took them to his house and began to think on his way back. 'Why has Mohan tied a piece of chundari cloth at his waist. Why did dacoits not make a thorough search of his person.'

Observing their apparent plight and poverty, neither Panda nor his servants was amazed —for many a prosperous person went on pilgrimage in tattered clothes so as to avoid falling a prey to pick-pockets. Noorbai did not wish to disclose the incident of robbery to Panda's servant.

With a view to arrange food, Shubrati said, 'I am going to Maratha canmtonment and shall come back after making some arrangement.'

Mohan raised his doubt — it's a mere hearsay; suppose there is no such encampment here.'

Shubrati allayed his doubt.

'Let me go and check at least.'

---

112. Panda – A freelance priest unattached to a temple, who takes care of pilgrims' needs at holy places of Hindus.

Noorbai also wished the same. When they were left in the house all by themselves, Noorbai told him, 'Let me take out a few rupees from your pouch. We shall buy some things, clothes and a few utensils.'

'May be, wc shall regain some strength by tomorrow. The swelling on the shoulder had reduced a little. If Ramrao does not bring some thing with him, we shall send him again to fetch it.'

'Our secret is likely to be out. I shall go out myself.'

'Of course, you can go but will not your features and complexion beg loo many questions? Don't you realise that your back is bare and your belly exposed? If I had a gun, I would have seen to it that you were not driven to this state.'

'All right, all right, keep silent. I will not go. But, brother will, otherwise too, come to know that we are left with something still. He will ask from where we got all that money.'

I shall tell him that this has come from the same source which gave us rupees one thousand. In fact we committed the mistake in the beginning. If I had told him earlier who you are, this fabricating of lies would not have been necessary; to make good one lie ten more have to be fabricated.'

'No, don't do it, What I am, in reality, I am standing before you and him. It's no use digging up my past.'

'I won't tell him; I alone know your real identity and it is not likely that any other person would be able to make out. Come closer and massage my head.'

Mohan's eyes were full of tears.

Noorbai placed her hand beneath his head to serve as a pillow and began to massage with the other. Her eyes also welled up with tears and her throat was choked with emotion. She tried to overcome it and said,

'This is not proper. Please do not shed any more tears. We have not come here for this.'

Mohan replied, 'There is nothing else to it. My heart wells up and makes me penitent. A piece of wrapper! Half-naked body! Dust in the hair!'

"Go on... go on. Don't tell me that my Kanhaiya is present before me and Kanhaiya's master, 'Kanhaiya' is playing hide and seek somewhere around here —that Kanhaiya in whose honour, the saints and the great spiritual leaders go on singing songs about Brij region's glory and do not feel weary of reciting them. Some people sprinkle a little dust over their head—the same dust lies sprinkled on my head, of its own."

'You must be having many songs on your finger tips?'

'Yes I have and should sing them for you. I shall sing so long that you would forget and lose your entity. You must laugh now. You should laugh by recalling the name of Kali Kamli Wale.'[113]

Mohan looked into her loving eyes with his own full of tears, as if trying to mingle his ownself into hers. He tried to laugh but could force only a weak smile.

Mohan pointed towards his waist and said, 'Untie and take out coins. Remove the piece of wrapper and wrap yourself again. When brother comes back, you would get a good one. It is now unbearable to see you in tatters.'

She said, 'Not a good one, —an ordinary one will do. I have seen many a poor who do not possess even such rags. Did you not see the shepherd who had brought us milk last night? He was not wearing even such a torn piece on his waist. He had given us his entire day's earnings without showing off! He was a great man —a saint indeed!'

'You are a Gopi, you can elevate a person to any height.'

'Hm... Hm', humming thus, Noorbai brought her forehead closer to Mohan's temple, touching it in turn. Withdrawing it

113. Kali Kamli Wale – An appellation of Lord Krishna : (Literally one who carried black blanket to cover oneself up at some point of time.)

after a moment, she said, 'Oh, I have smeared my dust on your cheek!'

'Yes... Yes, it is the sacred dust of Brij land for you and mere dust for me!'

'It is beyond me to argue with you.'

Noorbai burst into laughter. She kept smiling, her smile shimmering like particles of mica against sunrays. She united the piece of wrapper from Mohan's waist, opened the pouch and took out a few rupees. She tightened the girdle on the waist again. She joined the two pieces of wrapper to cover herself but was able to wrap herself up only partially.

Shubrati came back after some time. He was very sad. He reported on arrival, 'Maratha cantonment has shifted to Vrindavan. They departed only today. What to do now?'

With her back towards them, Noorbai said, 'Don't worry, brother. I have some money, here take it. Bring some food, utensils and clothes.'

Shubrati was amazed and expressed his wide-eyed surprise, 'What!' and added with joy, 'This younger brother of mine is good for nothing. He never understood you properly. How goddess Laxmi[114] like is my sister!'

Mohan said with a smile, 'Laxmi sings very well.'

Noorbai knitting her eyebrows turned back her head.

Shubrati replied, 'The same old subject matter of quarrel! She will start off' quarrel on the old pattern and then I will side with her.'

Roni's face flashed before Mohan like lightning and vanished.

Noorbai said, 'You are still limping, my brother. But hungry as you must be, you may go to market, have something to eat, and bring back something for us too. Bring a tumbler full of milk, one or two clothes and a couple of metal bowls.'

114. Laxmi – In Hindu mythology, goddess of wealth and property.

Shubrati was in a fix—'How could Mohan eat things touched by him?' He said, 'We shall not let him eat food prepared in the market. I shall fetch some milk besides a few other things.'

Mohan said, 'Bring some small change of coins. We'll be required to make payment here.'

Shubrati went out with money. Mohan said, 'We shall leave here for Vrindavan soon.'

'Well! We have seen nothing here? We shall see temples. Meanwhile, you would have recovered.'

'Brother may be in a hurry to join his platoon. He will get some rest there. Hence it is not proper to get stuck here. Vrindavan is more beautiful and a more sacred place for pilgrims. Krishna had performed his superb divine ballet there only. Besides there is the bank of the Kalindi,[115] the river in which the Kaliyadeh,[116] destruction of the Kaliya Serpent by the Lord was accomplished. Besides, there are the groves of Kadamb-trees.'

Ras[117] Lila, singing of psalms, the religious prayer gatherings, saints and monks —all these are in plenty and more numerous there as compared to this place. Let us leave here, day after, if not tomorrow itself. Meanwhile, let us go and see temples here.'

'I would not go out anywhere all by myself. I shall be accompanied by you wherever I have to go. Let us go to Vrindavan. We should visit places in Mathura some other time.'

—❋—

56

All of them went to Vrindavan by a hired cart. On the way, they came across throngs of pilgrims. Most of them wore thick,

115. Kalindi – River Yamuna is also called Kalindi because of its dark complexion.
116. Kalihyadeh – The legend has it that Lord Krishna killed the demon—snake Kaliya in the river Yamuna near Vrindavan.
117. Ras – The dramatic performance staged by Lord Krishna and his Gopis symbolizing gaiety and romance of life.

rough and old clothes; some were healthy while others weak-looking; there were old men with bent-bodies, wilted young women like buds swept by hot lashing wind. But all of them had eagerness, a yearning writ large on their faces, betraying an ardour like a flame sparkling through a layer of dust and sweat. Noorbai was watching all this through the veil of her newly acquired thick, colourful wrapper —she could observe more of that flame than the overlay of dust on their bodies.

The day had advanced towards forenoon by the time they arrived near the large temple. Loud sounds made by instrumental music came piercing from inside the temple. People forming a few psalm — singing groups were dancing and singing devotional songs with small drums hanging from their necks. 'What a sacred land it is! Here every speck of dust seems to be keenly rising above the ground to lose itself in singing. When I see Gope[118] and Gopies[119] of this town, who are devoted to Kanhaiya, I can't imagine what would happen to my intellect and conscious being — she felt a little commotion within her inner self.

The driver said, 'It is a famous temple dedicated to God. The priest lives close by. Why don't you seek a place to stay here?'

'Yes... Yes, we agree!'

The driver wished to get rid of them rather easily and then return home. No sooner had he halted the cart than the priests and their servants surrounded them.'

'Where have you come from, our pilgrim-guests?'

'Please come to our place? Which village do you hail from?'

'We come from Fatehpur Sikri.'

'Folks from that place do stay with us; come and have a look at the entries of seven generations of ascendants made in this register.'

'Our temple of God is larger than theirs.'

---

118. Gope – Milkmen who kept company of Lord Krishna.
119. Gopis – Milkwomen who danced and sang in merriment with Lord Krishna.

'We would offer you all facilities. You would get no amenity at their place?'

'A broken cot — full of bedbugs! The Mother Yamuna flows far away from here.'

Shubrati put them a question, 'Has any Maratha squadron arrived in the neighbourhood here?'

One of them replied instantly, 'Yes... yes, it has come. Baburao Malhar is commanding it. His squadron is stationed near my house. Come, I shall take you there.'

'How will you take them there? We have a certain claim on the pilgrims who hail from Fatehpur Sikri', one of them shouted. The conversation became hotter with heads likely to receive batter.

Noorbai said in a sharp, piercing voice, 'We shall stay at this priest's place which is close to this temple.'

'How, how can he lodge you?'

'We have Fatehpur Sikri under our charge and claim. We have inherited it from our ancestors. Brother, you would find all comfort at all our place. The river Yamuna is quite close by besides the thick grove of trees, the venue of Lord's dancing and merrymaking, the gay abandon of Gopis, the spot of Kaliyadeh, he could hardly complete the sentence.'

The very mention of Fatehpur Sikri brought flashing in Mohan's mind the familiar village with the hut, the trees, the buffalo, Roni, Tota, etc. It struck him that he should not opt for staying at that priest's place. The second alternative presented itself with greater weight — the bank of river Yamuna, the groves, Kaliyadeh, venue of Kanhaiya's dancing and merriment. He told Noorbai, 'Please settle the place to stay.'

Noorbai uncovered her veil. The priest who was bent upon picking up a fight watched her exquisite, unique beauty. They were able to make out that the pilgrims were rich people. Then ensued a duel, tactical twists and bouts of wrestling. The duellists found themselves licking the dust.

Noorbai thought, 'All this too takes place in Kanhaiya's Vrindavan. It must be for a a while only; besides it is not the real Brij area.' With all her strength, she blurted, 'We shall stay with the priest whose place is nearby.'

Mohanlal also raised his voice and said, 'Wc don't want to go to the priest who has claims on Fatehpur Sikri. We are sepoy — Jat sepoys, we are not bonded labour. Stop this fight.'

Shubrati also aired his views, 'And I shall proceed towards Maratha cantonment. I don't have to stay with any priest.'

This duel proved of no avail. It might be taking place every day and would be of no use like-wise. The cart was driven to that nearby priest's place. The driver having received his dues turned homewards.

All of them were amazed to observe the physique of the priest —his height and bulk were almost identical; the abdomen bulged so heavily and his thighs were so thick, plump and fleshy that one could not figure out how he managed to walk. He was all courtesy and brimming with sweetness all over.

Mohan disclosed his intention in the course of conversation thus, 'We shall stay here until the rainy season lasts. We are prepared to pay the rent. Please take us to a house where we can offer prayers without being disturbed by any one.'

The priest led them to a smalll house adjacent to his own, which served to lodge pilgrims during fairs and festivals.

Shubrati sought lodgings in Maratha contonment. The injury in Mohan's shoulder did not pain too much and he started walking around on his own. He brought articles for preparing food and clothings for bed-spread and wrapping the body.

Noorbai insisted on cooking food, 'I shall cook the meals. If you keep on doing all this, I shall remain a rustic for ever'.

Mohan thought, 'Rustic!' He added, 'Who prevents you from doing it? I would get time to roam about and an opportunity to land a good job. Also a chance to get a glimpse of God!'

'I should also like to go for offering prayers in the temple.'

'Yes, of course, you should accompany me.'

'There would be singing and playing of instruments in the temples.'

'Yes, quite so! Everywhere; in some temples, it goes on for hours.'

'I would listen attentively; I should see how they are able to please Lord Krishna. There must be Gopis too!'

'Gopis keep Krishna's company. In some places they must be dancing too.'

'I shall watch their performance as well.'

'But I shall watch my Gopi's performance here.'

'What! Would I dance here?'

'All right, would you sing or not?'

'Of course, 1 wouid sing. You would not have to tell me to sing. We need not fear the appearance of the priest here as he is unable to walk presumably.'

Noorbai laughed. Mohan too joined her.

Mohan said, 'Even so, he would be boasting of his skill in wrestling.'

Noorbai expressed surprise, 'Wrestling! The same style of wrestling which we saw a little while ago? If this priest falls on someone, he would be completely smashed.'

—*—

57

Just after twilight, both of them proceeded to have a glimpse of the deities in various temples.

Since the time the ruler of Jaipur had conferred the title of 'Brij Raj', the king of Brij area, on Raja Badan Singh of Bharatpur, the temples of the region of Brij acquired an added air of freedom in recital of 'Bhajan'[120], in worship, in the

120. Bhajan – Devotional song.

evening prayer with the lighted lamp, in the playing of large cymbals, blowing of conch accompanied with drum – beating, instrumental music and singing and in the performance of 'Raas', the dance reminiscent of Lord Krishna and his Gopis. Monks and mendicants had always frequented that area which, then, witnessed gala fairs and festivals on a large scale. Nadir Shah had mounted his assault on Delhi around the time of the Holi festival[121] which, until then, had been described vividly only in religious books or handed down by oral tradition and had come alive in celebrations during that period. But that particular year, the Holi festival was not celebrated with the gusto associated with it because of Nadir Shah's campaign against Delhi. After his departure, the clouds, portent of ill-omen and disaster broke up and gave rise to the commotion of pilgrimage. Groups of people thronged the place from the area around although it was not the usual season of a festival, just to be in time for pilgrimage before the onsent of rains.

People swarmed the temples as during days of the fair. Noorbai and Mohan also went in. Mohan's heart swelled with devotion while curiosity coupled with desire to dedicate herself at the feet of God — welled up in Noorbai's heart.

As soon as Noorbai entered the temple premises, she lifted her veil. There was no need to go about veiled in the temple. She had 'Darshan' (full view) of the deity to her heart's content and also watched the ostentatious and gorgeous adornment around the figure of the deity blending inio the devoted spectators' unfathomable faith, coupled with the priest's aura of humility and spirited devotion.

It was the image of Lord Krishna (Kanhaiya). Whatever could be encompassed by the man's bounded fancy and imaginative power had shaped the idol, illumined with the halo and aura reflecting the glory of God. Whoever it may be — be it the man

121. Holi – op. cit 2, p. 15.

deeply hurt in life, a man with a broken heart or a person with a distracted mind, a poor, homeless downtrodden or shelterless or a person wounded and groaning — each one could observe and gather some solace in his chest at the feet of the Lord. If we do not accept this spiritual approach and pronounce the idol to be just a piece of rock from a hillside, carved out and given shape, how we can fathom the bottomless depths of the Unseen Power? How will the people with the smouldering spirit extinguish the fire within by splashing cold water? Who will support and lovingly stroke the heads of all those who undergo sufferings and pain day in and day out and get no respite or sleep of those who shiver out of fear, in every pore of their body or those who are unable to drink deep at the fountain of life or read into its meaning because of the the threat of awesome death hanging like Damocles' Sword and are not at peace with themselves even at deathbed or who are just the same throughout all seasons, never able to distinguish between the light of happiness or the darkness surrounding their lives or the twilight zone between the two? Who will transform the half-broken thorns embedded in their flesh into bearable ones? One, who reveals himself at times or smiles in their dreams or sings sweet rhythmic strains in their ears evermore — Noorbai was immersed in thinking about all this.

Noorbai saw a smile playing on the lips of the Lord Krishna, which seemed to inspire and fill the flute with immortal music and undying rhythms. Noorbai was thrilled to the core and tears welled up in her eyes. It struck her that the flute-player's harmonious cadence was unique in that no learned musician of great stature could ever have grasped its spirit. It seemed as if the flute-player danced His way into the devotees' heart. Playing on the flute, He seemed to suggest that even if high barriers or mountains impeded the way or the gusty, stormy winds blowed to sweep them off their feet or the flames of fire leapt to reduce them to ashes or create havoc for them, devotees should not give in. He stood by them shoulder to shoulder; He (God) was behind them, in front of them and was to be found everywhere with his flute flowing in harmomious musical strains.

Noorbai wished to dance with the flute playing Lord and tell him that He should continue to give her 'Darshan' just like that. When she was about to balance herself on her toes, tears welled up. Everything around her became hazy. Noorbai wiped her tears. She observed that some people were staring at her, wide-eyed while others ogled with side glance and yet a few others lowered their eyes as they tried to catch a glimpse of her beauty. Conches, cymbals, drums were sounded in full fury.

She questioned herself impatiently, 'The strange strains of music played by the flute-player which I listened to, the captivating smile which I saw just now — where has all this vanished? Has all this been absorbed by the loud instrumental music? Where is it gone? Where? In those moments, no instrument was being played and nothing else was heard then.'

Another question arose in her mind, 'I can see now, so this is your unique style of performance. You were used to stealing butter and Gopis' ' clothes. You raised a big commotion with your pranks with a view to tease your fans and devotees! Well! I shall see later.'

She watched one spectator paying obeisance to deity with folded hands but looking at her at the same time. Noorbai did not dislike it —let him go on looking. What would he gain? He was not looking at her Kanhaiya who too would not be watching him. Mohan stood beside her with hands folded in adoration. Her own Mohan was watching that other Mohan who belonged to them both.

Mohan's attention was diverted, He said, 'Let's go to another temple.' 'Stay for a while', she said and tried to recall, without success, in her mind's eye that very scene so as to hear the same music. She made up her mind, 'I'II come back here again. I'll see Him again.'

Both of them found their way into many other temples and met with the same commotion everywhere.

At the last place, Noorbai told Mohan in undertones, 'This noise is piercing my ears. Let's go from here.'

'You call it noise? They are instruments accompanying the worship.'

'No, all this is noise. How can you call it the harmony and music dedicated to worship?'

Mohan accompanied her to the place of stay.

Noorbai's eyes were dazed and swollen out of sheer joy and eagerness as if she had seen only a part of the whole and something remained unseen as if she had heard only a portion and the rest was unheard. It seemed, she did not look for the invisible and whatever had come into her grip she held on to it firmly, having quenched her thirst partly and remaining unsatiated thereby.

Mohan felt contented and wished to go to sleep. Wavering between contentment and sleep, he kept on looking at Noorbai.

Noorbai said, 'Shall I sing a devotional song for you? I feel like singing.'

He nodded in assent, 'I shall listen and go to sleep while doing so. The pilgrims usually sing, hence, il will not appear to be odd."

Noorbai sang one of Soordas's[122] devotional songs, translated as follows:

'I bow to the lotus feet of Hari, my lord!
His grace Almighty when showers
The lame crosses mountains high,
The blind sees all around
The deaf hears, the mute speaks

122. Soordas – A great classical poet of Hindi literature, who sang devotional songs dedicated to Lord Krishna.

The pauper wears a royal crown;
Such is the Lord of Soordas
Kindest and compassionate,
Million, million bows to His feet.'

Mohan's sleep deserted him and a sense of satisfaction was reflected in his eyes. Noorbai, absorbed as she was in her singing, lost sight of her own 'Self'. Both of them found themselves in a state of ecstasy.

'May I tell you what I saw and heard in the first temple we went to? I think, may be, I shall lose, by expressing, whatever I had gained there. All right, I shall tell you. Speaking will only add to the capital because you were also lost in meditation then.'

'Surely, you must tell me.'

'I saw Kanhaiya's smile and listened to the strains of music produced by the flute. In those moments, I saw no one nor heard any loud sound produced by the instruments.'

'Noise! The same noise again!'

'Yes, a peculiar, terrible noise in which the harmonious music of the flute-player was drowned and his smile also faded. I could not see or hear the same despite my repeated efforts.'

'You saw and heard, indeed! Did you?'

'Yes... my... '

Noorbai's throat was choked with emotion. She began to sob but somehow managed to smile through the contorted lips. Mohan had placed her hand on her shoulders.

Keeping her cool and self-control, she said, 'Whatever little I gained there, I shall enlarge the same. What did you absorb there? You must tell me, don't be secretive!'

Mohan cleared his throat and replied, "You are a Gopi! Krishna will reveal Himself in 'darshan' to you first. I am a farmer and soldier too; may be, I would also be enabled to see Him sooner or later. I should make an effort. Even the illiterate, rustic poor did get a chance to have his 'darshan', I am told."

Noorbai clasped his cheeks in her palm and said, 'Again, the same remark repeated! Don't utter it again, I have told you several times. When you were praying to God quite a few learned Pandits started looking at me, which I found out as soon as my attention was distracted.'

Knitting his brows, Mohan could not resist remarking, 'Phew .... Such mean fellows!'

Noorbai instantly put her fingers on his lips and replied, 'I did not mind that. They must be making hullabaloo the whole day and would be expecting to hear the same there also — I do wish to sing some day in a temple so as to please Lord Kanhaiya, and in doing so, would bring home to those learned people how they should concentrate themselves in meditation.'

Mohan's mind raised a query, 'May be, the tale of your beauty and personable qualities would reach Agra and Delhi.'

She replied, 'If the beloved Flute-player and Protector of the world bestows His blessings on me, what harm can Delhi do to me? I have no fears now,.'

'I can't say no, now. All people sing and play music in temples. Shall I talk to Panda about it?'

'Oh no! One needs no aide or mediator to have communion with God. Whenever I feel like, I shall burst into singing.'

'Yes, this is how it should be.'

'And I would dance as well. Don't worry, I shall not dance in the midst of milling crowds. I shall dance at the bank of the Yamuna amidst cappris and Kadamba[123] groves, in shades and glades and to this end, I have learnt the songs by heart. Only you and Lord Flute-player will be there to watch me. I would dance.... dance and keep on dancing so that He will cherish the memory of my dance for ever.'

'Take care lest you should turn crazy.'

'If you call it craziness, how would you label Nand Das,

123. Kadamba – Favourite tree of Lord Krishna under which he palyed on his flute and his Gopis performed dances.

Soordas, Swami Hari Das and Tansen? I stand nowhere in comparison to these great poet stalwarts.'

'I think we have come here to go crazy. If I could share an iota of that frenzy, I would deem it to be more than enough. Winning your love gives me the feeling of communion with God.'

'Oh yes! Winning your love has inspired me to seek and yearn for His benediction.'

'My fair lady.'

'My beloved Mohan!'

—✵—

58

Roni and Tota joined a group of pilgrims making their way from Bharatpur to Mathura-Vrindavan. The formation of that large group had taken quite some time. At first that band went to Mathura. They had no worries about farming and related activities. Hence they struck upon the idea of touring and staying away from home. Roni had left behind her buffalo in the care of that old man's son and did not bother too much about the resultant loss of butter which, she conceded, would accumulate a little more. On the other hand, she was determined to call for its detailed account to the last penny.

Roni prayed to God in all temples visited by her,

'O God, May you be pleased to bestow peace to the ghost of the dead. Fill our family coffers with money and riches.'

She prayed for fulfilment of her wish,

'If my wishes are fulfilled, I shall come back again in my own bullock-cart and make an offering of money in every temple during next festival season.'

After doing the round of Mathura, this group of travellers proceeded towards Vrindavan. Before they could reach the big temple, they were surrounded by priests and representatives of the religious sects. But this time, there arose no occasion for a wrestling bout. As soon as the preist got to know that the members of that group hailed from the particular localities of Bharatpur, he opened his register of entries and started collaring and catching, by elbows, the visitors. One of the priests pointed towards Roni and asked, 'Where is the entry or the code signifying registration of this mother's ancestors in your book?'

One of the residents of Bharatpur and a member of the pilgrims' group replied,

'Does not matter at all! She has come with us.'

The priest asked, "Where do they hail from?'

Pat came the reply, 'She is from Fatehpur Sikri.'

'So what?' the rejoinder came from one of the priests who carried a thick account book in his hand. He jumped to the front of the crowd and said, 'They are our guest-clients. All the guests of Fatehpur Sikri come to stay with us.'

The other fellow taunted, "And the man who came the other day, accompanied by a 'motherly-lady' like this one —he is also a resident of Fatehpur Sikri. Why couldn't you succeed in escorting them to your place? That day also you carried your account book tucked under your arm."

'That day I gave you a fight in a wrestling bout at this very spot. Let us have it again. One round of it!'

Roni stood there with her veil uncovered. She said in a sharp tone, 'Wherever our companions go, we shall follow them there.'

Tota asked, 'Who were they, from Fatehpur Sikri? What was the name? Do you know?'

One of them replied —

'Such an occasion did not arise that one could ask for name and get a reply. This Panda was licking dust here after the bout and they went and stayed with a Panda who lives nearby. There lies the house which belongs to that fat, old Maharaj.[124] There were two men and a lady.'

Tota added in a tremulous voice, 'I recognise every resident of Fatehpur Sikri. We shall see to it later. We are going to stay together at one place.'

124. Maharaj – op. cit 41, p. 112.

That band of pilgrims made their way to the house of that priest who was incharge of pilgrims from Bharatpur. That apprehension and discovery which had terrified Tota now gnawed his mind. He tried to console himself.

'The ghost can't follow us to this holy place; besides, they were three in a group. Even so, I shall make enquiries some other time to find out their identity at the fat Panda's place.'

The group from Bharatpur chose their convenience in making trips to the temples. Its members enjoyed the sound of sharp and loud-sounding instruments, the full-throated singing of psalms and the jostling crowd and all this made them spend hours in each temple.

Tota had overheard others mention that there were quite a few Pandas with an obese constitution and physique. Among them, this 'fatty' Maharaj had a special place because of his girth and dimensions. What he looked like became a matter of curiosity to Tota. He told one of his companions, 'Apart from the temples, let us also have a look at some other things of this place.'

'What?'

"Oh, I hear that the fat-bellied Panda looks like a wooden oil grinding mill. Why don't you go and see him?"

'Have a look but don't take anyone with you. If a whole crowd turns up to see him, the Panda will make out our intention. May be, he will fly into temper and pick up fight—who can anticipate? These Pandas are very quarrelsome.'

'All right, we shall also find out, as to who has come from Bharatpur. We shall enquire about the crop and the conditions back home.'

'Let's go.'

Both of them went to that Panda's house. Tota asked his servant, 'Where is Panda Maharaj?'

The servant replied, 'He is inside, what is your business?'

Tota replied, "I have some business to transact with him only. We shall seek his blessings by 'darshan'. We have to inquire too whether someone from Fatehpur Sikri is staying here."

The servant replied, 'Yes, they are staying in that house which is nearby. They are husband-wife. They are good devotees. If you wish to have Maharaj's darshan, follow me inside. There he is.'

Tota asked him 'Do you know the name of the person from Fatehpur Sikri?'

The servant replied, 'Yes... Yes. He is a Jat, Mohanlal by name.'

Tota's complexion faded. His whole body was shivering. He asked in an undertone, 'Is he inside?'

The servant said, 'I don't know. He was seen in the morning.'

Tota was stupefied and dumb founded.

The servant resumed, "Why are you standing here? You may come in. Please give one paisa in offering—you will earn benediction and religious merit besides 'darshan' of Panda Maharaj."

'I shall come back', said Tota and headed backwards with a staggering gait.

His companion urged him to see the 'fat Panda' but Tota did not agree to this. Both of them left the place.

At the earliest opportunity, Tota gave the news to Roni. Roni told him,

'You are unnecessarily worrying! Ghosts do not visit the place of pilgrimage nor do they cohabit with a woman. One cannot see them in daylight.' Tota insisted, 'There is none else in Fatehpur Sikri with this name.' Roni said, 'You think you can vouchsafe for the entire Fatehpur Sikri. Who knows how many do bear this name?'

Tota replied with an air of indifference, "We'll see; there is no hurry about it. First of all, let us do the round of all 'Darshans' and then we'll look into such trifles."

Tota consoled himself but his nagging curiosity persisted.

—✻—

59

The day had not dawned yet. The crimson clouds in various sizes and shapes had not appeared in the sky. The birds had not begun to chirp. The drowsy priests of temples could not help belching due to indigestion caused by over-eating. Beetles droned while cool breeze wafted the air all around. It was slightly warm and cool at the same time before the end of winter and onset of summer.

Noorbai, still in bed, was awakened. She gazed wide-eyed at the stars without stretching her arms or heaving a yawn. She felt herself in the presence of someone all smiles, someone playing music. She jumped out of bed. Mohan was still asleep. Waking him up she said, 'Come, let's go and have a dip in the Yamuna.'

Rubbing his eyes, Mohan replied 'It is not morning yet!'

Shaking him, she said, 'By the time we bathe ourselves, there will be daylight. It will be exhilarating indeed. We shall roam about in groves and shrubs after bathing.'

Shaking off his laziness, Mohan was up and accompanied her. As he paced along, he regained his strength and smartness. Noorbai frisked forward like a fawn.

A placid Yamuna flowed quietly. Standing on its bank, Noorbai asked amidst her laughter, if you take away my clothes and perch on a Kadamb tree while I am having a dip, what would I do?'

'If I carried a flute, I would have given you a befitting reply.'

'Yes, indeed, you should buy a flute and learn how to play on it.'

'Who will make me learn?'

'I will.'

'Then I shall go and sit on some Kadamba tree to play on it.'

'On an acacia tree! On a Cappris tree! Name Kadamba-Kadamba only-otherwise, God will mind it.'

'He has created all-acacia or kareel or whatever. Why did he create them?'

Noorbai instantly recalled and then forgot a quartrain from Omar Khayyam, the substance of which is as follows —

'Why do you label the juice produced by a plant, as poison? If that juice were poison, why was it created at all and by whom? She was absorbed in her thoughts again. She mused; He must have created acacia and cappris to hook up the long stretches of the apparel of Gopis.'

After they had bathed, day had already dawned.

Noorbai entreated, 'Let's go in a distant grove.'

'Why?' Mohan asked.

She replied, 'To look for Kali Kamli Wale,[125] the flute player.'

Mohan sighed and added, "You cannot commune with Him this way. We'll get 'Darshan' in temple."

She said, 'We'll find him in groves of Kadamba trees, under shades of trees and in lonely places, when I am dancing.'

Mohan agreed with her, 'All right, you may?.'

Both of them went on and on until they arrived at a spot where, probably, no one was likely to intrude — a thick grove on the bank of Yamuna. They spread their clothes to dry on a bush. Noorbai lifted a pinch of dust and put it as a round mark in the middle of forehead at the parting of hair — Mohan seated himself at the base of a tree. The rays of the sun burst forth. Noorbai sang a song composed by the poet Raskhan[125A] which is translated as follows:

'Were I to be born as a human being, would love to live amongst the cowherds of Gokul in Brij, yearns Raskhan,[125A]

Were I an animal, would love grazing every day in the midst of the cows of Nand, [125B]

Were I a stone, would love to be part of the mountain which was held in hand as an umbrella against torrent of Indra,

Were I a bird, would love to nest on the branch of a Kadamba tree on the banks of the river Yamuna.

Mohan had never heard such sweet and melodious singing. After the song was over, Noorbai rendered a dance-performance of the same. She wore no ornaments and had a few bangles only on her wrists and anklets made of brass. That is all! She wore a colourful and dotted blouse covered by thick, colourful wrapper. The sun was riding high by then. The rays filtering

---

125. Kali Kamli Wale – op. cit. 113, p. 291.

125A. Raskhan Muslim poet (1548-1628) devotee of Lord Krishna

125B. Nand op cit125B- Foster Father of infant Lord Krishna handed over user to him by Devki-Vasudev, the natural parents

through branches and trees playfully reflected on her, as she danced her steps and numbers. Her fawn-like eyes, at times, expressed her amazement or her blushing coyness, while she smiled, immersing herself in intoxicating joy alternately.

Her hands, fingers, feet —the entire body seemed to be adorned with flowers— at least so it seemed to Mohan.

While keeping her steps in dancing, Noorbai was making gestures as if she was looking for someone. She alternately expressed her joy, eagerness or the gesture of being misled by mirage, her anxiety or total surrender to God. Sunrays appeared to be helping in her search while the shade of bushes seemingly betrayed obduracy in hiding the already 'hidden one'. The rays of the sun reflected in the slowly rising waves of Yamuna, playing hide and seek, glimmered and wavered as if it was endowed with certain eagerness to witness this communion. She was eagerly looking for someone who revealed Himself in the darkness against light and in the light topping darkness but could not be grasped between the encircling movement of fingers. As she danced, she began to peer through the bushes. Suddenly, she was thrilled to the core and stopped dancing. Putting up a skein of fingers over her eyes, she spoke in a quivering voice. 'I have seen and absorbed Him within myself. Now I'll not let him go anywhere, never!'

Mohan was thrilled. He also closed his eyes and felt within as if he had also seen something. When he opened his eyes, he found Noorbai standing still and calm. The round mark of dust on the forehead glistened due to shimmering and falling sunrays. Her eyes also reflected the playful sunrays. To him, Noorbai had never appeared to be so beautiful, lovely and gloriously dignified. He believed, he had really gained something. He stood up. He wished to convey something but could not. With a great effort, he could bring himself to say, 'Saroopa, my fair lady!'

She knew not what she was looking at or what she was listening to. Mohan closed his eyes, again saw that there was someone moving about, someone dropped some thing with a thud and Noorbai uttered a cry, 'I have the ornaments, here with me. Release my Lord!' Mohan opened his eyes. Tears which had trickled from Noor's eyes glistened like pearls against the rays of the sun while the mark of dust shone in the parting of hair.

Mohan's throat gurgled up in a quivering tone, 'Saroopa!'

'What!' She uttered in surprise and wiped her tears. Mohan dashed towards her and put his hand on her shoulder. He asked, 'What did you see?'

She told him in a sweet, soft tone, 'Whatever I saw can, at best, be described by a thousand tongues. That handsome face, That flute! That musical intonation! That plasticity.'

Noorbai reclined herself against Mohan's shoulder. Some moments slipped by and then raising her head, she looked at Mohan. Mohan said, 'Supposing Shubrati turns up here!' Noorbai separated herself instantly. She replied, 'Let Shubrati or someone else come here. I fear no one. I have gained everything. I have come upon Mohan and thereby also won you over.'

Laughing, he added, 'I am called Mohan... it is me here.'

She burst into laughter and said, 'He is a thief, stealing butter, He is the thief of Brij area, thief of the whole world, thief of sun, thief of moon and stars, a thief who steals away the sorrows of the suffering. You are also a thief... a disciple of that thief -my Mohan. Let me sit down for a while, I feel tired.'

Noorbai seated herself resting against the base of a tree and closed her eyes. After some time she said, 'Let us go now' and started moving. Mohan stopped her, 'For whom are you leaving behind these clothes.'

Noorbai was surprised, 'Oh, I had forgot all about them.'

—✵—

60

Mohan and Noorbai had finished their meal by the time it struck eight o'clock.

Mohan replied 'If you agree, I shall go and see Shubrati. I haven't met him since that day.'

"Soon it will be quite hot followed by blowing of hot winds. Take some rest and go out in the afternoon, a little before 'Aarti'[126] and prayer time."

'In that case you would sing!'

'Then you would ask me to dance also.'

"How will you dance after the meals when you would feel a heaviness in the belly. And why should I urge you for that? All right. Come here and be seated. Put a 'Bindi'[127] mark on your forehead and I should keep on looking at you."

'If I had a set of small tinkling bells for my ankles, I would certainly dance.'

'Shall I bring a set of them from the market.'

'Not from the market but from any temple where some one would have performed wearing them in the presence of Kanhaiya.'

'How do you distinguish between the two?'

'I don't know but I won't wear the ones from the market. Ofcourse, you may buy, give it as an offering to the temple and then request for its return to you.'

'I am at a loss to make out its import.'

'Let it be! This is just a whim of mine. I would dance even otherwise. If I were to dance in a temple, I would wear them.'

'This morning while dancing I did not miss the absence of jingling bells. How did you like my dancing?'

'Do not dance in the temple premises.'

'Wherefore?'

'For I am telling you not to.'

'All right, I agree but what about dancing when we are all by ourselves? I would always crave for that. What about my performance this morning?'

'Don't ask me! Words fail me in describing it. To me, you appeared to be a Gopi. I too was transformed into something else.'

---

126. Aarti – Evening prayer and worship in which an earthen or brass lamp is lit and moved by hand around the deity accompanied by psalm singing and music of instruments.
127. Bindi – A red mark applied by Hindu married women as a mark of marital status and loyalty to husband.

'I saw the flute-player several times; since then, I am feeling intoxicated and transported. We may or may not go to temples but we must go to that spot. It seemed that there existed a temple without a temple structure.'

'If we still possessed those jewels and diamonds, I would adorn you with them and then dance with you.'

Noorbai was startled and looked at him wide-eyed. She said, 'Why do you mention it? God was gracious to have removed these unholy things from us. The gay abandon we have gained cannot be bought by exchanging jewels and diamonds worth crores of rupees. I wish you to shake off the burden of your girdle pouch and offer the same in temples or disburse them among the poor.'

A little awed, Mohan replied, 'You are right —we have to eke out our living by these rupees until I have found work on wages. Then I won't keep them anymore with me. Even so, I wish to see you dressed up in befitting and beautiful clothes but this will be possible only when I get my own earnings and this I would certainly accomplish.'

Noorbai smiled, and replied, 'Now as it is, how do I look?'

He said, 'There is no one like you in this world but I feel like doing that —after all, it is my intuitive inner desire.'

Noorbai said, 'Never make a mention of those jewels henceforth.'

Mohan fondly replied, 'I am not attached to them but the way they were snatched from us has been gnawing my mind. You were forced to take off your clothes in their presence! Oh!'

'I was not stark naked; I was wearing the long skirt but even if I was made to strip myself completely, what would it come to? They would have watched my body made of clay; even wind passing over them would be unable to touch my pure, unravished soul.'

'I could see nothing. Listened to something indistinctly. I can guess by their height and physique that they were Jats by caste, but I would not recognise any one.'

'I could recognise them.'

'I suspect they were members of Chintaman's gang-those who held consultations that night among themselves.'

'Chintaman was accompanying them.'

'O! Did he?'

'Undoubtedly, he was there!'

'How did you come to know!'

'By his voice and by his eyes. It takes little time for a woman to make out.'

'If we were carrying guns, we would have made them lick dust. If ever I have one, I would do it to them.'

'Oh! Oh! What are you saying? Work hard and pray to God. Do not nurse that grudge, that thorn in your mind.'

'Yes!'

"Would you see me dance? I shall dance with 'ta thei' steps and numbers of dance."

'With bellyfull of food! No!'

Both of them heard footsteps at the door, and leant their ears to the same. Someone was knocking.

Mohan shouted, 'Coming!'

Opening the door, he found Shubrati standing there. He said, 'What were you doing? I had to knock for long. Were you sleeping? You are getting cooked food without problems —isn't it?'

Mohan laughed and said, 'I was thinking of going out to see you but then we began to talk.'

Shubrati taunted, 'It is the charm and aroma of the romance of Brij area, dear fellow! And why not?'

Both of them burst into laughter. Mohan ushered him into the room without closing the door behind him.

He told Noorbai, 'There he is, your elder brother. He tells me that I did not go to see him while he enjoyed himself in the cantonment.'

Noorbai smiled as she spread a piece of cloth for Shubrati to sit and she herself sat in a corner.

The first thing mentioned by Mohan was, 'The gang of dacoits we ran into the other day, was led by Chintaman.'

Shubrati was amazed, 'That day too! That they had attacked a Maratha squad was brought to our knowledge in that very village but how did you know that they had committed this robbery too?'

Pointing towards Noorbai, Mohan replied, 'She has told me just now. She had recognised them.'

Noorbai softly intervened, 'I found out by Chintaman's voice.' Shubrati's eyes were lit up with anger. He said in a deep, hoarse voice,

'I have conveyed the name and address of the village to the emissary. He has vowed to take revenge. On return, I shall incite him further. The entire village is full of dacoits. It will be reduced to ashes.'

Noorbai was reminded of that old lady who had helped her in drawing water from the well. It shook her completely; she said softly, 'Don't do that, brother, there are old men and women besides children in that village.'

Shubrati flew into rage, 'They are all rascals.'

Mohan rose from his seat. He heard someone talking in the porch. He heard someone saying, 'They live in this very house. They are talking. You may call them outside.'

Mohan came out in the courtyard, remarking, 'Let me see who is there in the courtyard.'

On seeing Mohan, Panda's servant accosted 'Mohanlalji, these people from Bharatpur are looking for you.'

Roni and Tota were in the porch. Mohan recognised them instantly. Roni was standing with her face uncovered. Scared, she drew the veil on her face. Tota with a choked throat gurgled the monosyllables, 'Hey Ram[128] and as he retreated fast, he collided with the Panda's servant who was standing behind him.

Mohan anxious and hurt said softly, 'I am not a ghost nor is it the time of night! Don't feel terrified, Tota!'

The servant went away. Roni was trembling all over. Mohan asked, 'Tell me, what has brought you here?'

Tota was stupefied and speechless. Roni advanced to touch Mohan's feet. Mohan shouted, 'No!'

Shubrati came and stood at the doorway. He asked, 'What is the matter?'

Mohan could give no answer anyway. From the courtyard, he proceeded towards the room. Roni followed him. Roni stood on the floor of the courtyard which was quite hot in the scorching sun. Tota still stood in the porch.

Noorbai standing behind Mohan and Shubrati said, 'Sister, come here. Your feet must be getting scorched there?'

Shubrati also repeated it. Mohan kept silent. Shubrati tried to read Mohan's face.

Noorbai raising her voice exclaimed, 'Sister, come near me, here. What's the matter?'

Roni advanced a little further towards the interior and immediately knelt at Mohan's feet. She burst into tears and began to cry aloud. Tota too arrived there.

Shubrati cleared his throat and asked her, 'Brother. What's all this? Who is this wretched woman?'

Mohan replied in a relentless tone, 'It is she against whom I gave vent to my grievance while talking to you in Poona and whose witchcraft made me desert my home and hearth.'

'And who is the other one?' Shubrati could not help asking Mohan, pointing towards Noorbai.

Mohan answered, 'The one who is making such a hullabaloo is my spouse by marriage in this present life and the other one who is going to make me a human being belongs to me since my previous birth.'

Shubrati was perplexed and began to scratch his head.

Mohan angrily growled at Tota, 'Wherefore, lad, did you escort her to this place?'

Tota too clutched his feet in obeisance and cried, 'Brother, we are innocent.'

Mohan said, 'Ain't I a ghost? A fool too!'

Roni stood up. Her veil was half-uplifted; tears trickled down her face and her eyes were bloodshot with tears. Her face

---

128. Hey Ram – Oh! God Rama!—An exclamation generally pronounced by a person just before death or under threat of death.

which was ruddy and sun-burnt betrayed signs of struggle in life. Noorbai fancied that woman to be a beauty too.

In a tremulous, tear-jerking tone, Roni exclaimed, 'I am as pure and mnocent as the water of the Ganges,[129] so is Tota. We have come on pilgrimage here. That is all!'

Noorbai consoled, 'Sister, calm yourself, keep cool and be seated here.'

Roni shouted intercepting her voice, 'What a fine woman is she who addresses me as her sister. He is my husband and master. Who are you? Where do you hail from and where are you coming from, now?'

Mohan remonstrated her harshly, 'Get out from here! Go wherever you wish to.'

Noorbai was face to face with Mohan, her hands folded in supplication. She spoke spontaneously, 'Surely, she is as pure as the water of the Ganges so is this brother too. I say, cool down and keep calm.' She turned to Roni and told her, 'Sister, you should serve him well. I am leaving; I shall go to some temple and settle there.'

Mohan looked at her, wide-eyed in amazement. He said, 'What do you say, Saroopa? Where will you go leaving me behind? Did you save my life from the dacoits that day only to desert me today?'

Noorbai felt a lump in her throat as she stood there with folded hands. He was choked in emotion. Tota said, 'Brother, forgive me. I have done many other misdeeds —theft, robbery, etc., but I haven't brought dishonour to you.'

Roni, her eyes still lowered, looked at Noorbai who was calm and quiet and felt awed.

Mohan spoke to Noorbai in a tone expressive of his authority over her, 'Be seated there! You said, you would go away! How dare you go away until I am alive and kicking.' Turning to Roni, he said, 'Go away from here and don't show me your face. Don't hurt and burn my inner self.'

129. Ganges – The most sacred river, according to Hindu scriptures, held in reverence all over India.

Shubrati said, 'Hold on, brother Mohan.'

Mohan told him, 'Brother, you don't know this woman. She is like a whirlwind and a rising storm. She is like a stack of burnt ash. I don't wish to see her face anymore.'

Roni dropped down at his feet and clutched them.

Speechless and stupefied, Noorbai seemed to be begging without speaking any words apparently suggesting 'Enough! Don't torture her anymore.'

The spectacle of the puppet back home flashed in Shubrati's mind and he became wistful and penitent about his own helplessness. He said, 'In the situation that has arisen, is it not possible that both women may live like sisters in the same house.'

Roni softly assented 'Yes.'

Noorbai raised Roni from the floor close to Mohan's feet, where she was seated and embraced her. She said, 'You are my elder sister; I shall serve you.'

Roni again uttered, 'Yes.'

Tota said, 'Brother, I shall keep holding your feet in my hands.'

Mohan had regained his cool by then. There was some hustle and bustle in the porch; a few people were coughing too. Mohan peeped from behind the door. There was the fat Panda escorted by his servant.

Mohan invited him in a suppressed tone, 'Come Maharaj'! The fat Panda came in followed by his servant who seemed to be a little ant compared to the obese body of his master.'

Panda exerted himself to get into the room where they were sitting. The doorway was too narrow for him. The heat was scorching enough. After his abdomen found its way through the door, his thighs seemed to give way. As the thighs twisted and managed to get in, his shoulders stuck against the door panels. Breathless as he was, his throat seemed to be choked. Panda said in a broken, stammering voice, 'I have come into this wretched, small room after years; so it seems, the door has shrunk a bit.'

Panda appeared to be taking cover in laughter to hide his embarrassment. Noorbai smiled. Roni started laughing after drawing her veil. Shubrati observed Roni's laughter closely and thought her to be an uncouth woman. Mohan having regained his calm, engaged himself in pulling Panda inside the room and finally succeeded in his labours after Panda's servant had extended his helping hand from the side of the courtyard. Breathless as he was, Panda seated himself with a thud and questioned Mohan, 'What caused this commotion and crying?'

Shubrati said, 'Oh Saroopa, spread a cloth for Panda Maharaj.'

'No brother,' the fat Panda replied.

'I shall return just now. Have come to ask what is this row about?'

Shubrati replied, 'Nothing, Maharaj. We belong to the same family. There was some argument and family row, which resulted into provocation here too. There is absolutely nothing now. You took this trouble needlessly.'

Both women were smiling and seemed to be figuring out the cause of Panda's unwieldy obesity and bulk. The incident of past few moments still cast its lingering shadows in their minds.

Panda in an improved tone and voice told them, 'Let me tell you one thing. You should resume singing songs as before. Don't quarrel among yourselves, my guests! I swear, it is extremely hot here. Let me go now.'

Shubrati added a cool, satirical repartee, 'Yes, Maharaj, hurry up lest the door of the room should shrink more.'

Panda, himself a man of humour, burst into peals of laughter. It seemed that many a bellow were pumped with air which blowed in and out. His entire body was shaking with laughter. He was about to move. As he made an effort to rise, he had to go through a strenuous exercise in resting his hand, in panting, breathing and in withdrawing his thighs. The servant helped him in all this.

Roni nearly twisted her body while laughing. Noorbai pursed her lips in an effort to check the laughing bout. Shubrati was about to burst into guffaw while Tota too seemed to join him in that.

Panda simulated a sombre face with sober gestures and told them, 'I still do my press-up and push-up exercise and can go jogging too. Don't take me to be a commoner.'

Shubrati said, 'Yes Maharaj, for miles. You can run miles, on the sandy banks of the mother Yamuna.'

Panda too joined in the laughter.

He had to go through the same sequence and motion in an effort to make his exit from that room. This time the servant pulled him from outside and Mohan pushed him from inside. The Panda went away blessing all of them in response to their 'palangon'[130] in touching his feet.

Shubrati remarked after Panda had left, 'See how carefree he is, this Panda!'

Mohan asserted, 'Carefree he is, surely, for he gets enough to eat without working at all.'

Peals of laughter vanished from that room as fast as it had made itself felt. For a while, all of them were immersed in thinking what to do?

Shubrati ventured a solution. He said, 'All of you should go back to Fatehpur. Manage your household and farm and take a vow not to quarrel again among yourselves.'

Roni spoke first, 'I had made over the farm and the household too to an acquaintance. Land revenue has become overdue for payment. Who knows what must have happened there? I have left behind the buffalo at Bharatpur.'

'Damn your buffalo' Mohan retorted, 'I'll work hard, earn wages and live happily hereafter on the bank of Yamuna.'

Roni's thought spurred her, 'Why not....why not, enjoy yourself in her company. The holy place is meant for all this', as she turned to gaze towards Noorbai. Noorbai did not bat an eyelid and her eyes reflected an eagerness which lay embedded in her declining, raving beauty. Roni pondered, 'Has she taken some intoxicant?'

Tota, seemingly about to cry, prayed, 'No, Brother, let's go home. I shall work and you too.'

Mohan said aloud and sharply, 'Yes....Yes and may go on robbery outings also. You too had joined Chintaman in that looting ! Ha, now you go away long distances for working. Your feet also had pressed my chest ! If it were not for this goddess-like lady, my friend and I would have been killed.'

Roni was amazed to hear, 'That lady is a Devi.'

Tota stammered the words, 'Brother, I was not there that day. I do not know anything about that day's incident, I swear by the rivers, Ganges and Yamuna. Of course, I was there when you were brandishing and fighting with your sword in that culvert. I apologise for that lapse. Incited by the sister-in-law, I had started taking part in looting and robbing. We had followed those five men as we did not recognise them. We could never anticipate your being among them.'

Roni's face became red with anger.

Mohan was provoked. He said, 'She tries to put us to harm, which is better left unsaid. After turning me out of home she would have made up her mind to get you killed.' Roni flew into easy-to-provoke rage and said, 'O lad Tota, did I tell you to go about robbing others? Speak out, when did I tell you to do so?' Tota was about to burst forth.

Mohan interjected, 'Shut up and keep mum! Don't enter into argument.'

Noorbai, taking a cover behind something said, 'Why are you losing temper on them? Let bygones be bygones. Let's think of things which lie ahead.'

Taking cue from her, Shubrati said, 'Take home this boy and these two ladies too. Saroopa is such a gentle and good-natured lady that she would get along with all.'

Tota expressed his firm determination, 'I won't go anywhere from here. A place where I get work and happiness, that is my home,'

Roni responded quickly, 'I have no possession, no one at Bharatpur whom I can call mine. I'll bring the buffalo and look after it here besides working for wages.'

Roni ogled sideways at Noorbai and mused, 'Her body is as soft as butter. She can't work for wages. She will keep lying in bed and eat all by herself.'

130. Palangon – A form of respectful address to priests which means 'I touch your feet respectfully'.

Mohan argued, 'Buffalo and buffalo! She has nothing else to look to except the buffalo.'

Noorbai spoke in a melodious note like a cuckoo, 'If you men can follow everything that we women plan to do, there will be no trouble at all.' Roni seemed to like Noorbai's sympathetic words. With her veil drawn, Roni turned to Noorbai and uttered in a tremulous voice, 'God damn me and burn my tongue! My soul is not at all like that, Sister!'

All of them liked her form of address.

Shubrati spoke in a supplicating tone, "Sister, you have addressed Saroopa' as your sister today; you should continue to do so in future. Won't you do it?"

Roni could only muster to say 'yes' but that too with a certain force injected in her tone.

Mohan asked Tota, 'When did you arrive here and wherefore?' Tota replied, 'We had set out two-three days ago. Misled by the impression that you were no more, sister-in law came here to perform the rites related with death in this holy place.' Mohan smiled spontaneously and responded, 'It would have occurred to her that she was cursing me all the time in life and now after my death she would cool my spirit by holy waters.'

Roni clutched his feet and began to weep. Noorbai helped her rise from the sitting posture. Noorbai raised her voice, 'Hold on, Sister! Be seated there. I shall touch and clasp his feet now.'

Noorbai could not clasp the feet as Mohan had moved away a little. He said. 'What... What's this you are doing? I swear I would follow you and abide by your desire in the manner you want but I won't go back to Fatehpur and would not leave Vrindavan for one year. Brother, I have discovered the real Saroopa today. This morning, she had a glimpse of God. Neither she nor I will leave Brij area presently.'

Shubrati could not make out what sort of glimpse he was alluding to.

Roni thought that such a slim, tender woman had saved him from tne robbers —that is why he became fond of her. 'She must be more terrible than me to deal with.'

Roni urged thus in such a respectful vein of which Mohan had no earlier experience, 'Shall, I, then, bring the buffalo from Bharatpur?'

Shubrati answered immediately, 'Yes, do bring it. Why ask him at all?'

Roni turned and looked at Mohan from behind her veil. Mohan saw tears welling up in her eyes. He said, 'Am I restraining her? Brother Shubrati has already permitted. Saroopa's expressive eyes have spoken volumes for her. What do you want Tota?'

Tota replied 'Brother, who is mine in this world except you? I shall always remain with you under your care and shelter. I will not go back to Bharatpur now.'

Shubrati asked, 'Who will, then, go with the sister-in-law to fetch buffalo here?'

Tota replied between sobs, 'Someone else may go there; I won't accompany her even if you cut me into pieces.'

Roni sadly gurgled up words after a moment's pause in a soft tone, 'Well, I shall go with those who are here to take part in the fair and would come back with a servant.'

Noorbai entreated Tota, 'Please do go with her.'

Tota said firmly, 'No, sister-in-law! I won't go to Bharatpur with her. Like a devil, she would devour me.'

Roni replied in a suppressed tone, 'No, I won't curse you henceforth.'

Tota repeated his firm decision, 'I will not go at any cost.'

Noorbai on being addressed as sister-in-law felt herself to be in a trance.

Shubrati said, T shall take two-three days' leave and escort sister-in-law to Bharatpur. I shall come back with bag and baggage besides the buffalo.'

Roni firmly replied, 'If the sister can fight the dacoits, couldn't I bring my own baggage and the buffalo? Let Tota, the damned fellow, not accompany me,' and intercepted her tongue from speaking further. Shubrati laughed. Noorbai smiled. Tota felt embarrassed and his wistful face reflected it.

Mohan said in an apparently serious but betraying a lighter

vein, 'You all observed how determined she is to keep her vow? It is hardly a moment that she said she would not abuse anymore.' Roni, her head bowed, said in an undertone, 'I did not take a vow. Today, I will do so in Baldau's[131] temple.'

Mohan told her, 'Go and take vow just now.' Roni made a move to rise.

Noorbai intervened, 'Be seated, sister; don't go anywhere in this scorching heat of the afternoon. Wherever you are able to resolve firmly and pray in your heart, the place becomes as sacred as a temple.'

Roni arose and seated herself close to Noorbai. She wished to know who she was and where she came from and how. Both of them began to converse in a whispering tone.

Shubrati said, 'Our squad has to make move towards the Deccan. They would like to return home before the onset of monsoon'

Mohan asked, 'When would you be back?'

He replied, 'We shall stir again after the Dussehra. I hope we shall meet again, at least once more within this lifetime. We have to punish that Chintaman and also take on other Chintaman of this area, who might have only heard of Marathas so far. Nadir Shah has swept, like a whirlwind, the Hindu kingdoms of the North. I hear that the Rana of Udaipur is being offered the throne of Delhi. Marathas cannot lie low and unmindful. They would march towards Agra. My squad will also take part in the campaign. I shall look for you in Fatehpur Sikri on arrival there.'

Mohan said, 'I shall see you here. I don't intend to go home for one year.'

Shubrati remonstrated, 'How obstinate are you? If you find the place uninteresting, would you still continue to loiter and not go home?' Mohan began to ponder.

In the meantime, Roni came to know from Noorbai's replies that the latter belonged to an upper class family and had escaped from Delhi to save her life immediately after Nadir Shah's attack.

131. Baldeu – op. cit. 105, p. 268.

By sheer coincidence, she met Mohan and fought against dacoits. She could not harm the dacoits in any way, but Lord Krishna came to her rescue and gave chase to the dacoits. She related to Roni the incident when Mohan had lost his consciousness. Shubrati observed that both the young ladies were making friends. He liked all this.

Mohan, after pondering for a while, told him, 'Brother, I give you my word that as soon as I get bored here, I shall go back to Fatehpur. Let people there also come to know that I am not dead nor have I become a ghost.'

Noorbai intercepted, 'Again, the same story!'

Mohan said, 'I had gone to Fatehpur. When I reached home at night, people there mistook me for a ghost.'

Shubrati blamed him, 'You never told me.'

Mohan set him at rest, 'There was nothing much to convey. I never told anyone.'

Shubrati asked him, 'Anyway! Now tell me how long do you intend to stay here?'

Mohan told him, "We have seen here almost nothing till now. We have not had 'Darshan' in many temples. I should seek blessings of monks and saints too and above all, I shall go for a walk, early in the morning, in those groves and bushes where Saroopa had a glimpse of God. When my yearning is fulfilled, I shall do something to exterminate Chintaman's gang. Thereafter, I shall go back to Fatehpur to look after my farm and to sing devotional songs in the honour of God."

Shubrati remarked, 'Leave Chintaman and his kind for us to deal with.'

Noorbai said in soft undertone, 'There may not be any other holy place which can surpass Vrindavan as holiest among holy places, to devote ourselves in singing psalms dedicated to God. Somewhere around this place, it should be possible for us to do a bit of farming too. All of us shall work here.'

Shubrati thought, 'This innocent-looking, beautiful lady has persuaded poor Mohan to be obdurate. Hence it would be futile to talk to him about anything else.' He added, however, 'There is no comparison between repeating the name of God, Rama and the drudgery of daily life, nothing to compare between Vrindavan and Fatehpur Sikri. After all a home is a home.'

Noorbai was, again and again, wiping her perspiring body and Roni too was sitting a little withdrawn.

Shubrati propossed, 'Let's go into the porch to pass the afternoon and let the ladies also rest a while.'

Mohan, Shubrati and Tota went into the porch. Noorbai and Roni uncovered their head and stretched themselves full length, to rest.

Noorbai observed anger floating in the big, black eyes of Roni and also that her physique was sound, strong and hefty. Roni guessed that there was something bewitching in the intoxicating eyes and body of Noorbai.

Noorbai said, 'You must be tired; let me press and massage your body.'

Roni thought, 'May be, she would try to play some trick or magic on me and then God knows what would befall me.' Hence she declined her offer. She said, 'Let's talk of something and while talking thus, we shall embrace sleep.'

'All right, start!'

'Have you ever milked a cow?'

'No.'

'Did you ever harvest a field?'

'No.'

'Did you ever make dung-cakes?'

'Yes.'

'Have you ever drawn water from a well?'

'Yes!'

'You must be a good cook.'

'No!'

'How about grinding flour in grinding-stones?'

'No!'

'Were you, then, wasting time for nothing?'

Noorbai burst into peals of laughter. Roni observed that Noorbai's teeth were extremely pretty and shining.

Noorbai said amidst laughter, 'Indeed, I was wasting time doing nothing until now. I shall engage myself in singing devotional songs, doing righteous duties followed by psalm-singing.'

Roni too laughed. Noorbai observed that Roni was a simple, rustic and beautiful farmer woman. Roni replied, 'One can do only one thing at a time —either sing devotional songs or do one's duties.'

Noorbai said, 'Shall do both.'

Roni was enthusiastic, 'You can do precious little. That you are a white complexioned woman hardly matters. Your legs and hands are like those of Raas-performers.'

Roni was overwhelmed. Those intoxicating eyes, the tale of how she overcame dacoits by her sheer strength or God's help becalmed Roni. She said, 'We shall share work between us. I shall keep myself busy in chores and you would sing hymns. Besides, listen, you should take care of 'him', for he has gone crazy. Earlier, he behaved like a pussy cat haying a suppressed personality like a real cat.'

Noorbai laughed so much that she felt cramps in her stomach. Roni joined her in laughing and remarked, 'Sister, look at that Panda, how bulky he is! Must be eating a maund of foodgrains daily. How breathless he was —seemed some storm was, blowing! What eatables would he be taking to make him buffalo-like? Restraining her laughter, Noorbai said, 'Shouldn't we ask him about it?'

Roni was provoked as if ignited by that remark, 'You would talk to that damned, burntout leper who has no son of his own.'

Noorbai again burst into peals of laughter which filled that room and spilled over to the porch as well. Shubrati said, 'Your problems are over. Both will live together as companions. There will be no row at home, I am quite confident now.'

Mohan said, 'God knows! I can only say that I have always observed her knitting brows and getting angry. Today all this happiness is Saroopa's gift to us —you may take it from me.'

Shubrati said, 'I am glad that you would no longer be unhappy. I may, however, caution you not to seek the company of Chintaman and his kind. We shall pay him back in the same coin and much more for his wrongs. Marathas don't ever forget good deeds done to them nor do they shut their eyes to the wrongs meted out to them. All right, take some rest now. I shall return to the barracks by the evening.'

Both of them stretched themselves and sleep overcame them soon. The peals of laughter resounding in the room warmed up into prolonged conversation which tapered off and all became quiet.

Noorbai said, 'You promised not to utter an abuse thenceforth.' Roni replied, 'Well I did not abuse Tota or anyone else, and, for that matter, I have yet to take the vow in the Baldeu's temple. Please come with me to the temple.' Noorbai agreed and said, 'We'll all go.'

Roni said, 'Two of us will do. Men have their own group, we two form another.'

'I don't think it proper.'

'Why? Will someone take us into custody?'

'Suppose anyone does?'

'I will be with you, of course. I shall give him kicks.'

Both of them burst into laughter. They had already stretched themselves and snatched naps in between talking and keeping awake.

Late in the afternoon, Mohan and Shubrati woke-up. Before his departure, Shubrati told him 'Remember what I have told you already. I shall see you soon after return from the Deccan.'

—❋—

61

Roni and Tota brought their baggage to the ce where Mohan and Noorbai were staying. All of them set out to have 'darshan' in the temples. Large crowds thronged the big temples. Roni wanted to penetrate the crowd to get into the sanctum sanctoram. Noorbai urged them to proceed to other temples only after observing the vast expanse and the large structures of the temple. Mohan endorsed her view. At last, they came across a temple which had much less crowd. Mass prayer and singing called Kirtan[132] accompanied by instrumental music was in full swing. They entered and seated themselves.

Roni liked the instruments of music which seemed quite interesting to her while Noorbai judged the high pitch of male voice leading Kirtan to be in disharmony and against the spirit of music.

She diverted her attention from the music to the idols and made an effort to concentrate her thoughts on them. The disharmony of Kirtan music lingered in her mind. She closed her eyes but could not focus her concentration on the idols. She imagined and recalled the scene — Shubrati was lying while travelling in a bullock-cart and Chintaman's gang surrounded him with their swords drawn and sticks uplifted to hit him. Somehow her imagination warded it off but she saw that Chintaman's Chaudharin wife was going into the room to collect her clothes. Noorbai then tried to recapture the rapturous experience which she had gone through in the grove —to have just one glimpse of that but it was all in vain. Noorbai opened her eyes and saw two buxom country bumpkins staring at her. Exasperated, she turned her eyes towards those who were singing in chorus. They were intermittently looking at her while paying obeisance to the idols.

Sitting by her side, Roni whispered in her ears, 'How nice is all this?'

Noorbai said, 'It is no good; they are singing in a hoarse manner.'

Roni asked, 'Could you sing like this?'

She replied, 'Listen to it when we are back home.'

On seeing the two women whispering between themselves the Kirten singers gazed at them more intently.

The spectators thought, 'She was a beauty, nonpareil. The face of the other woman too has sharp and well-shaped features.'

Roni said in the same vein, 'May the goddess Kali[133] kill and devour all these damned fellows. All of them may die and leave

132. Kirtan – Mass prayer and singing accompanied by instrumental music of sorts.

133. Kali – One of the several goddesses worshipped by Hindus. Kali killed several demons and came to symbolise the great strength and destructive power against demons and evil spirits.

skeletons behind. See, how they are ogling and staring at us?'

Noorbai said, 'Come, sister; let's go there from here.'

Roni insisted, 'My dear, sit a little longer and enjoy the music; it is all so endearing.'

Noorbai stood up followed by Mohan. The spectators had a chance to have a good look at them. She drew her veil and made it more lengthy. Mohan quickly grasped the reason why Noorbai stood up suddenly.

Mohan told Roni and Tota, 'Let's go.' They too stood up and all of them went out.

On arrival at the lodgings, Roni told Noorbai, 'You spoilt everything. How interesting and endearing was the music being played on the instruments! What an excellent hymn-singing was going on!'

Noorbai exclaimed, 'What do they know of singing and playing on the instruments.'

Roni replied in a hurt, sad tone, 'You are a great expert! You must be able to sing one or two romantic songs and you are already boasting about your singing. When you are about to sing, you will seek the help of your father who has his abode in heaven.'

Noorbai tried to pacify 'I shall sing to you for I have listened to much better songs than these.'

All this was exchanged in a low tone. Roni raised her hoarse voice, 'While living in Delhi, you thought you were the queen of the Emperor.'

To Noorbai it came piercing like an arrow. Even so, she maintained her equanimity and humbly prayed to her, 'Sister, don't be angry with me — I have learnt by heart certain devotional songs which I shall sing to you some day.'

Roni loudly expressed her desire to listen to them, 'All right, sing here and now. You escorted me out, against my will, from the temples by telling me this very thing.'

Mohan sensed that there was something wrong. He told them harshly, 'Go to sleep and stop this noisy nonsense' and then added softly, 'Saroopa, we have to get up early in the morning. After bath we have to go back to the same arbour and groves.'

Noorbai avidly expressed her agreement, 'All right!'

After a moment's pause, Mohan again spoke a little harshly, 'Listen, please go back to Bharatpur in the morning if you wish to fetch your buffalo or send Tota for the same.'

Roni had hidden, under the earth, a few rupees, back in Bharatpur; she had to recover her dues of the sale of butter oil and also ventilate her grievance against Mohan to her acquaintances. She said, 'I'll go myself tomorrow morning or day after, before daybreak.'

—✵—

62

Noorbai and Mohan went to take bath while Roni was asleep.

A gusty wind was blowing all over. It was pleasant and cool. When they arrived at the bank of Yamuna, the birds swarming and nestling in the groves of trees flapped their wings in fear and became still. Beetle-drone became more piercing to the ears for a while before it was wafted down to the quietly flowing river Yamuna. Both of them stood at the bank. A draught of west wind untied Noorbai's wavy, long-flowing saree and the curly plaits of hair and floated them in the windy gust. Mohan looked at her and then turned his eyes towards the gliding flow of Yamuna-water.

Noorbai moved and reached for him as a creeper waves its way to seek sustenance from a tree.

Mohan drew her close to his shoulder in an embrace and remarked, 'My own Saroopa!'

His receptive ears seemed full of ardour to receive the appellation, 'My Mohan!' But Noorbai burst into tearful cries.

In a quivering voice Mohan asked, 'What's the matter?' Noorbai managed to say between hiccups, 'Let me cry and pour out my heart first.'

Mohan's shoulder was wet with Noorbai's tears and her gasps warmed his chest. Mohanlal seated himself, snuggling her in his lap.

Collecting her wits and trying to keep cool, Noorbai said between her sobs, 'Where can I go now from here, leaving you behind except to drown myself in the current of mother Yamuna.'

Mohan held her body in full embrace against his broad chest. He fumbled for words befitting to the occasion, 'How to express himself? Irresistibly, he could only say: 'Not to the flowing current of river Yamuna but into the gaping, bleeding chasm of my heart.'

Noorbai blurted in reply as she tried, with a jerk, to separate herself from his body, 'What! What nonsense did you utter just now?'

'Am I wrong? You would drown yourself in the river Yamuna and I would remain a mute spectator!'

'How dare you say that? Have you lost sight of the fact that you are a man and I am a mere woman? And what sort of woman? One who was made to learn the art of dancing and singing merely to make her sell herself finally, one who offered her body to those who made the highest bid to buy her; one who could not protect herself against Nadir Shah's tyranny.'

Noorbai who firmly held on to Mohan's neck, her hands clasping it, loosened her grip as her entire body felt relaxed. Her voice vying with and rising above the buzzing of the beetle became faint and was hardly audible. Mohan, completely shaken, was shivering. Noorbai seemed to faint.

'My dearest Noor... '

He could not complete the sentence. Lightning seemed to charge her whole body as it shook off all its stupor and languor.

Noorbai retorted harshly, 'You tried to unearth that dead body! You resurrected that rotten corpse! Why are you determined to dig up the grave?'

Mohan was mortifed by the harshness of her voice. Earlier, he had only once heard such a harsh tone which was not as piercing as in that moment—that was vague, indistinct, diffused and faint while he was on the verge of unconsciousness and his ears had received the words, 'Spare my master!'

'Pardon me, Saroopa! My Saroopa, if ever I utter these words again, I shall cut apart my own tongue.'

'Being a manly person, you derive pleasure in teasing me.'

'Of course, you do seek pleasure in mouthing such words and in remonstrating me. Tell me, why you wept at all. How did I offend you?'

'All right, let me put it straight to you as I would like to be clear on this now.'

'Ask me and I shall not withhold anything from you.'

"Wherefore? What could I do? There was no chance to talk to you nor could I have any fun in your company. How many people were there in that courtyard? I too could go to sleep quite late after turning sides in bed.'

Noorbai laughed —it seemed sunrays had formed a rainbow, in airy nothing, out of showers. An image of a simple, unsuspecting and honest farmer Sepoy was framed in Noorbai's eyes and vanished soon after.

Shaking Mohan with her arms, she said, 'You are unlike yourself; come on, you took me otherwise. I did not mean that.'

Mohan asked fondly, 'What, after all, is the matter?'

'Has my sister been informed of my past?'

'Who would tell her?'

'I am not aware of that.'

'What did she say?'

'She remarked, as I had lived in Delhi, I imagined myself to be the queen of the Emperor.'

'Oh, that bumpkin told you all that! What else did she remark and what was the occasion?'

'It was in the course of conversation.'

'What conversation? Tell me its beginning and end!'

"When singing and instrumental music were in full swing in the temple, the sister told me it was all very good. When I told her that it was quite crude and without the essential symphony, she taunted and challenged me to sing. I told her I could surpass that singing, on which she flared up and said, 'Having been in Delhi, you imagine yourself to be the queen of the Emperor?' Did you drop some hint to her?"

Mohan heaved a sigh of relief. He said, 'Even if I am a farmer, I could make out but for all your knowledge, learning and sharp intelligence, you could not follow her remarks. Did you gauge her nature or not?'

Noorbai replied with the usual indifference, 'Yes, she is quite used to abusing.'

'And a variety of abuses too?'

'Yes, like Damned, God-damned, issueless, leper, etc'

'Futile to count, for the treasury of her abuses can't be put to count. Whatever she told you is also in the form of an abuse, a small gift from that treasury. But I would put it this way that she has dispensed you her offering made to God. My regret is that if I had a chance to talk to you, you would not have been made to keep awake through the night nor would you have gone through this agony as now.'

'Oh! What a fool I am! Now I can see that!'

'Even so, she should be silenced, I'll see to it.'

'What will you see? You will remonstrate with her.'

'The devil should have her due which she deserves.'

'If you strike her with your leg, it will give a blow to my heart. Give up this idea, swear by my head.'

'I shall not swear! I promise!'

'I'll not accept it.'

Mohan had to take an oath.

Noorbai said, 'She promised to take oath in a temple that she would not abuse thenceforth.'

Mohan replied hastily, 'Even if she swears by all the temples of Vrindavan and Mathura, I should not trust her.'

'I am confident, of course? I vow here and now at the bank of Yamuna that I would not take amiss any remark of hers,' said Noorbai.

Mohan was reassured and said, 'I trust you would be able to get along with her.'

Mohan patted all over her back, 'Come, have your bath first, it is close to daybreak now.'

'It seems, I have had bath already.'

'You would feel it all the more when I steal your clothes, then, go and sit on some tree; there you will come to beg of me, with folded hands, to get back your clothes.'

Go and bathe, I shall pay you back for your ignorance.

'Don't tease me indeed.'

'Hm.'

'All right, I am folding my hands to beg your pardon, in anticipation.'

'Not in anticipation like this! I accept a deal in cash. Pay by this hand and take it by the other.'

'Not now, my dear Mohan!'

All right, I release you; you may go.'

—❋—

63

The frolic delayed them a little. The rays of the sun had already lit up the whole place filling and blending everything with their hue and shimmer when they reached the arbour after bathing themselves in the river.

Light played upon Noorbai's cheerful and exquisite face. She neatly lifted a pinch of dust and thereby put a round mark on her forehead right above the middle of her eyebrows.

Noorbai said, 'My heart spurs me to burst into singing here and now, and if my heart swells in a temple prompting me to sing, I would not resist at all and, may be, would step on to dance too.'

A puzzled Mohan replied, 'Don't ever do it! This is a wicked world. Last night when you were meditating with closed eyes, some ruffians were staring at you with evil designs. My shoulders swelled in desperation to crush them.'

Noorbai said in a detached manner, 'People carry dregs of their heart and evil desires even to temples!'

Mohan's temper showed as he expressed, 'I have found out that in the past few days, many persons smear the black tar of their heart on their face when they come here.'

Noorbai, 'You may be right! But the temples are still pious and pure!'

'As it is, this spot itself is a pious place. It instantly transformed itself into a haunt of Krishna's flute playing when you began to sing. Won't you sing now?'

Noorbai responded, 'Why not —today my heart is yearning to immerse myself in singing for the Lord.'

Noorbai sang a devotional song. The arbour seemed to swing in harmony with her sweet, exciting and rhythmical recital. Sunrays shimmered, in keeping with the rhythm of her song. To Noorbai, the waves of Yamuna seemed to ring with peals of laughter while they swept their way towards her with her Lord Kanhaiya, bedecked with flowers riding their crest and playing on his flute. Noorbai began to dance. As she advanced towards the bank of Yamuna, she found herself in full sunshine. Mohan closed his eyes. The cadence of song echoed in his ears and the image of a Gopi flashed into mind's eye which witnessed a haloed and bright tableau before he opened his eyes. Noorbai's footsteps raised dust particles which encircled her body as wind swept them in air. Sunrays reflected themselves in the smallest particles and filled them with a heavenly halo. To Mohan, Noorbai bathed in light herself appeared to be a source of haloed and accumulated illumination.

Mohan approached her and entreated, 'Let's go in the shade —it is hot here in the sun.'

Noorbai lost her concentration and said, 'Oh! What was all this?'

Holding her hand, Mohan escorted her to the arbour. Noorbai's eyes were full of tears. She stammered out the words. 'What an image did I see? Indeed, Kanhaiya comes here leaving the temples behind. If someone sings to him, even for once, the song which he likes, it makes him follow that person everywhere. What a vision I had today—saw everything! My beloved Mohan, it was you who revealed to me all wonderful things.'

A hoarse voice piercing to ears came from behind a tree, 'She has started calling him by his name. How proud is she about her beauty!'

Roni came out and stood before them. Noorbai's face did not change its expression or make any grimace.

She smiled and said, 'You did not abuse me at all, sister!'

Roni was speechless. Mohan asked her, 'Why have you come here?' 'To leave for Bharatpur after a bath.'

'How did you get to know we were here?'

'A majority of people in Vrindavan know it already. This song could be heard from a long distance. Many people turned to this direction and I too joined them.'

'Where are the others? What about Tota?'

'I have left behind others standing at some distance. Tota is not there among them. I had recognised you both from a distance.'

Noorbai asked, 'How did you like the song, sister.'

'I liked it! Others too said the same thing. But I did not like the way you swayed and bent your body during dance movements. Besides, didn't you feel ashamed while calling your paramour by his name! I felt, it was not in good taste.'

'I had invoked God by His name, sister.'

'He is God! Oh, my grandma!'

'You don't know Him really. You can see Him from a distance, of course. But you must discover Him at close quarters.'

Roni burst into laughter as she said, 'He is God! I don't recognise Him!'

Mohan also laughed and said, 'If you take me and her to be human beings it will suffice. If you give up cursing, it will be a greater accomplishment. Did you take a vow in the temple or not?'

She replied, 'I shall take a vow now but ask her not to call you by your name.' And she turned coquettish in her demeanour.

Noorbai began to laugh. Mohan made an interesting point when he remarked, 'If you give up cursing, I shall pay you two rupees every month.'

'Do I yearn for money so much? You may or may not give it; I promise, I shall never abuse anyone in future. I shall take a vow in the temple too. Well, you would pay me every month thereafter.'

Mohan laughed but Noorbai wore a sombre look. Roni blushed as Mohan promised, 'I shall!'

Noorbai ran to Roni and hugged her. She said, 'If, at all, you so wish, you may curse. I shall never misunderstand you.'

Roni relented and said, 'Last night, I could not help muttering, if ever you sat for singing you would be reminded of your dead father. I uttered no more. But taking offence you came away with him to take bath here and did not wake me!'

Mohan remarked, 'You came to offer prayers to this holy place trusting others to help you. So you must pick up some worldly wisdom on your own.'

Roni coquettishly remarked, 'Does she possess only the talent of singing or something else! I have the skill to keep cows and do farming too, which serves me well. But Sister, I liked your devotional song which was praised very much by those standing there. It must be appealing. You possess some wisdom which I came to know just now.' Both of them burst into laughter.

Roni said, 'Let me bring my buffalo and other things and, then, you would see how I work—I would work and you would sing!' Mohan said, 'When are you going to Bharatpur?'

Noorbai replied, 'Not today! She will go at her convenience and she will not go alone.'

As they turned to go back to the place of stay, all three of them observed that beyond the distant part of the arbour, a few persons were marching back hastily.

—❋—

64

Shubrati was back home when his squad dispersed before the onset of monsoon. Most of the Maratha soldiers engaged themselves in agricultural operation. But before laying hands on their plough, they had acquired control of Bassein fort[133A] by dislodging the Portuguese, in a grim battle, from the Bassein island. Some of the chieftains who were engrossed in internal feud and strife became a source of anxiety to Baji Rao.

After monsoon was over, the task of overcoming Nizam had fallen on Baji Rao's shoulders. After the departure of Nadir Shah from India, Nizam returned to the Deccan and passed away. There were conspiracies, murders and skirmishes galore among his sons and nephews. Baji Rao had to wage a battle against one faction among them.

In north India, the strength of Badan Singh, the Raja of Bharatpur had increased rapidly. Sikhs too had become a force to reckon with. Rajputs were deriving satisfaction by indulging in envious feuds and mutual rivalry. The contemporary history of India being shaped then included the stubborn British diplomacy, the new weapons of war, the sharpened edge of the ploughs belonging to Marathas, Jats and farmers, hoofs of horses, swords of Sikhs and the bottles of wine drained by the Moghul Emperor.

The pace and progress of social history of Maharashtra was thwarted and hindered by people belonging to higher strata, entangled and choked as it was in their thorny and orthodox predilection. It was the occasion of 'Yagyopavit'[134] ceremony of Baji Rao's younger son. Mastani, the mistress of Baji Rao was already there in Shaniwar Mahal at Poona. How was the 'Yagyopavit' ceremony going to be organised successfully? If Bajirao were to participate in the celebrations Mastani would certainly join the same and play some role therein. As there seemed no alternative to it, Bajirao sought excuse to absent and extricate himself from that situation. Nizam's crisis was creating problem at the threshold of Poona. Bajirao set out at the head of

133A. op.cit Vasai Fort in Maharashtra known as Bassein under Portuguese rule.

134. Yagyopavit – Sacred thread traditionally worn among Hindus, especially Brahmans as a mark of religiosity. A ceremony is held early in life, in which a young boy is given the sacred thread after chanting of 'mantras.'

a large army to resolve and overcome that crisis. But he could not take Mastani with him. Mastani stayed back in Poona itself.

Bajirao defeated Nizam in a fierce battle. At the same time, he received the news that Mastani was forcibly taken into custody and interned away from Poona. Bajirao was deeply hurt but found himself quite helpless. When he heard that it was the handiwork of his brother Chimnaji Aapa and his elder son Balaji, he was shattered completely. The same Bajirao, who had been inspired by Mastani's smiles mingled with the brandishing of her sword as she rode the horse with him during his Delhi expedition, felt as if his heart was drained of blood, his eyes devoid of zeal and his hand missing the sword. He consumed more and more of liquor in order to forget his and Mastani's miseries. After a few days, he suffered from a high fever and died of the same after a short interval soon after the spring was over. The demands of casteism and the distinction between the high and the low seemed to have been fulfilled. No sooner had Mastani received the news of Baji Rao's death, she also passed away to join him in his heavenly abode by repeating his name to the dance time and after ending the rhythm and harmony of life.

Shubrati was at Poona when both met their death. When he got the news of Bajirao's death, a question arose in his mind, 'How was Mohanlal? By God's grace he should be all right.'

When he received the news of Mastani's death his heart welled up with the question, 'How was Saroopa? God may grant Mohan and Saroopa a long life.'

—✵—

65

Roni brought from Bharatpur a buffalo, some hidden money, butter-oil and a few clothes. Mohan took lodgings not far from the bank of the river Yamuna on the outskirts of Vrindavan and bought some land for cultivation. Tota began to live at Fatchpur Sikri. Roni's buffalo had gone dry after monsoon was over. Mohan procured a milch buffalo. Roni had the knack of working hard and of enlarging the range of her activities. Noorbai tried her best to partake her share in work. She made dung-cakes, fetched drinking water and helped in cooking but grinding flour was beyond her. Roni did most of the work. She did not like others remarking that she had some one to help her. She told Noorbai at times, 'All this is beyond your capacity! You are worthless. You should go on singing and playing on music! But she no longer used abusive language, or she thought so, because she received two rupees every month. They visited temples only on some very important occasions or celebrations.

Noorbai and Mohan pondered and remarked, 'We have temples here at our home within our hearts.' Noorbai escorted by Mohanlal, projected and discovered, in the clear weather, her own unsullied and unflinching faith in the gay abandon of cool, overshadowing groves under the open sky. Noorbai had acquired a single-string musical instrument which she played as she sang hymns at night. Keen listeners and lovers of music from neighbourhood as also from distant places used to lend their ears at the outer wall of her lodgings. Her singing and outings in the groves cast her spell over a large and widespread area. Someone remarked, 'She is a Gopi from her previous birth.'

Another person joined in, "She has communion with God, the flule player'."

'How pretty and delicate-framed she is! Seems, her limbs are made of roses!'

'Mohanlal has kidnapped her from a royal palace, for he has that shrew as his wife, the one whose temper shows too often.'

'Mohanlal is an honest, hardworking and devoted person —it's impossible!'

'We have known many a devotee! They all fall for a woman.'
'But he meddles with no one.'

'From where does he get money to maintain two women.'

'Does some one from the upper class gentry frequent their house to listen to her singing through the night.'

'No one has watched this. 1 tried to probe, but could discover nobody.'

'If there was someone, he would be seen among the groves too.'

'What could be the reason for her outburst in singing? Where did she learn singing so well?'

'The female disciples of the great exponents of music from Delhi alone can sing so well matching her style and rhythm. I suspect, she may be a dancing girl or a prostitute?'

'If she was a prostitute, Mohanlal would not eat food cooked by her; he would have provided her lodgings in a different house.'

'But Jats are capable of swallowing everything like this.'

'Oh no; no Jat farmer would ever do this —it's altogether a different fare for the Rajas and nobles.'

'May be, Mohanlal is a Raja or noble in disguise, who has come to the Brij area to devote himself to penance.'

'No! If it were so, why should he bear the burden of a household, farming and the tending of cattle.'

'Saroopa must be the incarnation of an angel. She has come here to bide the period of curse on her head. She makes dung-cakes in day-time and sings like a cuckoo at night.'

'People say, God reveals himself to her in those groves, which makes her abstain from going to temples.'

'Some sinners had ogled at her with evil intent, in the temples.'

'She is the bride of a Jat, and thus has saved herself. If it was someone else, she would have landed where, no one can predict.'

Mohan also lent his ears to such gossip at times. He relished the idea of Noorbai being an embodiment of her original self of Gopi or an angel—all other gossip made him sullen and sulky.

He would muse at times: 'if those jewels and diamonds he possessed still, he would raise an army of his own, establish his rule in some fief and crush the dacoits. But his attention would veer round to the flashback vision of the marauders, who had crushed him beneath their feet and in whose presence, Noorbai had been forced to go half-naked. All this was the mischief of Chintaman. He would indulge in a monologue, 'if I did not make Chintaman lick dust, I would call myself a nincompoop. Shubrati's squad had not returned. Who knows whether Shubrati was spared and still alive and kicking. What a distance between Poona and Vrindavan! How long do I stay here at Vrindavan? Why can't I start mobilising the Jats of the neighbourhood myself? We poor farmers and wage-workers can accomplish a great deal by our collective strength. But where do we get our finance from? From the booty of the dacoity? Fie....oh no!! What, do I smear and soil myself with the same dirt and slush which I want to remove? No, never! But, then, where will the money come from? There is a lot of money in the temples of Vrindavan. We shall be able to protect the temples from the assaults of aliens, the field of farmers, the honour of our women and of the waves of the mother Yamuna and the groves once frequented by Gope and Gopis in a far better manner than the stout priests. We shall kill the marauders and die at their hands. God will back and support us throughout. But why should the temple priests part with their money for us? Then, shall we go and ally ourselves with some chieftain. May be, we join the forces of Badan Singh! Oh, no! We, as against our will, have to toe the line of others while serving them as vassal. Let me rest content with the number of farmers and workers who agree to fall in line with me.'

Mohan was ill at ease and his mind fidgety. He broached the subject among the religious-minded farmers and workers who flocked there. They looked upon Mohan as a devotee of God. A few among them who came closer to him resolved that they would not demur in sacrificing their lives in face of danger or trouble. The authorities of temples too viewed it with favour as it would ensure the safety of their property alongwith temples. Even so, they did not contribute a single paise towards building up this organisation.

Mohan's objective found publicity outside the township too but the nobles turned a deaf ear to it. Factions of fighting Jats were indifferent to such a move. But Badan Singh was sagacious, alert and mischievous. Although the title of 'Brij-Raj' had been conferred upon him, he had not been able to mobilise solid and necessary resources for defence. On receiving the exaggerated and distorted version of the news about Mohan's objectives and efforts made thereof until then, he struck upon the idea of assimilating him and his comrades in his overall strategy and plan. Mohanlal received and despatched his emissaries. He was not prepared to work at Bharatpur on payment as a servant. The messengers related to Badan Singh the inimitable beauty of Noorbai and the above average looks of Roni.

—※—

66

Mohan had gone to the city centre. Noorbai was making dung-cakes. Roni returned from the Yamuna after a bath and having finished her washing, she carried her 'saree' on her shoulder. When Roni took her turn at making dung-cakes, Noorbai would be up pretty early for a bath in the river and would take a round of one grove or the other on her way back. Putting her pot of water on the ground, Roni began to spread her wet 'saree' for drying. With large and thick turbans tied on their head matched with wide, rectangular and colourful mark on their forehead, two men arrived and seated themselves in the courtyard. Noorbai turned her back towards them. Roni drew forth her veil a little and asked them 'Where do you come from? What brings you here?'

One of them replied, 'We have come to see the Thakur. Where is he gone to?'

'He has gone to the village on business.'

'When will he come back?'

'He will be back by mid-day. What is your purpose?'

'We have very important business with him. Won't he come back before mid-day?'

'No!'

'Please give us water to drink.'

Roni offered them some water and waited to see them depart. She turned to have a look at the red mark on their forehead.

One of them said, 'We have to discuss something and now let us talk it over with you both.'

Roni responded, 'Let us know what it is.'

Noorbai resumed the work of making dung-cakes.

'We know Mohanlal very well. He is a deeply religious person.'

'All right! Proceed further!'

'And you are the very embodiment of Gopi. When you sing hymns at night, God playing on his flute stands outside listening to it with rapt attention.'

'Yes.'

Noorbai stopped making the cakes. Facing them, she lent her ears to their conversation. Her profile from one side and side-glance was enough to impress them but when they observed her whole body face-to-face they were amazed. One of them remarked, 'What a beauty you are, and what a place to live in! And are these lovely hands meant to make dung-cakes?'

Noorbai smiled gently and questioned them in a simple manner, 'What else are they meant for?'

And the other person butted in, 'Are these hands meant for drawing water from the well. Gold ornaments studded with diamonds should adorn them.'

Roni did not take it amiss as she quickly glanced at her hands devoid of ornaments. Noorbai replied effortlessly, 'This is part of our chores.'

'You are born to rule, over a kingdom, and to command maid-servants.'

'Which kingdom?'

'Any one will do for you —it would be so easy for you.'

'Our home and hearth is our kingdom. Making dung-cakes which I am doing now and drawing water from well, in which she is busy, constitute our affairs of state. Please disclose why you are staying on.'

'Have you ever heard of Badan Singh?'

'Yes, we have! Well!'

'One ruler of Brij is in heaven above and the other one on earth is Raja Badan Singh. Gopis of God Brijraj have not been seen by anyone but the ones attached to the other Brijraj are living in Bharatpur fort, leading a gay and comfortable life adorned with ornaments made of pearls, diamonds, gold and silver.

'Is it so?'

'Of course! There is no dearth of food there nor does one feel want of costly clothes and ornaments. Gopis neither make dung-cakes nor do they go about recklessly drawing water in the earthen pots from a well. Both of you should have found place in the royal palace at Bharatpur. Would you go? At some distance, stands the chariot ready to leave with the passengers.'

Roni felt like spouting abuses and curses on them but as a measure of practising a different skill, she decided upon thrashing them with her legs. Then she thought of fleecing them first. Noorbai began to wash her dung-smeared hands.

Roni strained her mind to produce with restraint a remark full of wisdom, 'Do you have something in your girdle to give?' her tone betrayed harshness despite her effort.

With her hands partly washed up, an agitated Noorbai with a flushed face asked, 'What! What did you say?' She could utter nothing else as her throat felt choked.

Neither of the two visitors felt dismayed or embarrassed. One of them reached for his girdle. The other said, 'We did not start from home empty-handed. Take gold coins here for your husband, leave them here for him and follow us. There is no doubt about this lady. Badan Singh will like you too.'

Suspicious of the strength of her legs, Roni, wide-eyed looked around in the courtyard for a stick, a club or a piece of wood. Noorbai had a quick look at the earthen tiles of the roof.

Noorbai braced herself and managed to utter, 'You are a tale-bearer to Badan Singh despite being a man with a big coloured mark on your forehead. Go out from here!'

Roni exclaimed.'They won't go like this. Get me a stick and then I'll show these hounds of Badan Singh, the issueless Rajah what a Jat woman can do to them.'

Roni turned towards a corner of the courtyard, on the lookout for a stick. As both of them rose from their seat, their eyes were red with anger.

Clenching his fist, one of them remarked, 'If we had a mind to do it, we would have forcibly carried you away after thrusting a piece of cloth in your mouth but Chintaman has forbidden us to do so—the same Chintaman who had given you shelter and also saved you from being robbed. We'll see later.'

Roni rushed towards them with a long wooden piece and challenged, 'Let me see who has the guts to thrust cloth in our mouth!'

They came out of the house quickly. Roni watched them running away. There was no one around. Some people stood at a little distance, Roni shouted for help but nobody could hear her. Noorbai escorted her back inside the house by holding her hand.

Noorbai asked her in exasperation and anger, 'Why did you ask them whether they had something in their girdle?'

She replied with a lump in her throat, 'I indulged in a prank. I thought of fleecing them a little before kicking them out with legs.'

Noorbai calmly remonstrated, 'One should not play pranks like this. If you had accepted something from him, he would have become a claimant.'

—❋—

67

Roni related the whole incident to Mohan immediately on his arrival. She, however, held back the portion of prank. Mohan flared up and remarked angrily, 'You observed that demon! Even now you would ask me to forgive them. Attend to your chores and sing devotional songs. I take a vow that until I take revenge from Chintaman, I will not sleep on the cot and won't go to temple to seek a glimpse of God!'

An anxious Noorbai entreated him, 'All right! Now don't speak any more.'

Mohan gnashed his teeth and kept quiet for a while. Restraining himself under strict discipline, he said, 'God who revealed himself to you would protect us all and also stand guard for us. He had killed 'Kamsa',[135] likewise, could I not kill Chintaman?'

Noorbai urged, 'Please take some food.'

Mohan quietly finished his meal. After he had washed his hands and mouth, he remarked, 'I have a sizeable number of men at my command. I would take you to a Panda's place to be lodged there in the midst of a thickly-populated locality. The buffalo and cow will be left in the care of the neighbour and then I would set out to teach him a lesson.'

Roni had tucked away some money inside a hole in one corner of the house. How could she leave behind all that. She argued, 'We won't go anywhere deserting our home and hearth. Why are you frightened? Who would dare to touch and harm us here in any way?'

Noorbai asked, 'Who were these men? Where did they come from? How are they concerned with Chintaman?'

Mohan told her, 'They must be Badan Singh's talebearers. Chintaman too seems to have connections with Badan Singh. Badan Singh appears to have turned blind. He has, in his palace, too many women to keep their count or that of their progeny. Even so, he hunts and runs after wives and daughters of other people.'

Roni burst out, 'May God damn this blackfaced, shameless fellow; may jackals eat his corpse' and shut her mouth instantly, reminded as she was of the imminent loss of two rupees that month. Noorbai had a hearty laugh while Mohan smiled and said, 'Curses, weapon and hell have been invented for such fellows.'

Mohan enjoyed his siesta. Both women came up to him after

135. Kansa – op. cit. 22, p. 79.

finishing their meal. Mohan resumed the conversation. 'I would mobilise my men today itself and leave immediately to seek out Chintaman. You must take good care of the house. It will take me two-three days at best. God will protect you.'

Noorbai intervened, 'Chintaman certainly came to our rescue that night. These men hail from Bharatpur as I could make out from their conversation. They must be knowing Chintaman and would have sought his advice but he would have restrained them. Moreover, the Raja of Bharatpur rules this place too. If he was annoyed, we would be forced to flee this place also.'

Mohan replied, 'We would leave here for Gwalior and from there, we would proceed to Poona. There, neither the Moghul Emperor nor Badan Singh has his sway.'

Frightened out of wits, Roni asked, 'Poona! Where is Poona?'

Noorbai could not resist a reply, 'Poona is a city situated far away from here, where people belonging to high and noble families conspired to get Mastani killed.'

Mohan was startled. Roni asked, 'Who is this Mastani?'

Noorbai responded, 'A grief-stricken woman she was! I was given to understand this. Of course, I had no occasion or chance to meet her in person.'

Mohan could not suppress his surprise and asked, 'How can women get to know such news from places far away?'

Noorbai asserted, 'People come from distant places to centres of pilgrimage. They exchange views and news. Wretched women also come to know of happenings.'

Roni interrupted, 'If some calamity befalls us, we shall go to Fatehpur where Tota is already living and settled.'

Mohan's courage spurred him, 'No, we shall not be compelled to run away just like that. Lord Krishna reigns supreme here, not Badan Singh. If he turns up to inflict tyranny, he would be crushed outside the town.'

Noorbai entreated him sweetly, 'Now you should not invite trouble to yourself. Land has to be tilled for cultivation. Buy one or two wet buffaloes or cows. We shall have plenty of clarified butter and stacks of dung-cakes for the rainy season.'

Roni supported her, 'She is right.'

Mohan stared at them wide-eyed with vacant looks. He said, 'All right! We'll see all that in due course.'

Noorbai pondered, 'If this is put off now, it will get postponed for a long time.' The image of a stout buffalo flashed in Roni's imagination.

Noorbai said, 'It seems, Chintaman did not have a hand in today's incident.'

Mohan uttered, 'Hm' and went out.

—✵—

68

Noorbai did not sing devotional songs that night. Noorbai and Roni were asleep when Mohan armed with his weapons went out. At a little distance from the house, a crowd had collected. There was complete silence. Quietly, they turned and proceeded towards Chintaman's village. Avoiding villages and habitations on the way, they arrived in the vicinity of a village. This happened to be Chintaman's village. It was late at night. In this band of people, a few lay in ambush at the approaches of the village, while the others surrounded Chintaman's house. The doors of house were closed.

Mohan shouted, 'Chaudhary, open the doors.'

'Who is there?'

'Men on business' was the reply.

'We'll come out after finishing dinner.'

'So late at night! We have urgent business. Come out.'

Chaudharin responded from behind the crevices of the door, 'What men in hurry! He won't go out tonight. He has kept awake for the past few nights.'

Mohan spoke in a distorted, artificial tone, 'We are returning after mounting an assault; our throat is parched because of thirst.

We shall convey to him one important message before departing.'

'Tell me the message, I shall reply to you, myself. Who are you?'

'You will make out our identity soon enough. This house and village are going to be surrounded just now. The Emperor's force is following and we are all fleeing. Both of you should also run away.'

'I shall convey this to him.'

'There is something else, which I shall convey to him only. Let me get in. Unlatch the door.'

'Let me go and ask him.'

Chaudharin did not open the door. There was pin-drop silence. Suddenly, the sound made by the running on thatched roof at the back of the house was heard and it was followed by a thud and thumping noise. Members of Mohan's band were standing close to the house. Chaudharin and Chintaman were surrounded as soon as they jumped from the thatched roof. Mohan was standing in front of the house. His companions brought them in his presence.

Mohan roared, 'We are sepoys of the royal forces.'

Chintaman was shaken all over.

Mohan continued in the same vein, 'Chaudharin who is just like our mother, should stand aside. You must hand over the articles which you had come to possess by beating, robbing and extorting a guest of yours, a year back.'

'I was not among them.'

'Every thing has been found out. Tell us everything, otherwise, you will be cut to pieces; right now, here, out with it!'

Chintaman kept quiet. One of Mohan's companions, commanded, 'He will not come round like this? Strike him and mutilate his limbs.'

Mohan thought that night, Chintaman could have allowed Noorbai to be molested and dishonoured but he had urged others to refrain from it. For a moment, Mohan tried, in vain, to conjure up the image of Lord Krishna. The sound of being crushed under feet and Noorbai's cry 'Do not beat my Lord' flashed before him.

He shouted, 'Strip him and thrash his back. Then hack his arms and legs.'

Chintaman was stripped. There was something in his girdle.

One of the companions shouted, 'He has got something in his girdle.'

Chintaman said in a breathless tone, 'Don't torture me! Here take whatever I have!'

Mohan dipped his hand in his waist and untied two pouches.

Chintaman prayed for mercy, 'One of the pouches is the same and the other contains a collection of my earnings. Take both but have mercy on me, please.'

Chaudharin was crying. Mohan groped for valuables in the pouches. He tied one of them round his waist and carried the other in his hand. He said, 'Your limbs would not be injured, but you would certainly receive kicks with legs.'

Chintaman replied in an undertone 'Beat me up! What can I say?'

Chaudharin screamed as Mohan raised his leg to strike him but the leg remained uplifted in the air. The pouch carried in his hand contained coins.

Mohan said, 'Brothers! This pouch contains coins. What shall we do with them? We have to bear in mind that we are not dacoits.'

One of the companions replied, 'He is a dacoit, of course, but has not received any punishment so far.'

Mohan opened the pouch and poured out half the contents in the piece of cloth held out by the person accompanying him. He tied the rest of the coins. Barebodied, Chintaman was lying in dirt. Mohan dropped with a jerk the pouch on the shoulders of Chintaman and added, 'Marathas will carry this and whatever you earn in future too.'

Chintaman began to weep. Chaudharin was already crying. Mohan asked, 'Where are your comrades who had committed that highway robbery.'

'They have gone out.'

'Where to?' 'I don't know!' 'You don't know! Hm!'

On this interjection, 'Hm!' Chaudharin screamed. Mohan said, 'All right! Doesn't matter! Convey to Badan Singh, if he casts an evil eye on any woman of Mathura-Vrindavan, Bharatpur and Deeg, etc., he will be reduced to ashes. He is not the mighty lord of Brij area, God is the supreme ruler of the Brij.'

Chintaman moaned in an undertone 'Hm'. All of them left that place.

—✻—

69

Mohan returned home two days later in the evening. His face was writ large with happiness which showed through his weariness. Roni was eager to make enquiries but was perplexed as to what questions she should ask him. Noorbai feigned to be indifferent but wished to know whether Mohan had sustained any injury. However, she was trying to ward off her eagerness—for some time.

After the dinner was over, Mohan urged Noorbai, 'Please sing a hymn.'

Noorbai enquired, 'Did some one sustain any injury?'

Mohan said, 'Who received an injury?'

'You!'

'Not at all! And I spared him too.'

'Did he recognise you?'

'Perhaps not! Even if he did, I don't care.'

Roni wished to know, 'Did you bring something?'

Mohan replied, 'A little dust! Would you like to gulp it?'

Roni felt embarrassed and frightened and added, 'I had enquired by the way.'

Noorbai enquired, 'You remonstrated with her needlessly. I ask you what you fetched from there in a bundle? You left us around midnight. Both of us had an anxious time next day from morning until mid-day!'

Mohan replied amidst laughter,' What I have accomplished should gladden your hearts too. We surrounded the village and his house at night. Chaudharin did not open the door. Both of them wanted to flee by jumping from the thatched roof. I wanted to strike Chintaman's limbs but spared him on Chaudharin's prayer for mercy and help. He had tied a pouch in his girdle, which I untied and half of it, I flung on him. I disbursed the other half among my comrades.'

Roni's heart prompted her to ask as she could not resist it, 'And you did not retain anything for your own self.'

Mohan said tauntingly, 'Sew a bag for yourself but for that matter you don't need a bag. Make a hole in a corner of the house to keep things.'

Roni could not suppress her resentment and asked, 'Then what made you go away?'

Mohan replied, 'I had to drive home a message to Bharatpur that if anyone casts a glance at Vrindavan, he would be blinded by us. This is what I did there and managed, for my comrades, some money in the bargain. If anyone mounts an assault on this place of pilgrimage, they would withstand it with all their strength. Is it an insignificant achievement?'

Observing Mohan's joy, Noorbai could not believe that his strenuous outing and running about had resulted into such a small gain but she did not wish to discuss it. Instead, she said, 'You must be tired; please go to bed.'

Mohan said, 'Yes! Early in the morning, I shall go and have a bath.' Noorbai could make out everything. Mohan did not insist on her singing a hymn.

Mohan was up before dawn. Noorbai immediately rose from her bed on hearing a little commotion. Both of them walked to the distant bank of Yamuna, where they stopped and stood quietly. Mohan gleefully informed her. 'O, Kanhaiya's Gopi, What are you thinking?'

'That you should concentrate yourself in devotional music

and singing and not get lost in the mirage of materialistic world and wandering about. What were you pondering about, yourself.'

'I was weighing in my mind that lucre turns pious and dutiful men into cannnabis addicts and the poor sweat themselves out in hard work before they earn their wages, which is their Dharma.'

'Ha —Ha! Since when have you turned a poet?'

'Since the time I stripped Chintaman, left him naked and warned Badan Singh that he is an imposter in calling himself the Lord of Brij area and his will would not prevail against the real Brij Raj, the God Almighty.

'No tyrant's will would prevail against the supreme will of Brij Raj, the God.'

'I am trying to bring together the devotees of Brij Raj so as to face up to the tyrannical acts.'

'A vast majority among people do think on these lines and thus the days of tyranny are numbered.'

'In case people holding such views busy themselves in decorating and enriching palaces, nothing would come out of it.'

'Someone decorates his palace while another person beautifies a temple but no body can achieve anything without sublimating his mind and purifying his heart.'

'Won't you keep showering on me your affection, thus giving me a glimpse into your inner beauty.'

Noorbai embraced him and added, 'Whatever I possess has been bestowed upon me by you. I am in no position to give you anything. God who dispenses gifts to everyone would bestow the same on anyone if he prays to Him.'

Mohan kept quiet for some time and added, 'Now you may take bath; let's go to the arbour on the bank of the river. We have to talk about many things.'

Noorbai said, 'I wished to say the same thing.'

By the time they finished their bath and washing, day had dawned. Both of them went into a nearby arbour. Mohan urged in a sweet and affectionate tone, 'Sing a stanza and then sit by my side; I shall tell you something.'

Noorbai replied in a tone suffused with love, 'And what about dance?'

Mohan said enthusiastically, 'Dance; yes..... yes, of course but only after I have told you what I wish to.'

Noorbai picked up a pinch of dust and applied it to her shining forehead. She closed her eyes and opened them again. Mohan watched her eagerly. Noorbai came closer to him with a smiling face and placed her hand on his shoulder. She held his chin with fingers of one hand and replied, 'You did not tell me everything last night. Isn't it?'

Mohan said, 'Yes it is so! This is why I had hinted that we should take bath early in the morning. I wanted to tell you everything here in this arbour.'

'All right, tell me now whatever was left unsaid.'

'First of all please sing, a stanza of song now!'

'I would rather listen to your conversation first. My ears are agog with curiosity I shall sing after I have heard you fully.'

'All right!'

Mohan dipped his hand into his girdle and took out the pouch. Noorbai appeared cheerful but in a few moments, her face wore a dejected colourless look. She stood at some distance. Mohan untied the knot and emptied the pouch. It had neither pieces of gold nor pearls. There were small and flat pieces of gold studded with diamonds, emerald, rubies and topaz. He picked up a piece of gold studded with rubies in one hand and balanced another on the palm of the other hand. He rose from his seat and enthusiastically added, 'I shall adorn your hair with this piece here. When you dance, the rays of the sun will playfully reflect on this piece and the round mark on your forehead and then I would also join you in dancing with gusto.'

Noorbai's throat was brimful with emotion, 'What will you do with these pieces?'

'I shall watch your hair adorned with the gold piece and will raise a fighting force by exchanging the remaining valuables for money, for the protection of Vrindavan. I shall give as an offering one or two pieces in a temple.'

'You should raise the force with the sweat of your brow. The force mobilised with this gold will not be able to protect the Brij.'

'Shall I deposit all the pieces in temples as offerings?'

'Templs will be defiled.'

Mohan replied, 'I shall ponder and then see, what should be done.'

Placing the piece carried in the other palm in his turban, Mohan turned towards her. Noorbai's eyes flashed and reflected her fears like those of a doe encircled by hunters.

Mohan thought that Noorbai did not wish to wear diamonds and rubies in her hair out of her religious sentiments —they might diminish the value of the mark of dust imprinted on her forehead. But he nurtured a strong yearning to do so.

Mohan clasped her in his arms and she remained standstill. Mohan tried and fixed that gold plate in one or two plaits of Noor's flowing hair. He looked at her wistfully.

The soft, shimmering sunrays were filtering through the boughs of the trees in the arbour and played on her forehead which reflected the scintillating diamonds. Noorbai closed her eyes as her body remained unmoved and her lips quivered. Two big droplets of tears trickled from her closed eyes. Noor withheld them by deep breath, pursed her lips and opened her eyes. To her, everything appeared to be shaking —the rays of the sun, branches of the trees and Mohan's face. She wiped her about-to-trickle tears and cleared the mist in her eyes. She said, 'Let us go to the bank of the river.'

Mohan was surprised and asked her the reason for shedding tears. She replied, 'I'll tell you all this; let us go there.'

Mohan escorted her, carrying his turban in his hand. She was leading the way. Her unpleated hair was flowing behind her in the mild breeze. The diamonds and rubies were shining in those two locks of hair. As both of them stood at the bank, the river Yamuna flowed leisurely making a low, gurgling sound.

Noorbai took out the gold plate from the locks of her hair and kept it on the palm of her hand. Mohan advanced towards her. Noorbai warned him, 'There! Stand there, otherwise, I shall go and drown myself in the lap of the Yamuna.'

Mohan was stupefied and remained standstill. Noorbai withdrew herself a little. She said, 'You don't know how filthy is the story behind these diamonds and gold. Now tell me whether you love the unchaste Noorbai — the one who was buried in the grave or the other one, Saroopa, who stands here before you cleansed and purified in all ways.'

The quiet of that isolated spot was disturbed by these resounding words as if the silence had been set aflame into flying embers. Mohan's throat which had a lump, gurgled up the words, 'For Saroopa!'

Noorbai threw that studded plate of gold in the deep current of the river with full force and it sank with the sound of a low thud. Noorbai craned her neck to watch the bubbles raised by the sinking piece. It seemed as if the rays of the sun reflected in her face with a view to pry behind her flowing hair and exquisite eyes.

Mohan, brimming with deep respect, gazed at her intently and curiously watched the rising bubbles of water. To him, it appeared that eternity had absorbed, for ever, within itself the tenderness of her lips, the intoxication stillness of her eyes and the picture of peace that her profile and posture presented.

Mohan said, 'Let's go into the arbour!'

A smile played on her lips as Noorbai said, 'Let us go.'

❑❑❑